OFFSPRING

BECOMING A FAMILY FILLED WITH HERITAGE
AND HOPE

BY

NICHOLE MARCELL &
SHAWN MARCELL

Offspring

Copyright © 2022 by Nichole and Shawn Marcell

All rights reserved.

Unless otherwise indicated, all Scripture quotations are taken from THE HOLY BIBLE, NEW INTERNATIONAL VERSION®, NIV® Copyright © 1973, 1978, 1984, 2011 by Biblica, Inc.® Used by permission. All rights reserved worldwide.

Scripture quotations marked NLT are taken from the *Holy Bible*, New Living Translation, copyright © 1996, 2004, 2015 by Tyndale House Foundation. Used by permission of Tyndale House Publishers, Inc., Carol Stream, Illinois 60188. All rights reserved.

Scripture quotations marked MSG are taken from *THE MESSAGE*, copyright © 1993, 2002, 2018 by Eugene H. Peterson. Used by permission of NavPress. All rights reserved. Represented by Tyndale House Publishers, Inc.

Scripture quotations marked ESV are from The ESV® Bible (The Holy Bible, English Standard Version®), copyright © 2001 by Crossway, a publishing ministry of Good News Publishers. Used by permission. All rights reserved.

Scripture quotations marked by MSG are taken from The Message (MSG) Copyright © 1993, 2002,2018 by Eugene H. Peterson

Scripture quotations marked ESV are taken from The Holy Bible, English Standard Version. ESV® Text Edition: 2016. Copyright © 2001 by Crossway Bibles, a publishing ministry of Good News Publishers.

We dedicate this book to our four God-given gifts:
Autumn Brook, Tyler, Linzee Joy , and Josiah.

Outside of Jesus, you are everything to us.
We are so grateful that God chose to put us together as a family.

CONTENTS

Introduction   xi

Part I
GRACE AND SURRENDER
[THE CALLING OF TWO DISCIPLES]

1.1   3
See It
1.2   8
A Child, A Call, and Kiss Chase
1.3   11
The Devil's Playground
1.4   15
Falling in Love with God
1.5   19
Awakened Curiosity (Shawn)
1.6   22
Blessed Victim
1.7   24
The Breakup
1.8   28
A Tool of Satan
1.9   33
Sidebar on Dating
1.10   35
The Masked Seeker (Shawn)
1.11   37
That Pizza-by-Candlelight Night
1.12   40
Adam and Eve Ain't Got No Grandpa
1.13   42
Vow of Devotion
1.14   46
The Honeymoon is Over
1.15   51
Surprise
1.16   55
Ministry Success, Marriage Failure
1.17   61
You Do not Belong Here
1.18   66
The Frog and the Wicked Witch

1.19   68
Vortex (Shawn)

1.20   70
A Blue and White Checkered Couch

1.21   75
Lack

1.22   78
Jesus is Better Than a Pork Chop

Part II

THE ON-GOING PROCESS OF SURRENDER
[LETTING GO AND LETTING GOD]

2.1   83
The Genesis Narrative

2.2   87
By Design

2.3   90
No One Studies for a Marriage License

2.4   93
Regret

2.5   95
Love Fills Lack

2.6   99
Lord and Lover

2.7   103
Why Are You Driving Like That, Jesus?

2.8   106
Imaginary Arrows in Hand

2.9   110
Drawing Straws

2.10   112
When God Moves Through You to Move in You (Shawn)

2.11   115
Contentment (Shawn)

2.12   116
An Apology and a Prayer

2.13   118
Yuck

2.14   122
Confession

2.15   125
Redemption is a Broken Leg (Shawn)

2.16   128
Healing Takes Time

2.17   131
A Little Sparrow

2.18   136
Disappointed and Heartsick
2.19   140
Hope Is Not Lost
2.20   143
The Call of the Surrendered
2.21   147
Sometimes You Are the Answer (Shawn)

Part III

CROSSING BRIDGES AND BUILDING
[THE MAKING OF TWO DISCIPLES]

3.1   151
Bridges
3.2   155
Growing as a Disciple
3.3   158
Ralph Lauren Romance
3.4   164
Today, Life on the Other Side
3.5   166
God Speaks, We Echo
3.6   171
Build with God
3.7   174
Ask for What You Want

Part IV

TRANSFORMATION
[DEVELOPING NEW EVERYTHING]

4.1   181
Son of God/A New Man
4.2   186
Remember (Shawn)
4.3   189
Here I Am (Shawn)
4.4   193
Here I Am: Continual Counsel (Shawn)
4.5   196
I Do Not Know (Shawn)
4.6   199
Hold Fast to Her (Shawn)
4.7   203
Love Well
4.8   207
Daughter of God/A New Woman

4.9 210
Daughter Defined

4.10 216
God Did not Tell Adam to Name Eve

4.11 218
My BFF

4.12 220
Change Your Mind, Girl

4.13 222
Jesus and Women

4.14 227
Entrusted

4.15 230
His Art Exhibit

4.16 234
Honor

Part V

PASSING IT ON
[DISCIPLES MAKE DISCIPLES]

5.1 243
A, B, C—1, 2, 3

5.2 246
Storytime

5.3 251
Choices

5.4 254
Required Reading

5.5 260
He Does not Hide His Face

5.6 261
The Voice of God

5.7 264
Their Faith Journey, Not Yours

5.8 270
God-Confidence and Rejection

5.9 276
Community Blessings

5.10 282
Community Challenges

5.11 287
Discerning Spiritual Authority

5.12 289
Friends and Family

5.13 291
Homeschool

5.14   295
Sleepovers
5.15   298
Co-Mission
5.16   304
Covered
5.17   308
Let's Talk Sex
5.18   313
Our Hope

Notes   315

INTRODUCTION

Welcome!

It is a privilege to share our story with you. It's a story worth telling because it testifies to God's goodness, His faithfulness, and His restorative power. God took two broken, selfish people on the verge of divorce (who happened to be in ministry most of their adult lives) and made them one to reflect His restorative power and love. It is the story of how God faithfully brought to fruition a type of family He desires—one which produces Godly offspring.

Redemption, reconciliation, and restoration are beautiful things.

Why This Book?

My husband and I are often complimented on our children and asked how we have raised such good kids. My first response is always, "We are blessed. We know we are blessed. We have good kids, but Jesus made all the difference." Then the person normally proceeds to ask, "But, how? What did y'all do?"

The answer: We surrendered to God's grace and became disciples of Jesus Christ. How God parents us is how we parent our children. We do our best to treat our children like God treats us, utilizing everything God has taught us throughout our lives to love and lead our children well. We partner with God in parenting our children.

This book reveals a large portion of the process of "how" we did this and why.

How to Read This Book

The first part of this book tells the journey of a God who picked two people, Shawn and me (Nichole), to be His disciples. It is the story of His enduring faithfulness, even when we are unfaithful, and how He never let us go. In the second part, we share how we processed surrender, letting go, and letting God take over control of everything. Thirdly, we reveal what it was like for us to learn to live a new way developing new mentalities and new habits by becoming not just a follower but a disciple of Jesus Christ. Crossing over spiritual and relational bridges led us to find a good life on the other side.

It is often said, "It's 10,000 times more important what God does in you than what He does through you." In the fourth part of this book, we walk you through individual core changes Shawn and I underwent (in us), which led to the transformation of our family unit (through us).

And lastly, we share how God's impact on our lives directly impacted how we raised our children. We cannot write about all of them in one book, so we have shared what we have found to be fundamental in raising our children to be the offspring of the Lord. We share some of the strategies God gave us in parenting our children: Autumn Brook, Tyler, Linzee Joy, and Josiah. Our kids are evidence of God's richest goodness and blessing upon our lives.

Woven throughout is an eclectic composition of how Shawn and I became disciples of Jesus Christ. It is because we are disciples of Jesus Christ that we can even write this book. Jesus made the difference in our individual lives, marriage, and children. Our interactions with God, through prayer, are often written in a conversational format. (No, we do not hear an audible voice.) But we hope that you grasp just how engaged God desires to be in your day-to-day family life by hearing how active He is in ours. (Feel free to interpret the conversational format as you wish.)

Most of the book was written by me in first-person. Specific chapters and inserts which Shawn penned are identified by his name noted in parentheses and italic. If I inserted into a chapter Shawn wrote, my name is in parentheses.

Throughout this book, we share from a humble sense of "this is what we did" rather than "this is what you should do." We share insight—what we learned from the Holy Spirit (in God's Word) to do —as we became a family filled with heritage and Hope.

Again, I want you to understand we are not saying what we did is the only way to do things or that our way is right. We are simply sharing the insight we received from the Lord and how we applied it practically. We did not always do things well. We had success and failure. But we persevered in love with purpose, and today our whole family lives in the promises, pursuit, and purposes of God.

We hope you find inspiration, encouragement, and empowerment on the pages. Our prayer is that God transforms and blesses you and your family as He has ours. We pray He takes your big family mess (if you have one) and redeems and restores the mess out of it.

In Him,

Nichole and Shawn

PART I

GRACE AND SURRENDER

[THE CALLING OF TWO DISCIPLES]

"The thief comes only to steal and kill and destroy;
I have come that they may have life and have it to the full."
~John 10:10, Jesus

God does not let go. He never let go.
He is steadfast.
He fights for His sons and daughters.
His grace is ample.
Life in Him, abundant.
We, His two disciples, attest this is true.

1.1

SEE IT

Raising Godly children and building a God-honoring home is a cooperative effort. It is a joint mission between God and man. As a parent, you possess the privilege of partnering with the God of the universe in raising part of the human race. You have the ability not only to influence your child's life but also to impact people beyond your reach through the life of your child.

Let that sink in. How daunting! Yet, how exciting. As a parent, you have an opportunity to disciple a person for Jesus. From the moment they arrive on Earth, you are graced with a chance to affect nations by raising the one God entrusts to you. In the 21st century, it may seem impossible to produce children who love God. It may feel over-whelming to raise men and women who reflect His attributes. Let me assure you it is not impossible—for we work alongside *God*.

You can raise God-honoring kids. It is possible to have a Godly marriage and home. It is! You can build a family which carries and exemplifies a message of Hope. God desires this, and I believe you want this, or at least you want to desire this; otherwise, you would not sacrifice time and invest energy into reading this book.

Repellent

I yearned for this. I longed to honor God by building a family who would know His Name, honor Him, and love Him. To raise men and women who know they do not ever have to hide from God. People who understand they can run to Jesus no matter their failure or struggle. A group of disciples who delight in time with God and His Word. I wanted a peaceful home. A dwelling where everyone, with all their strengths and weaknesses in Christ, would be accepted and celebrated. A Godly, wonderful home.

However, I did not always wish for this. As a child, I witnessed the damaging effects divorce heaped on close friends. Disillusionment arose as I recognized that some marriages just exist as hollow shells. Some couples stay together just "for the kids." People settle. Some are discontent but too lazy to do anything about their relationship. Others simply cannot financially afford to split up. I witnessed marriages with no noticeable joy or life-giving force within their union. People were physically together, yet their souls appeared to be worlds apart.

For me, the many marital failures I observed served as a repellent. I often thought, "Why marry and be miserable? Why have kids when they are such a burden?" Nope. Not for me. Who wants misery? Not this girl!

Something to Believe In

In my mid-teens, something changed all that, or rather Someone. During prayer, God sparked and established a desire and hope for a Godly family inside of me. It is simply remarkable what spending time in the presence of God and His Word will do. The transformation that begins the second you encounter God's love is astonishing. The Dream Giver gave me an incredible dream to hope in and strive for.

Little pictures formed in my thoughts during prayer and tugged at my teenage heart. Images appeared of a family honoring God and one another. A community of loving and accepting people who know the privilege of their intimate relationships with each other. A home filled with people rooted in God's love and liberty.

Tiny glimpses invaded my mind. What I saw was foreign to me, yet so familiar. It felt like God's love. Pictures of His love, His grace, and His unity displayed through, well, people. Just the way He intended it to be. Not perfect, but peaceful. Not without flaw, but faithful. This dream may seem idealistic, but a natural order was taking place within me.

In His presence, I experienced love from the Creator of the world; I was alive in Him, and He awakened His will in me. Whereas the division, disunity, and dissatisfaction I saw in most marriages repelled me from wanting a family, what I saw in these divine peeks into a Godly family compelled me. Love drove me to want to build my people, reach out and love them, and teach my future children to do the same.

I wanted this then, and several decades later, I have it! But now, I hope for this to continue for my adult children as they marry and expand the family. I desire this for my grandchildren and all our descendants to come. And I want this for you!

Community That Expresses Divinity

Marriage and parenting are an effort of eternal effect for which I am passionate. Why? Because having a Godly family is like having a piece of Heaven on earth. And it is a powerful way to declare the Hope of Heaven on earth. God designed His people to carry His image. Each one contributes to reflect His glory through our collective diversity—a couple and their children: Community that expresses Divinity.

Maybe you want this but aren't sure *why* you want this. You desire to build a God-honoring home with a loving marriage and Godly children. I ask you, "What is your why?" Maybe you cannot pinpoint a time when this desire dropped in your heart from the Heavens or have a teenage tale like I do but allow me to suggest that the God of the universe placed this desire in you. People do not just naturally desire to build a Godly home. God breathes this within you. If you have even an inkling of this hope, God is already at work in your heart and home. Exciting, isn't it?!

It is important to recognize God is birthing something in you. Maybe He's giving you a new vision and hope for your future family and home, or perhaps He is reawakening a shelved hope in you while you are right smack dab in the middle of family dysfunction. When He gives you vision for a Godly home, His Spirit reminds you He is with you; you are not alone in this. He is sharing His heart with you. He is stirring in you to honor Him and bring to pass what He desires: Godly offspring for His glory. This is why we know having a Godly family is possible; it is His will for us. It is in Him and through Him a Godly family is born. Without Him, it cannot be made.[1]

No matter whom you have come from or what you have walked through, God desires you to have a Godly, loving family even more than you do. This is your "why"! It is our why!

Can You See It

As a teenager, I envisioned the family God forecasted for me. I saw a small community marked by love, unity, discipleship, building, honor, hospitality, generosity, compassion-led missional living, peace, and Hope. A family alive in Christ, living in His Kingdom Culture, very much a part of this world, yet passing through on a communal journey learning to love God and people as we roam Home.

Can you see it? Can you see this for your family? I could see it then, and we live it now. But it was quite the journey of crossing over and getting to where we are today. Our family's pilgrimage to become a Godly family is filled with

> default and design,
> lack and love,
> hope deferred and promise fulfilled,
> resistance and surrender,
> half-heartedness and intention,
> failing and victory,
> hypocrisy and sincerity,
> pride and humility,
> offense and forgiveness,
> lies and truth,
> idolatry and lordship,
> sickness and health,
> cursing and blessing,
> and disappointment and dreams.

Welcome to our story! The good and the bad. The hallelujahs and some hell. Sorrow and joy. One giant mess redeemed and restored into one Message of Hope. It begins very much like God started all our stories in Genesis:

with a man and a woman,
a boy and a girl,
Shawn and Nichole,
two individuals who became one in One.

1.2

A CHILD, A CALL, AND KISS CHASE

Before there was an us, there was a little girl and a little boy. Before our marriage existed and our four beautiful children were born into this world, there simply was Shawn and me. Individuals born to entirely different families who experienced distinct upbringings.

We all enter this world from the womb. With a bit of help from Mom and a few helpful attendants, we break down our first barrier to enter a new season of life, wide-eyed and curious, little sponges soaking up every sight, smell, and sound around us.

We are launched full of lack and need. We cannot survive without someone to hold us, feed us, change us, protect us, teach us, and love us. We are at the mercy of who, how, and what others want to invest in us. (How our caretakers choose to love us and what they decide to impart to us.) The dream of who we are lies dormant, waiting to be breathed upon, nurtured, and released by someone.

We are vulnerable, unable to contribute to the choices these caretakers make and how they will impact and mark us for a lifetime—mere recipients to the culmination of their choices. That is, until one day, we grow up and make our own choices and then become a choice-rendering caretaker for another. But first, we begin as a baby. Then we become a child.

. . .

My Childhood (Nichole)

Although the feeling of loneliness has attempted to be my companion since I was a little girl, I've always known I am not alone; God is with me. One of the strongest influential factors in my life is the sober awareness of God's near existence, which permeates my earliest memories. As crazy as it may seem, I remember being in a crib experiencing the presence of God and just talking with Jesus. As a little child, my mentality of worship and what a relationship with God is, was shaped as I sensed His presence, His listening ear, and His voice. He captivated my toddler thoughts.

Over four decades later, I realize I did not understand what an amazing prayer life I had as a small child. I practiced His presence. I spoke and sang to Jesus often. I knew Jesus to be kind, loving, and so very compassionate.

I was birthed to a young couple who did not know the Lord. However, as a little girl, I remember attending mass with my mother at the Catholic church down the street just a few blocks from our house. I found solace in the silence of the church and appreciated the beauty of the stained-glass windows. The ambiance was sacred, holy, and peaceful. However, I did not understand why we stood up and knelt so much during mass. It made my knees hurt, and I wondered how the old ladies could tolerate all that kneeling. And why in the world were handkerchiefs on their head? It is funny what you remember.

Around the time I was four years old, my father encountered Jesus Christ. I could see the effect of the power of Christ upon his countenance. His face looked different. I visibly saw what an encounter with Jesus does. Jesus makes a difference.

Kids detect things differently than adults; I could sense and see change. Good changes began to take place in our whole family. We attended a charismatic Spirit-filled church where worship included dance. God was present, and I was joyful. The beauty of being in a place where I could freely experience and express my love for God (with others) was not lost on this little girl. It was magnificent.

A Mission of Compassion

At five years old, I sat on a box and spoke with Jesus as I admired His handiwork in some rose bushes. During our conversation, God conveyed His desire to find the *runaways*. It seemed God was displeased because some people—who claimed to know Him—represented Him poorly. He isn't at all like they said He was. What they told the runaways drove them even further away from Him. He seemed to miss the runaways.

He was sharing with me the heart of what we often refer to as "The Great Commission."[1] The mission is to seek and save the lost. To introduce people to Jesus, teach them His ways, and tell them He is in love with them and wants them home with Him. To tell of His goodness and how He desires for all people to live in His love and liberty.

As I was chatting with God, my two-year-old little sister, Danielle, walked up and sat with me on the box. We just sat there a while looking at the roses as I pondered what the Lord was speaking to me. Then Miss Angelle, the old Cajun lady next door, laughed a wicked laugh out her window to scare my sister; she found joy in scaring my sister. Danielle took off running and screaming. Even though my sister was slightly traumatized, it is one of my best memories. God engaged, interrupting my thoughts with His on an ordinary summer day.

Kiss Chase

About a year later, I found myself learning more about worship during recess in a schoolyard. I was playing Kiss Chase. That's a game where a boy chases a girl and gets a kiss if he catches her. Well, it happened. A boy caught me. God whispered to me, "Just because he caught you does not mean he deserves your kiss." I thought, "I must reserve my attention and affection for those worthy." The One worthy! So, instead of kissing him, I just turned a cheek to him. In my enlightened six-year-old mind, I knew that not everything that captures you for a moment is worthy of your attention, affection, or adoration. The One who is steadfast, faithful, constant, and captivated with you, He deserves not only your attention but all that you are.

Those childhood years were a good season full of joy, peace, and learning. Prayer—an ongoing conversation with God—was as normal as breathing. I was living the most abundant life a little girl can live in Christ. However, it quickly came to an end.

1.3

THE DEVIL'S PLAYGROUND

I do not know exactly what happened, but I'm sure it's like what happens to most people before they leave "the church." Somebody got hurt over someone else's sin and became unwilling to continue gathering with their Christian brothers and sisters. Whatever it was, unforgiveness and bitterness set in. Our family no longer attended church, and negative changes occurred. From my perspective, our home began to be ruled by apathy, complacency, compromise, and bitterness.

This was the beginning of a spiritual and emotional downward spiral for me. God's image became distorted as adults used God's laws and rules to modify (through fear) my behavior. There was an acknowledgment of God and a form of godliness, but God's transforming power seemed lost.

Like so many families who experience offense, unforgiveness became a force of hindrance in our family's faith journey. My impression of God and church changed; both became undesirable. I perceived God as judgmental, critical, and just plain mean.

Unresolved Offense is The Devil's Playground
The power of unresolved offense has terrible effects on families, churches, and communities; therefore, contributing ill effects on the

children within these groups. An unforgiven offense is an invitation for an enemy attack. It isolates a person and their family, leaving them vulnerable prey in dangerous territory. If not appropriately dealt with, unforgiveness promotes bitterness, discouragement, and division— grieving the Holy Spirit. It is dreadful how the enemy works through hurts and wounds to destroy the people of God!

Ephesians 4 reminds us to

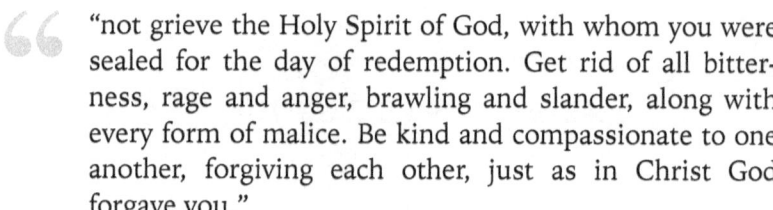

> "not grieve the Holy Spirit of God, with whom you were sealed for the day of redemption. Get rid of all bitterness, rage and anger, brawling and slander, along with every form of malice. Be kind and compassionate to one another, forgiving each other, just as in Christ God forgave you."

This instruction sounds wonderful when it means someone else must forgive me and be kind and tenderhearted toward me. When I am the one who should forgive and be kind, this Scripture isn't quite as palatable.

As a little girl, I learned that when we grip offense and are stingy with forgiveness, we look nothing like God's children. But when we forgive (and reconcile as much as possible), people can see Him in us. Jesus confirmed this in John 13:35. He states, "By this everyone will know that you are My disciples, if you love one another." When love is absent between God's people, it is impossible to see Jesus. His image will become distorted; it did in this girl.

Swings

Fast forward a few years. I remember an unusual breeze blew the rusting swings back and forth on a hot, humid day in south Louisiana. Focusing on my elementary teacher's voice was impossible. Like whimpering puppies, the swings begged me to play. I wanted to go outside and swing. High and free, reaching the heavens. But I was forbidden. "You may not swing anymore," my parents prohibited.

Blisters were the culprit for such a rule. The rubber seat of the swing had caused welts and bubbles to form on my thighs. I did not care; the feeling of flying overpowered any pain on my backside. I wanted to taste the cotton candy clouds in the sky.

Finally, my teacher quit talking, and Field Day began. Monkey bars, tug-of-war, races, and ribbons for first place all set the stage for possibly the most fantastic day ever. Life was good.

Eyeballing the swing set, I decided I could obey my parents while still obtaining the thrill I sought. I would lay on my stomach on the swing seat and spin until the chains could twirl no more, then let go and helicopter. I may not touch the skies, but I could feel the thrill of free-floating. I would not sit to swing; my blisters would not be irritated, but I could still have fun and be obedient. So, that's what I did, a few times, and it was fun.

Soon "monkey-see-monkey-do" ensued. My friends copied me. As I let go and began to whirl, the girl beside me did as well. Thunk! Our two heads collided only to catapult me in the opposite direction. Instantly, I felt a sober awareness and thickness in my brain. Then, bang! My teeth vibrated. I hit the steel pole of the swing set. Nausea and dizziness set in. I ceased helicoptering. I dizzy-walked in uneasy silence to my classroom and found a table where I could lay my head.

A fellow student slammed his hand on the table, jarring me awake. My eyes began to swell. When my teacher arrived, I tried to tell her what had occurred. She refused to listen. Hours later, someone called my mother to come to pick me up. When she arrived, she found me lying on the floor in the office area. (According to her, she let the staff know she was upset and what she thought.)

Later that day, I found myself in a hospital; I had a concussion. After the doctor finished examining me and left the room, someone reminded me about the consequences people face from God when they are disobedient; if something terrible happens to you, you must be rebellious or lack faith.

I was perplexed because I had not disobeyed. I did not swing and irritate the blisters. Was not that the intention of the rule? I was conflicted with what this person said: God was punishing me. I thought God should know what was in my mind and heart. I assumed He chose to punish me unfairly.

A Distorted Image Develops

God was cruel. I decided I did not want to serve this God. It was not the first time I thought God was cruel. This one event did not cause such a resolute opinion in my young self. According to people in authority over me, God punishes people every time they do something He, their parents, teachers, or leaders disapprove of. I began to believe God was the culprit of the many punishments I faced and why bad things happened to people.

Pleasing God seemed unattainable. I imagined a condescending God sitting on His high throne looking down on me, ready to pop me with a big stick if I did not do things just right. Or possibly, He would rain hail fire down on me, depending on His mood that day.

Someone suggested that when we sin, it's like this: If we are in a room with Jesus, He will leave the room when we disobey. Jesus must hide His face from us. Consequently, I imagined Jesus turning His eyes from me when I sinned because He could not be around unholiness. So, I developed a picture of Jesus suffering on the cross, bleeding for me, yet looking down on me with shame and frustration, having to turn His head and look away from me on a regular basis. After all, my sin nailed Him up there, and well, it was keeping Him on the cross.

I also thought God was cruel because He wouldn't fix whatever the issue was at church so we could get back to His house. How callous it was to dangle joy and allow me to experience church community, only to take it away! Being in God's house felt as natural to me as breathing. And, if I was in His house, I should be pleasing to Him and not get in so much trouble. Feeling disconnected, I grieved and simply did not understand.

1.4

FALLING IN LOVE WITH GOD

It may sound strange to you that a kid would have such deep thoughts about God, church, and spiritual things. Children are way more aware, perceptive, and thoughtful than we give them credit.

By eleven years old, I wanted to die; depression had set in. For various reasons, my spirit was crushed. Now, my life could have been far worse. I had a roof over my head, food on the table, and clothes on my back. I was not regularly physically or sexually abused. I was not living homeless on the streets. I lacked gratitude for the provision my parents provided. My physical needs were met, and that's a good thing. However, I struggled greatly spiritually and emotionally.

My soul lacked joy. My conversations with Jesus were nearly absent. Complaints, criticism, rules, and restrictions set the tone of my day. School, teachers, homework, watching tv, and bed for 8:00 pm each night were monotonous activities that filled my time. Children were to be seen and not heard. Women were to stay at home and not work outside the home. Submit to the man as the head of the household. Go to sleep, wake up, and repeat. Go to sleep, wake up, and repeat. Go to sleep, wake up, and repeat.

Mundane routine can be just as murderous as religion to the souls of people God created to be free.

Now that I'm older, I understand why people want to plop on the couch after working all day. Many times, I've done this. You're exhausted. I know why a working parent just wants a little silence at the end of a long day. Yet, children do not understand this; they want connectedness. I also understand why rigid routines form in families. Sometimes it's out of the sheer hope of survival in accomplishing everything on the schedule. However, children need the flexibility to breathe, play, and experience life, or the stiff system may crush their very soul.

Idolatry and Rebellion

Then in a blink, I was a teenager. I dabbled in the occult and eventually ran away, only to be picked up by the cops and brought right back to my parents' home the very same day. There is no other reason for running away and causing such a ruckus except for the chains of internal confinement I felt. It's like I could not breathe. I just needed to do something different, go somewhere—anywhere—and stop the pointless empty routines.

My heart longed for more than what I was experiencing. The Jesus I knew as a little girl was a faded memory. I knew God existed, but He just did not seem powerful. A gaping hole in my soul left me exposed to the elements around me. Vulnerable prey, I felt naked inside. This was a rough time. I did not doubt God's existence; I doubted His goodness and power. My view of God was perverse.

I was in a constant state of confusion, frustration, and depression. Around this time, I had a sobering moment during a crisis. In last-effort fashion, I cried out for the Hope I had lost. I called out to Jesus. I said, "Jesus, if you are the Jesus I knew as a small child, do not let me go." I hoped (with all my heart) that the hazy memories of who I perceived Jesus to be were true.

A Divine Encounter with Jesus

A couple of years later, my uncle Marty, who had encountered Jesus, brought me to church. I listened to the youth pastor preach. During the closing altar call, the pastor invited people to commit to Christ. I walked up to the front of the sanctuary and bowed my knee to God, humbly acknowledging His power and sovereignty; but I did not open my heart to Him. I was angry with God, or rather, with who I thought God was.

I had been pushing this distorted, fake, man-imagined God away for years, but God was not willing to allow this to continue any longer. The more I continued to push, the more the *real* God's presence permeated every aspect of my life.

An unexplainable compulsion inside me to read the Word sprouted from my inner being. I began to read the Bible for hours a day. Months later, I opened my heart back up to Jesus and prayed a prayer of surrender, acknowledging Him as my Savior. Quickly, I was made even more aware of the fact that He had never left me; I was never lost or abandoned by Him.

Memories of God intervening in situations and circumstances flooded my brain. I realized how He had pursued me my whole life. I viewed my life differently. I looked different. I knew God was with me, but I was confused about who He is. My journey with Jesus continued as I began to pursue Him more fervently. He did not let go. He never lets go.

He's Not Letting Go

God never lets go!

When you realize (when you really get it) that God has, is, and will always be by your side—well, that's a game-changer. He is present even when you feel lost, abandoned, confused, are grieving, or rebellious. Whether you understand who He is or not, the real God is with you.

This revelation opened my eyes to His abundant grace. God's presence is with me through joyous moments and hellish hours. Through my questioning and wandering. Through my anger and frustration. I cannot escape Him. Through distortion and despair, He is there.

And He does not love me more than He loves you. You may feel lost, but He knows right where you are. He sees and hears you!

He never lets go.
He never lets go.
Oh! How He never lets us go.

Self-Feeding

Even though my relationship with Jesus was rekindled, over the next couple of teenage years, I was punished from church for months at a time for various reasons. It was clear that I would mostly be on my own in my faith journey. Sometimes you must walk with God alone to walk with Him. You must "set your face like a flint"[1] and determine to pursue God's ways and trust Him.

No one celebrated or sought to help me in my walk with the Lord, but God worked it for my good. I learned to seek God by self-feeding on the Word of God; the Holy Spirit taught me to be a seeker.

Alone in Community

Every person's journey with God is individual yet simultaneously communal. You walk with God alone, but the community you are in affects you as well. You are alone yet always with others. Close community will either push you toward God or become a possible hindrance. God alone is faithful to draw you toward Himself.

To sum it up, the more I sought to know the God of the Bible, the more my affection grew for Him. I was ending my childhood and falling in love with God.

AWAKENED CURIOSITY (SHAWN)

My childhood is marked by the constant waiting for the "bottom to fall out." Like many, I am part of a divorced upbringing.

The Bible gives a clear description of what happens during a divorce. Malachi 2:16 warns that one who divorces does violence to the one he should protect. Divorce is violent; it is the dismembering of "one flesh." Destruction, division, and damage ooze from it and create despondency in the heart of a child. The chaos, physical and verbal abuse, and strife resulting from divorce within our family produced confusion, wounds, and internal conflict within me.

I bounced between two homes as a little boy, never feeling like I had a home. I was a weekend visitor at my dad's house; my mother had primary custody. Both of my parents tried to make the home "home." Yet I did not feel like an integral part of either new family unit; therefore, I did not feel like I belonged.

During the economic crash of the '80s, my mother and stepfather liquidated their assets and purchased a yacht. We lived on the water for several years and traveled to amazing destinations. To onlookers, we appeared to be a well-put-together family. We presented a prosperous image. We were a family of affluence, yet we were not thriving. It was a mixed bag. On display was considerable marketplace success, but substantial relational failures existed behind the scenes.

When a family has two faces —one which people outside the home see and one which people inside the home experience—it can create unhealthy things in a child's heart. I developed a defense mechanism to protect myself from the unpleasantness and abuse around me. I learned to hide the reality of what happened inside my heart and home.

I learned to be careful about what I said and did. Other family members were under incredible stress, and I did not want to be a burden. I felt a sense of responsibility and obligation to be okay, not bother others, and be a peacemaker. The anxiety and weight of performing so I'd appear to be doing well laid the tracks of an inevitable emotional train wreck to come.

A "boys will be boys" mentality was the norm in both homes. I was exposed to (and chose to expose myself to) inappropriate things. In a household mostly made up of boys, carnality was run-of-the-mill. No one ever mentioned God's design regarding sexuality; I do not know if it even was a thought.

Thankfully, my dad's house offered needed connection time. My father often took my siblings and me on camping trips and vacations. My father was a grounding force for me. He gave me an example of a nurturing and loving father. For most of my young life, my father was not a Christ-follower; however, my dad provided a moral compass in many ways. He taught me right from wrong and that a man should say what he means and mean what he says. He demonstrated that a man should work hard and be productive. Yet his house was not my home. The effects of divorce still prevailed.

From both sets of parents, I learned a strong work ethic; they worked incredibly hard. They taught me to bring my best self forward, which shaped my life tremendously.

To sum up this part of my childhood, I learned to take the good with the bad. It's all mixed; I have beautiful memories and unhappy ones. Good and evil coexist; this was my understanding of the way of life.

Traveling Evangelists

A defining moment where I felt a stirring inside of me for God occurred during an old-school revival crusade. Some of my family and I (just under ten years of age) attended a service where a traveling evangelist, R. W. Schambach, a Word of Faith minister, preached loud and on purpose. This was my first experience in a Pentecostal atmosphere. It was very different from Catholicism, my childhood religion.

A curiosity awakened in me, and I began to wonder about it all. Days after the meeting, my aunt and uncle visited my mom's side of the family. They spoke of things unfamiliar to me: the End Times, Jesus' Second Coming, and divine healing. I was fascinated. I took the information they gave me and began questioning my teachers at Catechism, a class where we learned the principles of the

Catholic religion. I wanted to know how it all worked. I no longer could grasp why we prayed to Mary or the Saints when we could pray to God.

My brother Todd encountered Jesus and "got saved" a few years later. I remember being sick and Todd "laying hands" on me to pray for healing. It surprised and shocked me that someone would lay hands on someone and pray for them. My curiosity of God continued to expand. Did He heal people? Were we able to have more significant interaction with God than just in a Sunday mass?

I understood God was the Creator of everything; He was good and judged bad people. And if you were good, you got into Heaven. But the implications of new things I was discovering made me wonder if there was more to God. I was intrigued.

A short time later, Todd invited my dad and our family to attend a service where another traveling evangelist, Jesse Duplantis, was scheduled to minister. We were all curious about the changes we saw in Todd, so we attended this powerful service. That night my dad decided to follow Christ.

We had an encounter with God, we had religion, and we possessed a moral compass of sorts. Now, we would add more of God to the equation. Some things changed, but not all things.

Sixteen

I was around sixteen years of age when I decided to surrender my life to Christ and attempt to walk out my faith. I clearly understood salvation, yet carnality and Christianity remained intertwined. I discovered more about God, but the depth of my sin and exposure to sin remained a force for reckoning. God forgave me, I made some changes, but there was much more in me God needed to transform.

At seventeen, I decided to break up with my girlfriend Nichole and attend a discipleship school to learn more about an intriguing God and His curious ways.

1.6

BLESSED VICTIM

Ah, other people's choices affect us all. How they live their lives impacts us. What our caregivers taught or did not teach us about God, ourselves, relationships, and life in general, frames our perspective and perception on just about everything.

The personal experiences you have when you are young impact your mentality, soul, and heart whether you want them to or not. At some level, we are all blessed, and we are all victims.

Blessed. We are all blessed to some degree. There is breath in our lungs. We are alive! God imagined us and sent us to be a gift to this world. We have good, privileged experiences. For many of us, people did the best they could for us, or at least they tried hard. What a blessing!

Victim. I do not even like to type that word out—it makes me feel blah! But we are all victims to some degree. People did things to us, we saw something our little eyes should not have seen, or we heard something our little ears should not have heard. Each of us has been hurt at some point by someone somewhere—a victim.

Cherish the blessings of life you received as a child. Hold on to them. Build upon the blessings and thank God for them. They strengthened and shaped a large part of who you are. But you must also acknowledge and deal with the "victim lessons" you learned. They will continue to govern your life well into adulthood if you do not.

They will haunt you, invading and controlling your thoughts, emotions, and choices. That is, until you say, "Enough!"

This is what Shawn and I experienced. It would be a decade into our relationship before we said, "Enough!" and believed and reached for something beyond what we had known and experienced.

1.7

THE BREAKUP

Shawn and I met in high school. When we first met, I thought he was much younger than me. What a babyface! Then one Friday night it happened: I noticed him. He arrived at a youth event. He seemed so full of God; he had just come from sharing his faith with people in town. The boldness he possessed and the anointing on his life hooked me; the anointing is an attractive thing.

I caught his eye too. He noticed how I worshiped unhindered during worship, and he liked that. He also was partial to the miniskirt I wore. We laugh today about which one he noticed first.

Our first typical teenage date was great. We went roller skating, ate cheeseburgers, and shared our first kiss at an echo chamber. We continued dating, attending church (when I was allowed), and participating in outreaches together for about two years. We had fun. We also had several breakups, which were not so fun.

Captivated by Shawn's Heart

The more I grew to know Shawn, the more his heart for his future children captivated me. We shared similar hopes for our kids. We desired to raise our children to know and love the Lord for who He is. We longed for them to live free in Christ. We did not want them to experience the bad things done to us or by us. And we definitely did not want them living in the effects of divorce or a miserable home. We wanted to propel our children to Jesus—not hinder them. Both of us had a vision of what it could be like to raise kids filled with heritage and Hope.

One night while leaning on the trunk of his car, Shawn shared his sixteen-year-old heart with me about this vision. He shared his experiences as a child living between two houses while lacking a home. (I knew he was not trying just to connect and tell me what I wanted to hear because he shared his heart before I ever shared mine.) What Shawn hoped for was important to me, and this heart in him was one of the things which made me love him and want to build a life with him. Also, he was bold and seemed confident. He was ambitious and a great communicator. He was compassionate to people even when he thought no one was watching. And bonus, he is a great kisser!

Breaking Up is Hard to Do

Sitting in his green Honda Accord, Shawn broke up with me to attend an eleven-month intensive discipleship school. Dating was not permitted while he was in this program, so breaking up was required. He felt this was what the Lord wanted him to do. He would give a year to the Lord free from distractions.

By biblical standards, our dating relationship was not perfect; we did not honor God at every point in our dating venture. We were both young in the Lord and needed discipleship, guidance, and personal discipline. We did have fun together and cared for each other. Even when we were on break, we often talked as friends. But now he was breaking up with me yet requesting I not date anyone for that year (if I believed we were to marry each other in the future).

Part of me was happy and admired His determination to pursue God. Another aspect of me felt sad and frustrated. But how could I argue with his reasoning? Who in her right mind would tell someone he is selfish, and it is a bad idea to pursue God in this full-hearted manner? I encouraged him to do what he believed the Lord wanted him to do. I surely did not want to discourage him from all God has for him.

I was heavy-hearted as I laid down to sleep that night, so I poured out my heart to Jesus. Afterward, the peace of God enveloped me and confirmed that Shawn's decision was right for him. But what about me? What should I be doing? Shawn put our relationship on the back burner, but he encouraged me to keep it a priority in my personal, relational decisions. Just weeks before this breakup, we discussed eventually marrying, yet at that moment, I was in limbo—suspended in an unexpected season.

Over the next few days, I sought the Lord. I felt increasingly challenged to draw nearer to God—urged to continue surrendering anything I thought or hoped for in my future. Prayers and confessions of faith I made to God as a small child circled in my thoughts. I had promised God everything. What I do and do not do—including my relationships.

My. Whole. Life.

I Give You Everything

Prayer is a powerful thing. Sometimes when we pray, we say things we do not understand. We pray bold things.

> God, use me for Your glory.
> Help me be more like You.
> Reveal Yourself to me.
> Be everything to me.
> Give me favor.
> Influence others through me.
> Use me.
> Be all I need.
> I give You everything.

Well, God does not let our words fall to the ground, no matter how old we are when we pray them.

I meant the prayers I prayed as a child. They are possibly some of the purest prayers I've ever prayed. I just did not realize where the answers to those prayers would take me.

I have learned that the purest prayers produce profound results.

God answers bold prayers. But the answer often comes through our self-denial and actual giving over of everything to God:

each relationship,

each desire,
each success, each failure,
what and how we use the gifts He has given us,
our offenses, our joy, our anger,
what we hold on to, what we let go of,
what work we do,
where we live,
and everything in between.

Daily surrendering what is to come or not to come. It is not mine to call the shots in my life; it is God's. Shawn and I broke up. I was single.

1.8

A TOOL OF SATAN

This year of singleness was particularly tough on me but extremely precious. God did a profound work in my heart and began dealing with the wrong mentalities I acquired throughout my childhood. It was an intensive spiritual boot camp just for me. And boy, did I need it! I was clueless about how much my upbringing and experiences affected my mentality and choices. You only know what you know. And I did not know what I did not know.

God shook things in me. He began tearing down the distorted images and views I had of Him. He challenged me to read His Word and what He said about Himself, urging me to quit believing the lies others taught. (It is sad how adults twist God's Word to modify behavior in kids or their congregation.) Over the next few months, the Holy Spirit taught me to worship from my depths and to pray over my future family and for the nations.

I removed Shawn from the equation in my mind and pursued God. I lived life as a single individual, building relationships with friends, obtaining a job, and attending church when I was allowed. I lived entirely in my season of life. I did not date anyone because there was simply no one I wanted to date.

I drew near to God, finding and embracing new freedoms in Christ. During this season, God increased my hunger for Him. I would pray for hours a day and search and memorize Scriptures. My friends and I would hold prayer meetings late into the night. Witnessing to others about God's grace was common.

I do not write all this to boast on myself; it was God. God pursued me. He put a fire inside of me to burn for Him. My understanding and love for God grew tremendously during that defining year of singleness.

A Distracting Demon

During this year, Shawn and I saw each other at church and had an occasional, quick conversation. Our communication was restricted due to the rules of the program. At one point, I was brought into an office by his leadership and told that Satan was using me to distract him. "Nichole, you are a tool of Satan in his life," is what the leader stated. At that point, I barely even saw or spoke with Shawn. I was confused.

Those words crushed and angered me. It was very frustrating; however, I did not want to make any waves, especially with pastors. After all, I thought they knew more about God and His ways than I did. Who was I to challenge them? (I now know leadership was out of line, but I did not know that then.)

Satan planted a lie in my mind and heart during this interaction. Shawn was worthy of discipleship; I was a distracting demon. I know this is extreme, but it's how I felt. I felt the church leadership was cruel to me. Those distorted images of God I developed when I was a child tried to resurrect themselves in my mind because of their careless words.

The struggle was real. On the one hand, the Word would go forth from the pulpit from this leadership, challenging and encouraging me to live for Jesus and change the world. On the other hand, behind the scenes, it felt like church leadership did not want me around.

The real "tool of Satan" is division. When a house is divided—when members of the body of Christ separate from each other—it is an obvious sign evil is at work for its purposes.

Words—A Divisive Weapon

For many years, "Nichole, you are a tool of Satan in his life" were words I allowed to speak louder than God's Word in my life. Long after they were said, those utterances affected me and our marriage.

However, words spoken over you should never trump what God's Word declares. Words are powerful. Proverbs 18:21 states, "Words kill; words give life; they're either poison or fruit— you choose" (MSG).

I am the one who chose to believe them even though I forgave the leadership for saying such a thing, which I know makes no sense. If I forgave, it means I knew what they said was wrong. However, just because your mind knows something is wrong does not mean it hasn't taken root in your heart and soul. I chose to let those words have life. I should have aborted them the moment they hit my hearing. I wish I had.

I'm not sure why we hand so much power over to other people, allowing them to define who we are. It puzzles me. What is it in the human heart which provokes us to believe lies over truth? Why do we find it so easy to believe bad things instead of good things?

When I talked to Jesus about it, He encouraged me to trust Him and what His Word said about me. Nevertheless, I began to battle with intimidation more. I thought I was so far behind (spiritually) I would drag Shawn down if we got back together. When I talked to Jesus, He would negate what the church leaders stated and often reinforce that I would marry Shawn and be a gift in his life. A gift—not a force of evil.

But how could I be a gift? According to church leadership, my very presence distracted him so much he could not grow in God. After all, he was allowed to speak to other girls, just not me. So, my perception became that it was not about a season free from dating and distractions in general—it was a season free from me, Nichole.

In the Pulpit and the Pew

Let there be no confusion. Church leadership is a good thing. My husband and I served in vocational ministry for over two decades. (We spent half of those years in leadership roles in a local church.) I've been on both sides: the pulpit and the pew.

It's a good thing to have people speaking into your life for counsel, guidance, encouragement, correction, and edification. People hold key God-given lead roles in the body of Christ. However, it is the body of Christ, and Christ is the head of this beautiful body. His Word trumps everyone else's. We can and should honor our leaders and submit to one another as we serve God's purposes. However, when a leader's words contradict God's, we must give precedence to God's Word. Leaders make mistakes; I know I have. Leaders learn as they go, just like everyone else; we all make mistakes.

The sad reality is that most of us have not read or diligently studied God's Word, so we take what our leaders say as Gospel Truth. When a leader's words are not in alignment with God's Word, this can be a significant stumbling block for a person young in faith. Therefore, it is of utmost importance we follow the wisdom of Scripture and "Be energetic in your life of salvation, reverent and sensitive before God. That energy is God's energy, an energy deep within you, God Himself willing and working at what will give Him the most pleasure" (Philippians 2:12b-13 MSG).

People are not God; they do not always speak the truth. And unfortunately, they do not always have your best interest at heart. You must work it out yourself. It's *your* faith journey. Learn and love His truth. Meditate on it and live in it, no matter what anyone else tells you.

The mishandling of me in that situation caused great conflict within me. Sadly, I began to understand how offense and unforgiveness toward church leadership could grip your heart and hinder you if you allow it to. I just kept talking to Jesus about it. And I reminded myself the same people who caused this grief are the same people God used to speak life into me as well. Ironic, isn't it?!

Words Kill or Give Life—You Choose

I want to stress that Shawn's year in discipleship school was crucial. Our whole family has drawn from what God did in and through Shawn in that time. The leadership over this program influenced, impacted, and still impacts our family in more good ways than we could explain. At the time, these pastors were young in leadership. They said and did ridiculous things like Shawn and I have done in ministry and life. It does not mean it's okay or right, but it is forgivable.

Forgiveness isn't saying, "It's okay." Forgiveness means it's not okay; it acknowledges a wrong. At one time, I believed to forgive meant to forget and act as if something never occurred, but this is not even logical. God forgives us, but the evidence and consequences of our good or bad choices and actions remain. Now, God does work things out for our good once we align ourselves to His ways, yet the consequences of stupid choices remain.

I knew the cost of holding on to unforgiveness and bitterness toward church leaders and members. I understood what the inability to let go, love, and forgive people could do. I decided to forgive, let it go, and move on. People make mistakes and say stupid-donkey stuff. This incident would not keep me from the house of God or my eternal community. I am so thankful that in Christ we do not have to remain offended.

1.9

SIDEBAR ON DATING

This whole offense came from the "no dating" policy of the discipleship program Shawn attended. After much reflection, the season of abstaining from dating was a blessing and beneficial. It's wise for young people to wait to date until they can sustain a serious relationship with someone. It protects people. So much emotional damage could be avoided by simply not prematurely engaging someone in a relationship. However, the presentation of this policy and accusations by leaders were disadvantageous for me and planted weed seed in my soul, which would later grow tall in our marriage.

Overall, that year was a good thing for both of us. There was hurt, but there was incredible growth. We shouldn't overlook the good in a hard season—eat the fish, spit out the bones.

What God did in and through me is astounding, and it has informed and formed part of the foundation of our family. There was so much good! I do not want that to get lost as you read through the not-so-good. We have included the yuck because the not-so-good things sometimes frame your life as much as or even more than the good.

Learn from the Good and the Bad

Sometimes you learn what to do from others. Sometimes you learn what not to do.

Both are valuable.
Both are guiding resources.
—Just learn.

My understanding of God increased through this time, but I had far from an accurate perception of myself in Christ. I also lacked understanding in the Church Institution's role in relationships.

It is *this* person who continued a relationship with Shawn. A woman seeking Jesus fiercely, growing in the Word and understanding of God's character. Also, a woman with meager self-love. A woman who gave way too much control over to others. An intimidated girl who felt lucky to possibly marry someone more spiritual than herself.

How you enter a relationship matters. When two become one, each person's experiences, upbringing, and mentalities affect the relationship. I brought all the good and not-so-good into my relationship with Shawn.

1.10

THE MASKED SEEKER (SHAWN)

Throughout this year of single focus, I grew in my understanding of the Word of God. Daily, I immersed myself in His Word: memorizing hundreds of Scriptures, reading through the whole Bible, and listening to Bible teaching. Godly people spoke into my life on a regular, welcomed basis. I had the privilege of preaching, continuing to witness to the lost, and traveling to other countries to proclaim the Good News of Jesus Christ. I grew in God. I realized a significant call existed on my life (and the life of each follower of Jesus Christ).

The Word of God was powerful to me in this season, yet I struggled with all the spiritual, mental, and emotional junk I inherited while growing up. The truth is I needed desperately to deal with all the effects of dysfunction and brokenness. Instead, I defaulted to the learned techniques of my childhood. I got good at looking like I was doing well. Nobody could see I had an inability to deal with the intense impairment inside of me. I continued masking what was inside while I sought God.

How could a seventeen-year-old even understand the depths of deficiencies he possesses, much less articulate them? Besides, the leaders of the program I attended were pastors and youth leaders, not psychologists or psychiatrists.

What this single-focus year of pressing into God did the most was set a hook in me. It planted the good seed of faith in God and His power. I knew I was not good; God is good. I began to understand He is powerful to deliver if you let Him.

What I did not give enough attention was the seriousness of the enemy's plan.

In John 10:10, Jesus revealed, "The thief comes only to steal and kill and destroy; I have come that they may have life, and have it to the full." I was beginning to understand God desired me to walk in "more"—His abundant life. I just did not fully appreciate the depth of destruction the enemy can wreak on you when you do not deal with your sin. When you just add more God to dysfunction, the enemy will exploit your vulnerabilities. I became good at being "good."

It was this person that continued a relationship with Nichole. A young man full of the Word of God, who believed in the power of God. But a man who gave little attention to the giants lurking inside him.

How you enter a relationship matters. When two become one, each person's experiences, upbringing, and mentalities affect the relationship. I brought all the good and not-so-good in me as I continued my relationship with Nichole.

THAT PIZZA-BY-CANDLELIGHT NIGHT

Graduation finally arrived. We made it! The night Shawn graduated from the discipleship program we began dating again. It was our new first date. Shawn booked a clubhouse. We ate pizza, danced, and talked. It was wonderful. We were a couple again.

During this night, Shawn presented me with a gift God would later use to impact our future more than we could ever know: three simple roses.

When Shawn presented flowers to me that pizza-by-candlelight night, he expressed several beautiful things. He described how two white roses and one red rose represented the Trinity: God the Father, the Holy Spirit, and the Son. In thoughtful detail he illustrated how the two white roses represented us and the red one represented Jesus. Shawn spoke about how Jesus makes all the difference. Us three together would be a cord not so easily broken.

We danced and did a little kissing. Okay, maybe a lot of kissing.

Things Were Different in the '90s

Whenever a person comes out of a discipleship school like the one Shawn attended, it is sometimes difficult for them to jump into the rhythms of family life and work. Shawn spent a year having people schedule his prayer time, teach Him about the Lord, and continuously challenge him to do amazing things. He lived in a community 24/7 with people who shared the same goal of passionately pursuing God.

As Shawn grew bolder in his faith and more confident in his actions, he became ministry minded. He began looking at things from a *working in a church* point of view. His goal was to be a youth pastor; I would be a youth pastor's wife if we married.

Some things are very different today than they were in the early nineties. Back then there was a definite pastor-wife mold within the affiliation we were involved in that one felt they must fit. I was super excited about ministry in whatever capacity the Lord would bring; however, being a pastor's wife came with a set of challenges for me.

One of the points Shawn discussed with me was how I dressed. It would have to change if we were to marry and work in a church. The question was, "Would I be willing to change the way I dressed?" I was also encouraged to keep my testimony more general and toned down because people might not understand the supernatural spiritual "stuff." Authenticity and individuality were not quite as celebrated then as it sometimes is now.

Even though parts of me were being deconstructed due to denominational preferences, I leaned on others' wisdom. Maybe they were right. I was young and had not attended church regularly. Who was I to argue with this? After all, clothes do not define a person.

These requests may make Shawn sound terrible, but he did not mean it unkindly. He was young and trying to figure things out too. We both wanted to be in ministry, so there were some outward things he felt I could tweak. The focus was on the outside, the presentation of things, which people looked most at in the church. Mostly, he followed the example, encouragement, and instruction of church leadership.

The '90s "freaky-style" was how I dressed. I looked different than most of the youth pastor wives we knew. My childhood does have a few supernatural elements some people may struggle with, question, or simply not believe to be true. So the requests sort of made sense.

I loved Jesus intensely, yet I did not love myself. I thought Shawn was this spiritual giant, and I was lucky to be his wife. I felt like God would allow me to marry him even though I was a distraction, a tool of Satan, and not worthy of discipleship. So I changed my dress and altered how I shared my testimony. I had not been discipled by a person, so who was I to question?

Looking back, I reeked with insecurities and intimidation, yet I had a solid heart to serve the people of God in His house. The calling and cause were more important than my comfort.

Our Engagement

A few days later, we were engaged. Our two-month engagement period was intense. Right after Shawn graduated, he secured a job as a youth pastor with the understanding he would marry quickly. The church's pastor was not keen on hiring a single youth pastor, so it was a mad dash to the altar. We were great with that; we were eager to marry.

We asked our pastors if we should attend marriage counseling before the wedding. They said no because it was enough that Shawn completed the discipleship program. This is where I wish I could go back in time and slap someone and shake myself for receiving and adhering to this instruction. We absolutely needed pre-marriage counseling. You just do not know what you do not know when you just do not know.

Looking back, I now see that church leaders planted many seeds in the garden of our lives. I did not realize how much Church leaders were entwined with our relationship until I wrote this book. The good seeds sprouted and produced good fruit; the bad seeds grew into weeds in our relationship. (And let's not forget the good seeds and the weed seeds planted in each of us when we were children.)

1.12

ADAM AND EVE AIN'T GOT NO GRANDPA

Interestingly, unlike Adam and Eve, each of us possesses a past filled with people. Think about it: Adam ain't got no Grandpa. Eve ain't got no Grandma. They didn't have parents or church leaders investing in or influencing their lives. But we do.

God plants seed into the fabric of a child. But parents, others in the community, and culture also plant seed into a child's mind and heart. We all had childhood connections and interactions. Experiences of our youth provided opportunities to explore and learn. Words spoken over us and to us planted "death and life" within us. Our observations and engagements contributed to memory-making and our perceived essence. Today, all of these combined inform and guide us. They advise our choices, what we do and do not do, our mentality, and even what we put up with from others. All the good and bad seeds integrate into one person—you.

A child is mainly at the mercy of those placed in authority over him; he cannot control the seed deposited into his soul. The seed grows together until a child grows up and begins to care for his life-garden. What people place in us affects us as we grow up, but it does not define us or determine our choices! The weed seed placed in you as a child may affect you tremendously because it is powerful, but it does not have the right to choke out your life. You can learn to weed the garden of your soul and heart.

Interestingly, Adam and Eve did not have a past filled with death words, violating experiences, or rejection. Things were GOOD for them. Their story teaches us that someone does not always make bad choices because of bad experiences.

There comes a point where you cannot blame your upbringing for your choices. I'm sure Adam and Eve would have condemned their mom and dad, grandma and grandpa, or leadership for their choices if they could. After all, they blamed everyone else possible when they made poor choices: each other, the snake, and God. But they could not blame their ancestors because they did not have a past; all they experienced was good.

The circumstances of your youth may influence you for many years; however, YOU get to decide what affects you today and in the future. As a Christ-follower, you are powerful, filled with the Spirit of God; you have the privilege of choosing a new life—a new way, a new everything. You have the power to choose how you allow another's choices to carry over and into the heritage you decide to leave your descendants.

1.13

VOW OF DEVOTION

On September 28, 1991, we married. We were followers of Christ, lovers of each other, and hopeful for our children. Three of us as one: Jesus, Shawn, and me.

Much was good, but we did not have it all together. We were Christians with problems. We were aware of some of the problems, but we did not acknowledge or address them. Others, we were oblivious to. We believed in Jesus. We knew we were sinners who needed a Savior. We thought just knowing Jesus and "being saved" could fix anything and everything. But we quickly found out we were wrong.

As our relationship continued, amazing and adverse things grew; weed seed camouflaged amongst the good seed. And that, my friend, is a paradox of life in Christ. God allows both seeds to develop and produce until He decides to deal with one of them, and we surrender our will and deal with it too.[1]

It seems like the moment—the exact moment—we said, "I do," weeds started sprouting faster than the fruit-bearing plants. Growing faster, wilder, and higher, the weeds began choking out the good buds of our life. The effects of our childhood journeys began colliding, and right from the start we learned that just knowing about Jesus and "being saved" does not fix everything.

. . .

Vows

When two Christians marry, they often pronounce their love for Christ and pledge their love to each other. They commit to love each other through sickness and health. A vow of devotion professed before God and proclaimed before family and friends encompasses words of allegiance, admiration, and adoration. They pledge faithfulness to God and one another, no matter what the unknown days ahead hold. Entering a covenant relationship of eternal value and influence, they commit to forsake all others and cherish only each other as they cling to Christ.

Each believes in Jesus. Each believes in the other. Their faith, coupled with their fellowship, fuels the smiles as they approach the future bright-eyed and dreamy, eager for the honeymoon. They have an electric expectancy for that night and anticipation for the future. Visions of growing old together occupy their minds. The two of them, hand in hand, standing against the difficulties and stresses hurled at them, as a team—as one.

I imagine most Christian couples anticipate difficult seasons occurring. After all, we state this reality during the marriage ceremony. We declare we will be devoted to one another while dealing with sickness and poor times. Yet when we make these vows, I do not think we fully appreciate how difficult certain circumstances and seasons will be.

Failing

Typically, what is not expected is that one or both of you will face a crisis of faith—a crossroads in life where one of you decides to take the road leading away from Christ. A time where Jesus is no longer the center of one spouse's life, nor is He the One in whom he/she seeks counsel. It's a season where someone embraces selfishness over solidarity and sacrifice. Poor choices are made, leaving the marriage and family heartsick and broken.

A place where no one is holding hands or standing together. Instead, each is left fending for themselves and, at times, standing against each other—fighting and barely surviving. A couple full of lack and untapped potential. Failing as a couple, as parents, and life in general.

This failing place is where Shawn and I were just a few years into our marriage—experiencing lots of failing.

Many of us find ourselves in this place. We wake up one day to discover we are not fulfilling our dreams because we are failing in our relationship with God and others. We cannot even seem to love the person standing right before us who we say we love.

Hater

1 John 4:20 says, "Whoever claims to love God yet hates a brother or sister is a liar. For whoever does not love their brother and sister, whom they have seen, cannot love God, whom they have not seen." The Greek translation *hate* in this Scripture means hate, detest, love less, and esteem less. If you want your marriage to fail, hate your spouse. Esteem and love them less than yourself. That's a guarantee for failure right there.

When I think about times when I place myself before Shawn, I do not like using the word hate to describe my actions; it seems like such a strong word. However, whether I like it or not, I must wrestle with this. With our words and actions, we build or tear down. We speak life or death. We encourage or discourage. We love or we hate.

Philippians 2:3-4 gives us wisdom. "Do nothing out of selfish ambition or vain conceit. Rather, in humility value others above yourselves, not looking to your own interests but each of you to the interests of the others."

Scripture reveals we can do this. Philippians 2:5-8 says,

"Think of yourselves the way Christ Jesus thought of Himself. He had equal status with God but did not think so much of Himself that He had to cling to the advantages of that status no matter what. Not at all. When the time came, He set aside the privileges of deity and took on the status of a slave, became human! Having become human, He stayed human. It was an incredibly humbling process. He did not claim special privileges. Instead, He lived a selfless, obedient life and then died a selfless, obedient death—and the worst kind of death at that—a crucifixion" (MSG).

Our marriage was filled with hate just a few years in. Maybe you find yourself in this situation right now. If you want a healthier marriage, begin by preferring your spouse. Honor your spouse above yourself by considering him/her and taking care of the things which concern him/her. Support and actively encourage him/her. Think highly of him/her. Jesus humbled Himself, even when He has rights to everything. If He can humble Himself, He will empower us to humble ourselves and love another.

What is common to all of us is that we all fail. Every single one of us! We may fail in different ways and degrees, but it's part of the relational experience, as noted in our wedding vows. No one escapes it. No one. You are not perfect, nor is your spouse.

Hate plagued our earlier marriage years. But how did we get there? How did we go from vows of devotion to indifference and hatred? Well, the weeds took over.

1.14

THE HONEYMOON IS OVER

Our first year of marriage was fantastic. We got along with each other. We worked and had enough money to pay bills plus some. That's a blessing for any young married couple. Can I get an "Amen!"?

The few arguments we did engage in centered around interactions with his former leadership and my inability to communicate. Some things were just out of whack, and it caused several issues in our relationship. Still, overall, it was a good year.

Through a series of unfortunate events, Shawn quit his youth pastor job toward the end of our first year of marriage. The youth group was going exceptionally well. Our students were growing in relationship with the Lord and quantity. However, lead staff changes at the church contributed to his decision to resign. It was a good learning experience. The whole church honored us on our last Sunday; it was a good departure with no bridges burned.

Shawn began work in the security department of a local hospital while I worked at our home church for the children's pastor. It was a good season in our marriage. Several months later, I felt a stirring in prayer. A transition was approaching. God spoke the words "Lake Charles" to me one afternoon. "Lake Charles? What's in Lake Charles?" I wondered. A few days later, we received a phone call which resulted in us working in a group home for boys right outside of Lake Charles, Louisiana.

Shawn and I worked side by side managing a group home for most of the next three years. We had up to twelve boys live with us at a time. (Over sixty boys lived with us within three years.) The boys ranged from the age of nine years old to eighteen. We were nineteen years old when we began working there. I'm not sure what possessed our employer to hire teenagers to parent these children and manage this home; however, I thank God he did.

This non-profit ministry opportunity was a privilege and blessing for us; we learned a tremendous amount. Our boss was and is an amazing Christian man we both admire. The job matured us in many areas, and our skills continued to develop. Giftings we did not even know we possessed surfaced and became strengths. The beautiful boys under our care blessed our lives. Our first daughter, Autumn Brook, was born during this time.

Lack of Community

It was during my pregnancy with Autumn I noticed a shift in Shawn. I did not know what started it or caused it. Looking back now, I realize the lack of Godly community and personal spiritual discipline was detrimental to both of us. Most of the people we worked with were Christians. We worked together and lived side by side on-site at this non-profit organization, but we did not live life together. The job schedule was very demanding, leaving little time off. We were so exhausted when we were off that Shawn slept most of the first day while I spent time with Autumn one on one. Then we would head to our hometown to spend time with friends and family. Shawn and I were rarely alone except for car rides.

Most of our community did not support our decision to work at this group home. They communicated that they strongly felt like Shawn was called to be a youth pastor in a church, so there was not much encouragement from them.

Some people did not feel like our daughter should be around "these kinds of boys." It's interesting because we were doing youth ministry. We were ministering to kids, some of which were orphans, who had never stepped into a church. We were on the front lines. Ministry was happening; it was just outside the church walls.

God did call us there; we know that. We obeyed. It was just weird not to have much support for our obedience from other Christians. We needed our community. It was a hard reality for me not to be part of a church community again. It felt like they abandoned us simply because we were not fulfilling their agenda. Even when we tried to communicate and ask for wisdom, friendly reminders that Shawn should be working in the church met our request.

God Knows What's Best

They say hindsight is 20/20. If that is true, then I know 100% we did not miss God by working at the home for boys, despite others who we deeply respect thinking we did.

When you do not receive the support or validation you expect from others, it causes you to question yourself and your motives. Questioning is good if you seek God for the answer. We did all the right things, such as seeking counsel from Godly advisors, parents, and Christian peers, as we decided on various ministry and marketplace opportunities. But for several assignments we embraced (including but not limited to working at the group home), some family and extended community met us with opposition. They said terrible things would happen—even going as far as to *prophecy* that one of our children would die if we took a particular ministry opportunity.

We have learned a few things:

- God knows best. Do what He has commissioned you to do.
- Seek godly counsel, listen to it, and then process it all in prayer. A different perspective may give insight and spare you from something awful. Yet, you must pray about what is said because sometimes even Godly people will allow their agenda to cloud their advice.
- If you submit yourself to God and trust His ways, there are times things do not make sense. He may lead you to places you feel unequipped for, but His presence will go before you and lead you every step of the way.
- Guard your mind and heart against fear. When people you respect use fear to discourage you, it can produce anxiety. Fear may attempt to grab hold of you, even if you obey

God's will. Pray for the peace of God to fill your heart as you trust Him with your life. Then just do whatever He asks you to do scared; peace will come.

- Sometimes, God takes people out of vocational church ministry, whose job is to "equip the saints to be ministry ready," and places them outside of church employment to be light in dark places and be ministry ready (available) themselves.

Do what God has designed for you to do! You can trust Him. Obey God even if you lack cheerleaders to cheer you on.

Lack of Disciplines

We were affected by a decline in our prayer lives and personal Bible study time, a demanding work schedule, a new baby, exhaustion, and lack of discipline. We were ministering daily to everyone around us, but we were not allowing God to minister to us.

That shifting I mentioned in Shawn concerned me, but honestly, focusing on myself was about all I could handle. We just could not connect spiritually. We worked well together. Shawn and I parented Autumn and the boys at the group home well together. We were excellent employees, yet we could not study the Bible, pray, or talk about the Word together. We did pray a small prayer together every night before going to sleep, but we did not *pray* together.

I began to be frustrated with Shawn. I thought, "Aren't men supposed to lead their families spiritually? Where is the spiritual giant I married?" I needed him to be full of God so I could pick some *fruit* off him. I was submitting and depending on Shawn for my God-nourishment. It just was not there.

It was during this time I noticed he had a wandering eye. I harassed him about it. I somewhat justified it because he is a guy, and do not all guys do this? Boys will be boys, even Christian ones.

You might be thinking that maybe the people in our lives were right and that we should have stayed working in the church. Perhaps these things would not have happened. I know I thought this then, but I do not believe that now. It is false. What is in a person will come out no matter where they work. It may camouflage better in different places, but it's still lurking. You are with you wherever you go. Location does not change who you are. Where you go, there you will be, and there will everything in you be—you cannot escape yourself.

1.15

SURPRISE

When we discontinued working at the group home for boys, we returned to our hometown. Shawn worked in construction; I worked as an office manager. We started attending our home church again. The weeds of our life suddenly looked like trees; our marriage began deteriorating.

This was when life and marriage became downright difficult. Really hard!

I unexpectedly became pregnant with our second child, Tyler. I wanted another child, just not at that moment because I knew our marriage was getting weaker by the day. When I told Shawn we were expecting, he said, "Congratulations." Then he just walked out of the room. I felt very lonely and depressed. I thought God was crazy to trust us with another young life; this kid deserved better. These feelings would last most of the pregnancy—I cried and prayed a lot during this pregnancy. [1]

Little Gift

God has used my son Tyler from the moment I found out he was in my womb until now to be my constant teacher. Profound revelations have entered my life because of his life.

He teaches me to look beyond what I see and believe. My capacity to love increased with his life. And the revelation to be "unapologetically who you are created to be" became foundational in my life through him. He reminds me that imagination is a tremendous gift to the body of Christ, which is sometimes underutilized. He reminds me of God's goodness and mercy. Tyler is a gift.

At times God bewilders me. He intrigues me. I think to myself, "What a curious God we have." He trusts flawed ridiculous humans with other humans. Seriously, what is He thinking?

Right in the middle of our deepest dysfunction of marriage, God said, "Here is Tyler, a second gift." Why? Why does God trust humans with other humans? I do not know, but I'm sure glad He entrusted us with ours.

Tyler entered the world.

What is Happening

Instead of attending church, Shawn went clubbing and drinking with family and friends. He was inattentive and neglectful. Nearly every night of the week, my husband kept himself busy. Yet Shawn was an exceptional dad for Autumn and Tyler. Each night he helped tuck them in and sang over them. (That absolutely must be mentioned here.)

Shawn would sing part of the song *Casual Christian* to Autumn and Tyler. The lyrics, "I don't wanna be, I don't wanna be a casual Christian. I don't wanna live, I don't wanna live a lukewarm life. 'Cause I wanna light up the night with an everlasting light. I don't wanna live a casual Christian life," rang out each night in our home.[2]

One night after he finished tucking the kids in bed, I asked Shawn if he wanted me to divorce him. There was silence. I wondered to myself, "What is happening?"

This life of contradiction just went on.

A Surprise Job

A few months later while I watched Shawn play softball, someone told me about a job opportunity at our area homeless shelter. The Lord spoke to me, saying Shawn should work at the shelter. It was like

God was sitting next to me on the bench. I thought this *conversation* was strange. Part of me imagined the Lord was angry with me. My marriage was a disaster, and my relationship with God felt strained. Yet He was speaking something very specific to me. So later that night I told Shawn about it.

Out of the Blue

God just shows up. SURPRISE! You are suddenly aware of His presence, and He whispers to you.

About thirty years ago, I read *The Practice of the Presence of God* —a collection of letters and recorded conversations with Brother Lawrence, a monk. This book reminds me to practice being aware of God's presence and goodness in everyday life. To exercise this, I quiet and direct myself to God, asking Him to make me aware of Him, what He is doing, and what He wants me to see and learn. Other times, God awakens me to His presence and His desires.

Sometimes—surprise! God interrupts your day-to-day with the extraordinary whisper, direction, feeling, and awareness. Listen to Him in these times, even if what He tells you does not make sense at first.

I have had incredible moments during corporate worship and prayer, but my favorite are these everyday encounters with God. They remind me that at one time God walked amongst us. He came down and took on the form of a man, becoming present in everyday life for His people to witness. And today He still walks among us or maybe sits beside us on a bench at a softball game.

Through various events, Shawn was offered a job at the homeless shelter. I also became employed at the same organization. It was an amazing time of learning, growing, and doing vocational ministry again. I wish I could find the words to convey to you how important it is to obey God even when you do not feel up to the task at hand.

Why in the world would God put us in ministry when we seemed so far from Him? Shawn was doing his own thing. I was still seeking God, but it felt strained. My desperate prayers consisted of asking God to keep me, not let me go, and help me. Sometimes the prayer was just, "Help me breathe." And I was so tired—just exhausted.

. . .

Breathe

Just the movement of air has life power.
Breathe in—breathe out—repeat.
God's very breath is in you.
There is life in you.
Do not discount this powerful force.
In.
Out.
Repeat.

Maybe all you feel you can do today is breathe, then, breathe.

MINISTRY SUCCESS, MARRIAGE FAILURE

God continued allowing us the privilege of serving people. He ministered through us even though our marriage was falling apart.

Shawn had great success at the shelter. A news article praised him for the success of a program he created to help people in recovery find jobs. Jesus transformed people's lives, and Shawn was instrumental in the changes. I also was doing well (at work), learning new skills and developing and strengthening ones I had. I regularly ministered to people. The non-profit arena was a good fit for us. Some of my greatest God moments happened in this season.

I hope you got what you just read. One of our marriage's weakest, most vulnerable seasons contained some of the greatest God-moments I've experienced. We saw people change because of Jesus. We saw people in poverty proclaim God's goodness. I learned a great deal, but that's for another book. What I want you to *hear* is God is faithful even when we are not. 2 Timothy 2:13 is true, "if we are faithless, He remains faithful." God still worked *through* us. He also attempted to work *in* us. However, we continued self-destructing even as God ministered through us to build others.

It may seem like we were hypocrites. I've thought and prayed about that. However, we were not telling people to do what we were not doing. We were just jacked up and trying to figure things out. We proclaimed Jesus and His Good News (hope to the hopeless) while desperately trying to figure out how to allow the power of Truth to keep transforming our lives.

Jesus referred to some of the Pharisees as hypocrites. What's interesting is the Pharisees were committed to the law they taught. Jesus acknowledged this. However, they were not dedicated to the heart of God's Word. Things like compassion, love for others, justice, and mercy escaped them. That's what Jesus called a hypocrite.

I was clinging to Jesus while in chaos. Shawn and I both knew He is the Way, the Truth, and the Life. To keep Good News (hope) from another, even if we were in sin or failing, seemed cruel and uncompassionate. After all, it was not God's failure that we kept making foolish choices and could not get our crap together. It was our failure, my failure. Not God's. So two sinners proclaimed what we knew to be true to others, even if we had a hard time allowing that truth to continue transforming our lives.

Love Covers a Multitude of Sin

By no means am I able to, or trying to, justify living a life of *hypocrisy*. It is good to walk the walk and talk the talk. Absolutely! Things are just not always so nice and tidy when you are trying to walk with God. People (including myself) make assumptions about who is worthy of being called, qualified, and acceptable to be "in ministry" to be "used by God." However, God's ways are not our ways. Why God chooses who He does when He does for what He does is beyond my understanding.

His Word says, "I will have mercy on whom I will have mercy, and I will have compassion on whom I will have compassion" (Exodus 33:19). ~ God

Jonah

Sometimes we forget about the outright screw-ups in the Bible. I am specifically speaking about people God worked through for His purposes. People like Jonah or the self-ambitious preachers that Paul and Timothy spoke about. Hello! Remember the whole nation of Israel?

In chapters one through three of Jonah, God commissioned Jonah to go to Nineveh, a great city that did much evil in the sight of the LORD. But Jonah responded with a big, "Nope!" and attempted to flee the Lord's presence.

After being humbled in the smelly belly of a big fish, Jonah became fish barf. Jonah obeyed (hopefully after taking a bath) and went to Nineveh. It took three days to cross the city of Nineveh. Jonah went about one journey day into the city and preached. From the least to the greatest, the people of Nineveh repented, and God was merciful. Jonah became angry with God for having mercy on such wicked people. If you read chapter four in Jonah, you will discover Jonah cared more about one plant which provided him shade than he did about 120,000 people. What an uncompassionate man!

The point is God chose to use Jonah, a man of such sin—one who did not love his neighbor or enemy. In chapter two of Jonah, we learn Jonah knew God to be a God who hears the cries of those in the depths of sin. Jonah recognized that if you remember God, He remembers you. Jonah acknowledged the role self-denial plays in a life of a child of God. He cried to a living God who was steadfast in His love. He sought personal salvation in the Lord. Yet Jonah did not love people.

God still moved in and through him. Uncompassionate Jonah, who delayed in obedience because of his lack of love, was the man God decided to partner with in sparing and changing a city. God could have picked any human on the earth at the time, but He selected Jonah for a work He prepared for him to do.

Self-Promoting Priests

In Philippians chapter one, Paul describes people in ministry with pure and impure motives, enlightening us with his conclusion concerning them. Verses 15-21 state,

 "It's true that some here preach Christ because with me (Paul) out of the way, they think they'll step right into the spotlight. But the others do it with the best heart in the world. One group is motivated by pure love, knowing that I am here defending the Message, wanting to help. The others, now that I'm out of the picture, are merely greedy, hoping to get something out of it for themselves. Their motives are bad. They see me as their competition, and so the worse it goes for me, the better —they think—for them. So how am I to respond? I've decided that I really do not care about their motives, whether mixed, bad, or indifferent. Every time one of them opens his mouth, Christ is proclaimed, so I just cheer them on!" (MSG)

Paul and Timothy mentioned people who ministered who displayed ungodly traits: pride, self-ambition, self-promotion, greed, and competitiveness. Paul and Timothy's conclusion, "We cheer them on!"

Paul

Let's look at Paul. Paul was a Jew with Roman citizenship who studied the Law under Rabbi Gamaliel. He was a man of conviction who witnessed the stoning of Stephen (known as the first Christ-following martyr). As a man who ravaged the early church, Paul put male and female followers of Christ in prison. He persecuted Jesus.

God chose Paul.

Acts, beginning in chapter nine, tells the story of how Jesus chose Paul (known as Saul at the time) to be His chosen instrument to carry His name before Gentiles, kings, and the children of Israel. Jesus decided to transform Paul, and the persecutor became the one persecuted. The one who set out to destroy the early church became one of the greatest builders of the Bride of Christ.

Israel

And let's not forget Israel—a group of people God chose to bless the world through by making His name known to and through them. In Isaiah 43:10, God tells the children of Israel, "You are my witnesses," declares the Lord, "and My servant whom I have chosen, that you may know and believe Me and understand that I am He. Before Me no god was formed, nor shall there be any after Me."

The people of Israel are one of the main subjects in many of the stories in the Bible. In these stories, we witness God's goodness and power. We also learn about actual living people. Real. Living. People. Sometimes when we read the Bible, we forget that the people we read about are made of flesh and blood. They dealt with significant failure and great success—the people God chose to minister to and through varied in degrees of sin and faithfulness.

What about people like Peter, who literally walked with Jesus and denied Him three times then died a martyr for Christ? And what about King David? He was an adulterer and murderer, yet he wrote about God and worshiped Him in authenticity. Not to mention Rahab, a prostitute who became a protector of God's messengers. And Noah, who got drunk yet built a boat which assisted in saving humanity.

God intentionally transformed these dysfunctional people as He fulfilled His purpose within and through them. He made them His servants, His sons, His daughters, and His witnesses. The ones He chose learned, understood, believed, and trusted that He is God. God worked through them, and they were part of His plan to preserve life and lead the world back to Him.

It's God's Choice

You should live what you preach; I'm not making a case that you shouldn't. But let's be honest. Especially if you are in leadership, you know no one except Jesus would ever preach the Gospel if we must wait until we have it all together.

Shawn and I had great sin, as well as great compassion for others, and we were "called." We just had to obey and be willing. God chooses who He wants, when He wants, to do what He wants to do through them. Who can know the mind of God? When you feel a prompting to share about Jesus, share; it does not matter if you have it all together or not. If you are waiting to be perfect, you'll be waiting your whole life. Your perfection does not define God's love for another human being, but you can withhold His love from someone because of your pride.

When you do not share the Good News with others because you aren't where you want to be, you glorify your lack of (perceived) perfection over God's grace and goodness. It's not about you. Let me repeat it for the people in the back, "It's not about you!" If He's trying to minister through you, then trust Him. Open your mouth and speak life to someone. Use your hands to serve someone. At least you'll be getting that right!

A Strange Time

So here we were serving people living with various difficulties: in addiction, in poverty, as homeless, and with mental illness with no medical care. Surrounded by need, we watched as God met the need. We struggled, but God worked through us to reveal Himself to others (and us) as we shared hope in Him.

It was a peculiar time—just strange.

YOU DO NOT BELONG HERE

Around this time, something shifted in Shawn and me. There is that word *shifting* again.

Shawn grew further and further away from pursuing God and our relationship. He was unkind. I became selfish. Temptation, loss of ministry, and betrayal entered our story.

I entered a season of clubbing and drinking. When I realized it was affecting my oldest daughter, Autumn, I stopped. There was a strong unction inside me that my child would know freedom and never taste the consequences of sin because of my life.

Autumn's Eyes

I remember the moment after Autumn was born. Swaddled tight to her nose, all I could see was her big dark eyes. I prayed in that sacred moment for God to burn her eyes into the fabric of my mind and heart so I would not forget. I thought to myself, "I will win and have victory because of her—for her." I did not want to hinder her walk with Jesus. God burned this within me.

When I saw the effect my foolish choices had on Autumn, a memory of her eyes peering up at me flashed through my mind. Also, I knew it was not profitable to go out and about to party, being careless with sobriety, nor did it please the Lord.

. . .

Do not Add Fuel to the Fire

During this foolish season, I did not want to turn from the Lord or be rebellious. I was exhausted and just wanted a carefree night. Also, I wanted to hang out with my husband. If that meant going out and drinking, then it's what I was going to do. (My motives do not justify my sin.)

Instead of having a carefree evening, I learned something: You will not win a spouse over by participating in the same sin they are committing. All you will do is fuel the sin and start a fire that will eventually burn you.

I've counseled several people who have confessed that they want to sin like their spouses have so that their spouses can feel like they do. If their spouses have cheated on them, they want to have an affair so that their spouses can feel the pain of betrayal. If their spouses live for themselves and neglect responsibility, they want to do this too, letting them worry about things for a change.

This irrational reasoning is a never-ending circle of destruction. If someone cheats on his/her spouse, he/she will not feel the same level of betrayal because he/she has already broken the pureness of the relationship. Just because you neglect responsibilities does not mean your spouse will pick up more responsibilities. If you continue this circle of destruction, more people will be impacted by your broken marriage. Also, there will be more consequences to deal with from lack of attention to matters.

When we do things like these, we take matters into our own hands. I know it's hard to trust God when your spouse is all over the place. It is hard! It is easier to try and do something. It's hard to be the recipient of unfair treatment. It is! So, what can we do?

Well, 1 Peter 3 encourages us to "in the same way" submit to our spouse so we may win them over. What does "in the same way" mean? You'll have to go back to 1 Peter 2:23 to understand what "in the same way" refers to. It suggests following Christ's example; He did not retaliate, made no threats, and "entrusted Himself to Him who judges justly."

What can we do to interrupt the circle of destruction? Entrust ourselves to God. Trust that He sees what you are dealing with and that He will deal with it! Be faithful to God. Do not play God in the situation. You are not God, and you very well may end up fueling fires you did not mean to, leaving your whole home in ashes.

Temptation

During this time, I faced another temptation. (Satan will always place someone, who seems better than what you have, before you.) A man I was attracted to was very kind to me. He told me all the right things. He appreciated my work efforts. I knew there was a potential danger with him, but I flirted and put the vibe out anyway.

I remember clearly how the Lord lovingly rebuked me one day while I was driving. I told God, "If you want me to stop pursuing this, you will have to remove him. My husband does not want me. And You will not change Shawn." The next day this guy quit his job because he was offered a job opportunity out of nowhere. Wow! I know the Lord removed him. I was relieved and angry all at the same time. I felt like Shawn could do what the hell he wanted to, but I could not.

I thought God was unfair, and I did not see the protection He provided. I was an ungrateful brat. Yet God used this situation to awaken me. Shawn did not seem to care, but God did. I began to seek the Lord a bit more. He began to speak to me more even though I was angry with Him. He would give me Scripture verses to write and encourage me; He pursued me way more than I pursued Him.

This very day as I type these words, those few months are marked as a crossroads in my mind. The best way to describe it is like a little cartoon where the devil is on one shoulder and an angel on the other, offering opposing paths. Then a bright light shines from the heavens as God speaks, shifting the scenario and changing everything.

During this time, I had Godly encounters, personal failures, God victories, frustrations, self-loathing, and moments of encouraging myself in the Lord and gaining new strength.

You Do not Belong Here

You cannot escape the "call" on your life. I remember when Shawn and I went to a club before I decided to stop participating in that foolishness. There were several people from our church there. One man walked up to me and said, "Why are you here?" We told him we were just out for the evening. He looked right at me and said, "You do not belong here."

I said, "Um, you are here." He said, "But *you* do not belong here." Then he looked at me with such a sad, disheartened, and disappointed face.

Those words affected me that night, and I remember them over twenty years later. When I asked the Lord about it, He reminded me that when He places a call on your life, it remains no matter where you go. Like Jonah, every person on the boat was affected by his behavior. Jonah caused other people problems because of his disobedient choice (Jonah 1).

The call remains. You have a choice to live it out well and bless others. You choose to bring goodness or withhold blessing, bringing good things or "bad" things upon others.

Children of Light

One of the Scriptures I kept as a focal point during this season was Ephesians 5:8-11. It states,

> "For you were once darkness, but now you are light in the Lord. Walk as children of light (for the fruit of the Spirit is in all goodness, righteousness, and truth), finding out what is acceptable to the Lord. And have no fellowship with the unfruitful works of darkness, but rather expose them."

At that time, people living in more *darkness* than *light*, who called themselves Christians, surrounded me. People leading ministry (around me) not only nurtured their sin, but they also boasted in it. Friends I had once looked to for Godly counsel encouraged me to have an affair; they had affairs.

Learn from Others

One of the most impactful moments of that season was when I watched a ministry leader lose his ministry because he would not repent of sexual immorality and pride. Part of my job was to record minutes for the meeting in which Godly people compassionately and graciously spoke to him, encouraging him to take a year-long paid sabbatical and rest, to receive counseling, and deal with his sin. Did you get that? PAID leave for a year! To my astonishment, he refused to yield. His behavior and choice shook me, and I awoke.

His peers were so gracious in confronting him; they wept before him, and still he refused to listen. He hurt many people. The pain on his wife's face was one of the most troubling things I've seen. It scared me. It motivated me to pray a specific prayer. I asked God to remove us from the leadership positions we were in before we hurt the people who looked up to us until we could live as people of light. I did not want to get so cold, callous, and selfish that I hurt people as this ministry leader did. I learned from him and his life.

Remember—She's Still Watching

Over and over, God reminded me of my children and how my actions would hinder or propel them toward Him. Every person will experience sin's effects, but I did not want to be the conduit by which my kids experienced it. That was more than my heart could bear.

As I mentioned before, I regularly reminded myself of Autumn's big brown eyes looking up at me moments after she was born that August day. "She is watching and absorbing everything you do and say, and she senses who you are in Christ." Right or wrong, this is how I began guarding my heart and choices.

1.18

THE FROG AND THE WICKED WITCH

It was also during this season (This season seems like a lifetime, doesn't it? But good times are coming, I promise!) that I became aware Shawn had crossed some physical boundaries with another woman. We considered separation, but we could not financially function apart; we needed both salaries to survive.

Shawn said he made a stupid mistake and promised it wouldn't happen again. I felt such loss; I felt robbed. Our first kiss was no longer his last first kiss. The fairy tale I hoped for was over; the Prince Charming I kissed on my wedding day was now a frog.

I was also self-righteous. After all, I did not continue to pursue an inappropriate relationship when I could have. However, I did not commit adultery because of God's intervention and because of Autumn and Tyler's influence in my life—not because of my vow to Shawn.

Echoes of the Past

Unfortunately, during that time, words of yesteryears began to echo strongly within me. I remembered what the church leaders said to me—over and over. I honestly thought some of Shawn's betrayal was my fault. After all, Shawn needed more than me. I obviously distracted him from God and could not give him what he wanted or needed. The church leaders' words haunted my heart. I was the tool Satan used to bring down this promising man of God.

Those tiny seeds of harsh words were now full grown and living in my head. It's hard for a wife to believe she is in the wrong marriage with the wrong man, especially if she is a Christian. And even more so when she thinks she is the cause of messing up the guy she married. I thought I probably was the cause somehow, someway for Shawn's lack. I also imagined Shawn thought his princess was a wicked witch in disguise. His discontentment with me and his life became a heavy disheartening weight strangling out the last breaths left in our relationship.

So many experiences played a role in the choices I made in that season: Scriptures, interactions in bars, divine deliverance by God from temptation, other leaders' failure and lack of repentance, Autumn and Tyler's watching eyes, betrayal, and echoes from the past were like bumper cars. God used them to bounce me around until He got me where I needed to be. I chose to forgive Shawn, and we committed to moving on.

1.19

VORTEX (SHAWN)

Modifying outer behavior is not the same as inner transformation through Jesus Christ. I, Shawn, was excellent at modifying my behavior and looking like I had it all together. However, as family life, work, and adult responsibilities began to rattle me, they forced what existed inside to surface. You cannot escape yourself. Lack of intentionality, authenticity, honesty, and vulnerability caught up with me.

I professed Christianity, and I trusted in Christ for salvation. Yet I was not allowing God to transform me and deal with the unhealthy appetites I fostered in me. Those appetites were growing as I fueled them. I had past offenses and hurt, and I had hurt people in the past. I did not know how to begin to deal with those things, and quite honestly, I did not want to. I continued to hide things.

It became second nature for me to outwardly put my best foot forward while still struggling within. Like my relationships growing up, the relationships in my young adult life seemed to be shallow. With the ones I should be most authentic —my wife, my kids, and the body of Christ, I could not. The truth is you can become a slave of your reputation to people and even the Church Institution and leadership. A slave to sin instead of Christ. There were more people with more expectations to disappoint if I dealt openly with my issues—well, rather my sin. "Issue" is a softer word for sin; I needed to deal with my sin.

If someone is new in the faith, people in the Christian community are often good with them being honest and authentic. But the further along you are in your journey with Christ, especially if you work within vocational ministry, the less these are appreciated. It's often okay to confess your struggle but confessing actual sin which entangles you and that you need deliverance from, well, that's another matter. Nobody actually wants that much genuineness. If you work in ministry, it could cost you your job.

The more I sinned, the more shame I had. The more shame, the more I sank into myself. Like a boat caught in a violent vortex (the kind you have seen in movies), I was pulled in and sucked beneath the "water." I felt like I was spinning round and round, dragged to the depths of despair. I was circling round and round, feeling the down-pull further and further.

I was undone.

A BLUE AND WHITE CHECKERED COUCH

Shawn and I moved on; I became pregnant with our third child, Linzee. Surprise! We used birth control, so we know God ordained her. I was happy about being pregnant. My second child, Tyler, who also took us by surprise, is such a gift. I knew although Shawn and I did not plan Linzee, she would be just as impressive as Tyler is because God planned her. I had joy immediately. Yet I had a concern. What would Shawn say?

I remember telling him the news a few days after I found out. He was happy; I was shocked. We had a fantastic family night that evening. We just sat in the living room watching the kids play. I felt happier than I had felt in years. It was such a good night.

The Lord instructed me to quit working outside the home during this pregnancy. After several months of disobedience, I finally obeyed. Shawn had already left employment at the homeless shelter and embarked on a new job opportunity.

What God did in me and through me throughout the time of this pregnancy is almost unbelievable. So much change occurred! One thing the Lord did was give me the heart to seek Him wholeheartedly. What did I want? I wanted Jesus. I always wanted Jesus. God showed me I was the biggest obstacle in my way to knowing Jesus more; not Shawn, but me. Not the lack at Church, but me. And not past words spoken; it was me.

God continued to deconstruct the faulty belief system which had developed in me. As I read the Word or studied something, He began showing me things throughout the text of the Word of God, specifically about women in the Bible.

Years before, I purposefully quit studying about women and wives in the Bible. The indoctrination I received regarding "women matters" was enough to last an eternity. What I did not know at the time was I received faulty doctrine. The teaching presented to me is very different from what God's Word teaches; I was astonished. God challenged me to believe what He said.

Believe God

Listen up! I challenge you to believe what God says above all else. If someone says something different from God's Word, even if they are your parents, a church leader, even your spouse, choose God's Word as your secure foundational belief system.

You may not understand why the ones who should love you the most do not. You may not understand why people say such nasty things. People may do their best but at times fail. And frankly, some people just suck at moments. You do not need to understand all the lies and why they did or did not do or say things for you to be whole and able to move on. You need to understand the truth—what God says about Himself and you! His Word makes you whole and enables you to move on and beyond.

I began to soak up the Word of God. God-confidence formed as I learned more about who I am as a daughter of God, believer, woman, wife, mother, and member of the Bride of Christ. He taught about family, parenting, children, heritage, and hope. He reminded me of a desire and vision I had before I was married—to raise a Godly family full of heritage and Hope. A family who loved the Lord and each other. He flooded my soul with remembrances of what He showed me as a teenager—tiny glimpses of Heaven pervading Earth through a community of believers, my family. I was in revival.

I was beginning to fall in love with myself.

Revival

Revival. Many images come to mind when one hears the word *revival*. Some people envision large crowds on their knees weeping and appealing for forgiveness. Some picture great outpourings of the Spirit in giftings like tongues, healing, and prophecy. Some see bold preachers of the Gospel on every corner proclaiming the Good News without reservation.

Malachi 4 speaks of one of the effects of revival, of what occurs when we remember and keep God's Words: Our hearts turn home, a father's heart to his children and the children to their parents. When God stirs up people, their response of repentance leads to greater care for other humans. Most importantly, they begin to turn toward their immediate community—their family. When all is made right, family relationships are restored and transformed.

Falling in love with God means falling in love with humans, yourself, and your family. Honoring God means honoring your humans. Revival is evident in repentance, rebirth, restoration, and recovery. Revival may include vast masses of people praying, being healed, and boldly preaching. Still, revival is also marked by restoration that is family-focused.

Couch Time

Toward the end of my pregnancy with Linzee, I was simply taking a moment to lean into God's Word. I was in survival mode one afternoon and just needed a word—any word from God.

Even though I was gaining revelation and insight as the Spirit led, all the other life stuff was taking its toll, and I was tired. Reclining on my blue and white checkered couch, I flipped open my Bible to Malachi. Crossing my fingers for something refreshing and easy to "get," I began reading. Then an unexpected moment happened.

The words of Malachi 2:15 burned within me as I read them. "Did He not make them one, with a portion of the Spirit in their union? And what was the one God seeking? Godly offspring. So guard yourselves in your spirit, and let none of you be faithless to the wife of your youth" (ESV).

I like how *The Message* paraphrases this scripture, "GOD, not you, made marriage. His Spirit inhabits even the smallest details of marriage. And what does He want from marriage? Children of God, that's what. So guard the spirit of marriage within you. Do not cheat on your spouse."

There was an electric surge in my spirit. I sprang up as energy flowed through me, and I paid attention. My eyes swelled with tears. "This is what You desire from me," I whispered to the Lord, "Godly offspring."

I wanted to give Him His desire.

What God already had done throughout my life and what He desired to do within and through my family, well, it humbled me. He impressed upon me what He wanted for my family. Attainable aspirations flooded my heart as He showed me a family who endured, had Hope, and walked in heritage—a family of eternal significance, marked and inhabited by the Spirit, producing Godly offspring.

He reminded me that He purposefully placed desires and hopes inside of me during my teenage years—longings conceived and birthed during prayer. Grasping onto bold assurances in God's Word, I committed never again to let go of these expectations on behalf of God, myself, my husband, and my children. To hold fast for those who are mine: my people, my tribe, my community.

Those wishes for my children were re-established and made strong. Solidified! Those personal promises I made to my kids before they were even born, the things I would do and not do to them or for them, circled within my thoughts. God told me all things are possible, through Him, in Him, and with Him (Matthew 19:26).

A boldness arose within me as I realized this was something I could do in honor of my King, my God. A calling of sorts. A co-mission. A joint effort with God. I must simply continue to partner with Him to raise Godly offspring. Children, disciples of Jesus Christ, filled with heritage and Hope. Image bearers of God who shine His light in dark places. Those who bless each other and others.

I had read the passage in Malachi before several times, but this time it glowed. It's like it was bold text, highlighted, and triple underlined on the page. God's Word and my former adolescent desires were coming into alignment. Wishes and hopes born out of personal lack, as well as promises rooted in His Word and grounded in His lavish love, were merging. A divine echo sounded over and over in my soul. All I hoped for my future family (before I was even married or a parent) He remembered. I remembered.

1.21

LACK

It is important to remember what God has placed in you. When we do not recall God and His ways, "bad" things happen because we are not functioning within His design.

Hosea 4:1-6 highlights what happens when people lack vision:

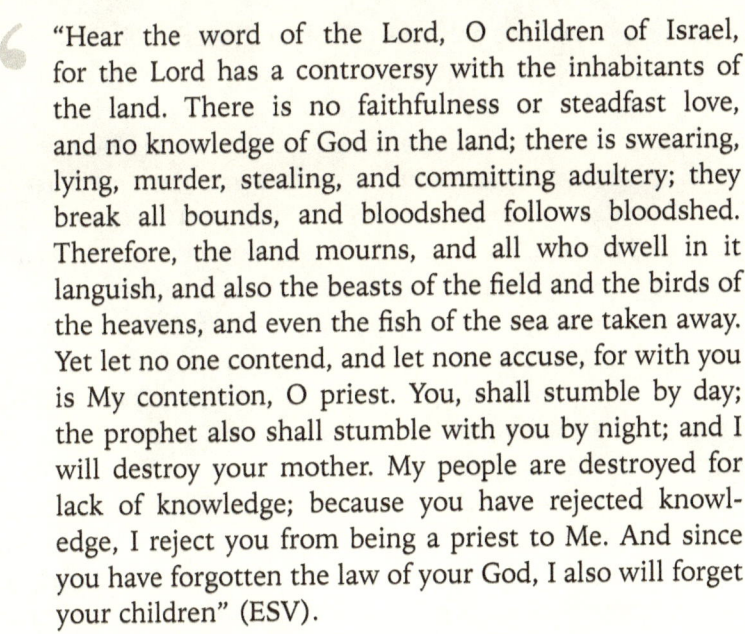

"Hear the word of the Lord, O children of Israel, for the Lord has a controversy with the inhabitants of the land. There is no faithfulness or steadfast love, and no knowledge of God in the land; there is swearing, lying, murder, stealing, and committing adultery; they break all bounds, and bloodshed follows bloodshed. Therefore, the land mourns, and all who dwell in it languish, and also the beasts of the field and the birds of the heavens, and even the fish of the sea are taken away. Yet let no one contend, and let none accuse, for with you is My contention, O priest. You, shall stumble by day; the prophet also shall stumble with you by night; and I will destroy your mother. My people are destroyed for lack of knowledge; because you have rejected knowledge, I reject you from being a priest to Me. And since you have forgotten the law of your God, I also will forget your children" (ESV).

The passage in Hosea was written primarily to the nation of Israel, but it reveals much to us. I've often heard the phrase, "People perish for lack of vision," preached in church; but more specifically, it states, "My people are destroyed for lack of knowledge; because you have rejected knowledge, I reject you from being a priest to me."

Let's take a closer look at four words in this passage from their Hebrew context.[1] The word *destroyed* indicates being cut off, ruined. *Lack* translates into a wearing out, unintentionally, unobserved. The word *knowledge* suggests knowledge, truth, concern. Lastly, let's look at the word *forgotten* toward the end of this passage where it states, "And since you have forgotten the law of your God, I also will forget your children." It does not mean to forget something like where you last put your set of car keys. *Forgotten* (in this context) means not to do and follow through with what you know. You know something but do not bring it into action. It is not a momentary mental lapse. It is when you do not acknowledge and apply God's knowledge in how you live out your life.

The lack of applied knowledge kills.

Let's probe a little more and take a look at Proverbs 29:18. It states, "Where there is no prophetic vision the people cast off restraint, but blessed is he who keeps the law" (ESV). Let's look at a couple of words from this text to understand their Hebrew origins better.

Vision means vision, the ability to see and imagine. *Cast off restraint* implies letting go. When we cannot envision what God has for us, we let go of God's way of life for us. We let go of the blessings meant for us, forfeiting the life meant for us and our children to live.[2]

From these passages, we can conclude God's people, His children, are cut off and ruined because they do not observe God's truth. They lack intentionality and follow-through in fulfilling God's concerns. Whether this is the consequence of sin or this passage gives us a description of what happens to a group of people when they do not pay attention or listen and do what God instructs isn't the point I want to focus on in this time. What I want to drive home in your heart is that when we do not walk in God's ways, it affects us poorly and, equally or more importantly, affects our children. God *forgets* them.

It does not mean He does not remember them like we cannot remember where the car keys are. It suggests He cannot bring about the blessings that living in His ways provides. It's not that He is vindictive and does not want to. Suppressed blessing results from us not living in obedience (actions testifying to our trust in Him).

Chaos conquers in the home. We live life from a defensive posture, always striving, never thriving. We become unhealthy and broken. All we see is what we are experiencing. Pervasive lying, unfulfilled vows, unmet unrealistic expectations of God and one another, lost victories, idolatrous and adulterous hearts, and an eye-for-an-eye mentality with little mercy and little grace fill our family. You treat me bad; I treat you bad.

Again, people do not perish for lack of vision for something great. They are left to ruin because they do not seek knowledge from God regarding His vision and ways to apply and live by them. Their actions lead them to have narrow sight and shrinking expectations. What they hope for in life becomes small. Much smaller than anything God ever dreamed for them.

One who lacks in applying God's knowledge is a destructive fool. However, one who applies God's wisdom is a triumphant ally of God. Instead of forgetting, we should grip onto the vision of God and hold tight to the established blessing God desires for us to walk in and then walk in it.

1.22

JESUS IS BETTER THAN A PORK CHOP

The afternoon I spent on our blue and white checkered couch
excited and sobered me. Enlightened by the illumination of
Scripture and the glimpses of what God showed me, I deeply desired
to raise Godly children who honor and love the Lord. God caught my
attention (again)—I was awake and alert. I reawakened to the vision
for a house—my house, His house.

I was falling in love with my husband and my children more than
ever.

Shawn and I were married about eight years when this reawakening moment occurred. Autumn was about seven years old, and Tyler
was about four years old. Linzee was still in the womb.

Why did God wait so long to rekindle the vision for our home? I do
not know. But my perception of my circumstances began to change
from a ruinous situation to seeing a righteous opportunity. I am
awestruck about how much He partnered with Shawn and me in
raising our children for His glory despite our complete dysfunction.
He covered, protected, and nurtured our children despite us. I
shouldn't be surprised by that though; they are in fact His children
first.

What Existed

I want you to understand that we prayed with our kids through the difficult early years of marriage and taught the Scriptures. The Word of God and talking to Jesus existed in our home. Once again, it may sound like we were hypocrites. Maybe we were. More accurate is that Shawn and I knew that knowledge of God and His ways was the best we could give our children. We knew His presence, His faithfulness, His love. How could we keep such a good thing from them? God exists. He is intriguing, you can talk to Him, and He talks back. We wanted our children to grasp this truth firmly.

Most importantly, God had and has them. Our children are His children, and He loves them even more than we do. God carried way more of the weight in the parenting partnership than we did or could ever carry. Early on He taught our kids astounding things. God's faithfulness to His desire for our family exists despite our failures. We trusted God with our children; we just found it difficult to trust Him with ourselves.

After God reawakened me to realize what life with my family-community could be, I diligently considered what and why I was doing things in my life with my spouse and kids. I turned to the Word of God for pretty much all circumstances in my life. I had some knowledge, but it was time to get more and apply it. Prayer was not a chore. It was an ongoing vital conversation. I quickly noticed how much of a worldly carnal mentality had crept into our home. It was time for it to go. I wanted more, and now I knew what *more* was.

Enough.

Get 'Dem Chops

I heard a story at a church conference that defined my thoughts at this time of life:

A young boy, Sam, rode his bike to the store every day. On his way, he would pass by a large but friendly dog called Moose. Chained to his doghouse, Moose wouldn't even bother getting up in acknowledgment of the young boy speeding by. He would just stare at him.

One Sunday afternoon, the boy's grandfather asked him to go to the store and buy pork chops for dinner. The boy obliged. After purchasing the pork chops, he placed them in the basket on the back of his bike and headed to Grandpa's house. Suddenly, "Whoof!! Whoof!!" Ka-plunk! Ka-plunk! Moose came running as fast as he could. He knocked Sam clear off his bike and attacked the pork chops. Moose had broken his chains. He wanted 'dem pork chops so bad he did what it took to break free from the chains keeping him from them. He was gonna get 'dem chops.

Well, Jesus is better than a pork chop. I wanted Him; I would break free from whatever kept me from more of Him. My husband is better than a pork chop; I would live free and seek God for Shawn's freedom, pulling on the chains that bound him through prayer and actions of love. My children, oh how precious. They are definitely better than pork chops! I would eat through chains if I had to for them. But more importantly, I would choose to live in such a way that my choices wouldn't chain them down.

Some chains were broken at this time in my life, but I had a few more to go. I bore witness that God was working within our family, but now we were about to enter a different season. A challenging season that could cripple us or propel us onward to seeing the fruition of this reawakened vision God had given me a decade before.

PART II

THE ON-GOING PROCESS OF SURRENDER

[LETTING GO AND LETTING GOD]

"A person standing alone can be attacked and defeated,
but two can stand back to back and conquer.
Three are even better, for a triple-braided cord
is not easily broken."
~Ecclesiastes 4:12 (NLT)

How do you let go and let God? Well, it's an ongoing process. Sometimes, the truth is you do not even know what you need to let go of. Sometimes you do know, but you just do not trust God with it.

In this part of the book, Shawn and I share how we let go and let God. When we look back at this season of life, we are ever grateful for God's patience, faithfulness, love, and tenderness.

On the path of surrender, we found hope,
redemption, and restoration.

2.1

THE GENESIS NARRATIVE

Before continuing with our story and sharing the hard season of our journey, I want to interject a little more biblical substance for raising a Godly family. Let's dive into the story of creation, which is at the beginning of all stories.

The opening book of the Holy Bible, Genesis, describes God's design and designation for families. (I encourage you to read Genesis chapters one and two before you go any further.) The narrative suggests planning, intention, and purpose while recounting the creation of the universe and everything in it, including man. Beautiful scripture-song gives a glimpse into the formation of the heavens and our home, Earth. Then the holy family of God emerges as God breathes life and fashions two to become one.

Genesis 1 states, "In the beginning God created the heavens and the earth. Now the earth was formless and empty, darkness was over the surface of the deep, and the Spirit of God was hovering over the waters." Wow! Did you catch that? God was present and active in the start of our earthy home as the Spirit hovered over the waters. God, Himself, was involved in the conception and construction of all things. He was, and is, close at hand. He purposefully created the world in which we all live.

God built a planet where He would be on display for future generations. Planet Earth, in all its majesty and beauty, was birthed and immersed in His presence, as He uttered life-giving words from His mouth. The remarks in John 1:1-3 confirm that all things came into being through the Word of God. It states,

> "In the beginning was the Word, and the Word was with God, and the Word was God. He was with God in the beginning. Through Him all things were made; without Him nothing was made that has been made."

Take a moment and imagine vibrant colors splashing across a bare sphere as continents surfaced from waters and plants and animals took shape. From the heavens to tiny hedgehogs, from mountains to the ant, from stars that light our night to glistening blinding sands, God displays His creativity and character in this world for all of us to behold.

God gave form to what was formless. He took what was empty and filled it. Seasons and time were established and launched by His hand. And then, right before He gave the gifts of time, work, and rest, we were made. Through distinct formation, mankind manifested. Both male and female awakened to bear His image.

Genesis goes on to give us additional insight into the formation of the first family. Let's stroll through that text to gather a little more detail about the formation of the family.

Genesis 1:27-28a states,

> "So God created mankind in His own image, in the image of God He created him; male and female He created them. God blessed them and said to them, 'Be fruitful and increase in number; fill the earth and subdue it.'"

Then in Genesis 2:7,

> "the Lord God formed the man from the dust of the ground and breathed into his nostrils the breath of life, and the man became a living being."

A few verses further along we gain knowledge regarding how the first female came to be. Genesis 2:21-22 reveals that

> "the Lord God caused the man to fall into a deep sleep; and while he was sleeping, He took one of the man's ribs and then closed up the place with flesh. Then the Lord God made a woman from the rib He had taken from out the man, and He brought her to the man."

I will not come close to dissecting the entirety of this insightful, in-depth text in Genesis. Mainly, I want to highlight that there is God, a man and a woman, and a blessing and a commission from the very beginning.

Born and Commissioned

Precious and priceless, the divinely designed family is a conduit for God's concepts and commission to flow to the world. God blessed a couple and called them to be caretakers, to be fruitful, and fill the earth. How astonishing! A primary part of God's first recorded desire is birthing and building people who bear His image.

God created humans to be part of a commissioned community created, called, and charged with the mission of acting like God and sharing His goodness with the world around us. For you, your family unit is the core heart of your community. You are called to the house —your house. Your home is where you belong and begin.

God chose to reflect Himself through a couple-led, commissioned community. Then He assigned them to raise a family. He established them to be in a unified relationship with each other that is second only to their relationship with God. There is considerable joy in community, and God simply could not withhold this blessing from us.

Another reason I believe God chose to reflect Himself through a family is because He knows that a family who loves and honors each other is a light in a dark world. A home filled with peace, safety, rest, and acceptance serves as a sanctuary for its members to recharge and receive encouragement. This type of home symbolizes what it's like to come home to Jesus.

In these dark times where divorce is rampant, where unforgiveness and selfishness seem to prevail at every turn, such a family is a powerful way for God to reveal Himself. A family filled with the forti-tude to fight on behalf of each other, not against each other, demon-strates unity. A family forged through the fire of forgiveness and faithfulness burns bright. It reflects devotion, unity, honor, and love—the very characteristics of God Himself.

How powerful a united couple raising a community of children in love with God is! They are carriers of connectedness and comfort to one another this world needs to witness. It is the beginning of the fulfillment of what we refer to as The Great Commission found in Matthew 28:18-20 and confirmed in Acts 1:8. It is the common call to disciple those near and far as disciples of Jesus Christ.

2.2

BY DESIGN

I had a rekindled vision and excitement. It was time to allow God to break patterns in my life and then for me to walk in the path of freedom He made available for me. It was time to let the transformation I experienced on the inside make its way outside. My actions needed to testify to freedom. It was time I moved from a follower of Jesus Christ to His disciple. My choices and habits should change and look different. My home should transform as I remembered God and His ways.

Even though I was doing *my* best in my circumstances, there were things I could change to be in and do *God's* best. I could trust God. Why didn't I trust Him? I had God-inspired vision and biblical backing to believe for such a family, but where was the trust?

Shawn and I fulfilled well the physical, emotional, and educational needs of our children. Yet we were both slacking in the spiritual department. By God's grace, I continued to pray with them daily, made sure they learned Scripture, and always pointed to God. I now did the spiritual things—me—Nichole, not us. However, my children were not experiencing a mom who had fully surrendered her family to God. They were not living with a father fully surrendered to God.

As I drew closer and closer to Christ, He taught me how to surrender and seek His best way for my marriage and children. He showed me how to align with Him and His mission to produce Godly offspring and not just raise good, well-behaved kids. Daily, I chose to align myself to His *design* and live intentionally, not just settle for a *defaulted* family existence. I refused to allow the devils of dissatisfaction in God and distrust in my spouse to run rampant throughout our lives.

Living by Design

Design is the purpose or intention behind something; it is to plan. When the Creator spoke the universe into existence, He created on purpose, with purpose, for purpose. God is an intentional God. He does not just do things off the cuff. He is a God of preparation. There is a reason you and your children are alive.

God dreams up each man and woman and gives them to the world as a gift, no matter the circumstance of their conception. We live in His imagination long before we grace this earth. That, my friend, is a powerful realization. Even if you were living like the devil when you fathered or conceived your child, it's God's grace and mercy that came your way in the bundle of a baby.

Psalm 139:13-18 gives such a beautiful explanation of God's design for each person.

> "For You created my inmost being; You knit me together in my mother's womb. I praise You because I am fearfully and wonderfully made; Your works are wonderful; I know that full well. My frame was not hidden from You when I was made in the secret place, when I was woven together in the depths of the earth. Your eyes saw my unformed body; all the days ordained for me were written in Your book before one of them came to be. How precious to me are Your thoughts, God! How vast is the sum of them! Were I to count them, they would outnumber the grains of sand—when I awake, I am still with You."

God is not surprised by your existence. You are His dream. Your children did not happen by accident; they live for a divine purpose. They are God's thoughts shaped into a gift for you, the body of Christ, and this world.

A Conversation

The first portion of Genesis 1:26 records a conversation the Godhead had regarding the creation of humankind. God states, "Let us make mankind in our image, in our likeness." Through this conversation, we understand that God thought about creating humanity and talked about it before He did it. The creation of mankind was purposeful. It was all planned. We bear the image of God together as one, being fruitful, increasing our community, and having dominion over much of creation—giving glory to God with our lives so radiantly that when others look upon us, they see the image of God.

Two Voices

Throughout Genesis chapter two, we learn even more details about the design of mankind. God breathed into the nostrils of Adam, formed from the dust of the ground. God positioned him in a garden to cultivate it. One day while Adam slept, God fashioned a person from his side. Then He introduced them to each other. God blessed this couple, giving them a cultural mandate. They were to "be fruitful and multiply and fill the earth and subdue it."

Two humans.
Two voices.
Two image-bearers.

The words of Malachi resound, "Did He not make them one, with a portion of the Spirit in their union? And what was the one God seeking? Godly offspring" (Malachi 2:15 ESV).

A man, a woman, and the Spirit (the intentionally created couple and Spirit partnered to raise and disciple sons and daughters of the Most High God) is a sacred union which has the potential to produce what several alternative attempts at relationships cannot: holy seed for God's glory.

NO ONE STUDIES FOR A MARRIAGE LICENSE

Remarkably, people enter God's design of marriage and family with little understanding of the magnitude and gloriousness their family can reflect. We give little forethought to the most important relationships we will ever have outside of our relationship with God. Then often because of the busyness of life and personal inadequacies, we continue to give little intention, investment, and planning to our spouse and kids. We neglect instead of nurture.

Think about how much time you prepared and planned regarding the type of home you wanted to make for your family. I am not talking about your wedding; lots of attention often is given regarding the wedding day. I'm asking about your home and family life. Most people spend months planning for one day but engage in little deliberation about how they will do life with the one they proclaim to love.

How many hours did you spend searching Scripture regarding being a spouse or a parent? How many hours studying and understanding God's Word regarding the design of marriage? Have you gleaned from books and other couples who have wisdom in these areas? Some of us studied more to get our driver's license than we did to get our marriage license.

We must understand that the relationships in our life, which God gives us to steward, nurture, cherish, and love, will exist by design or default. We choose. Unless we operate from a place of alignment in

God for our family, our marriage and children will be products of default.

Default

Default is to fail to fulfill an obligation. Also, default refers to an option assumed when there is nothing else specified. Within this context, it is not recognizing or remembering God's design and purposes for your family. Default is living in deferred hope.

A great sadness in the body of Christ is a defaulted family unit that does not fulfill the function in which God designed it. Marriages reflecting selfishness, strife, unforgiveness, and division (instead of representing the King of kings) fill our pews. Rather than producing Godly seed in unity with the Spirit, we give birth to children mirroring the world's culture.

Because God purposes marriage to represent Him, there is a designation in our relationship. Knowing that this covenant is not by accident or suggestion should lead us to ask essential questions about our marital relations. We must consider how our marriage reflects God.

Does your marriage emanate from the love of God? Do you, as a couple, reflect Him and His attributes? What do people see when they look at you as a couple? Do they know the effect of Jesus on you? Has your marriage fallen to default? Is it a shell of what God imagined and ordained it to be? Are your children wandering?

Often we align ourselves to selfish desires and expectations for self-fulfillment. In a Godly marriage, one benefit is that our spouse may meet many of our needs and wants. Marriage is a blessing and good. It can be thoroughly satisfying in many aspects. But do we align ourselves to what we are appointed as a couple by God first and foremost: two who are one radiating His image? Or are we more concerned with just getting along for the sake of quiet and absence of conflict? Do we prioritize getting what we want over our spouse?

Have we adopted the world's standards instead of God's for our family? Do we value individual success over interdependent stability? Are we focused on "getting ours" from God while our spouse struggles without encouragement or guidance? While we seek healing and wholeness from God, do we neglect our part in spiritually nourishing the child following us?

Whew! That's a lot of tough questions to meditate on. They can leave one feeling overwhelmed. However, they are important for our families' benefit to engage at some point. When we fail to consider these questions (and many more), we fail to pray, plan, and pursue the glory of God with the most consequential relationships we have. We are left feeling robbed of the goodness and glory found in God's design! Yet this does not have to be because it is not God's desire.

Do you feel your family has been stolen from? Is there forfeited or stolen peace, love, or encouragement? Have you realized you are living in a defaulted state and not in God's blessed design? Do you feel clueless about how to build a Godly family? If yes, I understand. We understand. This is precisely how I felt for years.

Unfortunately, my family found itself in this state of default. And did you get that? It was for years! I wish I could go back in time and make a prayerful plan to approach marriage and parenting. I had the heart to have a Godly family. Yet desire only carried us so far. My heart's ambition was strong, my prayers were strong, but my planning was weak. Most of my early marital conflicts and parenting choices were reactionary. They were defensive rather than initiated from a position of offense. Alas, like you, I cannot go back in time. I live today in my present, preparing for a tomorrow only God knows.

REGRET

Regret is a powerful thing. It can result from loss experienced due to poor personal choice or a disappointment over a missed opportunity. It leaves you feeling helpless because you are helpless; you cannot change the past. There is no redo for what we have done or not done.

But there is one thing that triumphs over regret. Redemption tramples over regret! When God redeems us, He redeems our whole life—past, present, and future. He holds it all in His hands.

Joel 2:25a states, "I will repay you the years the locusts have eaten." Over the years, I've heard sermons with this verse highlighted to encourage people. The preacher excitedly shouted, "When the Devil steals something from you, God will restore it back tenfold, a hundredfold!" Interestingly, what the Devil stole referred anywhere from a diagnosis robbing your health to a flat tire. It could be your lack of peace from an offense or just something out of your control like the electricity going out. "Whatever it is, God will give it back—somebody say Hallelujah!" You know all that "joy comes in the morning" hype that preaches well!

But I often wondered about what was forfeited, not stolen. What about what I chose to do or not do in my life, marriage, and parenting? Me, not the Devil or someone else—the things that are my regrettable choices. Does God redeem those things?

I testify He does! He has delivered me from my foolish choices. The past mistakes, failures, and lack remain in the past; they did not disappear. Although I cannot change any of them, God has done wonders with them. They have become learning tools in my life and my children's lives.

I encourage you to read Psalm 107 because it speaks to people who have behaved as fools with lives steeped in regret because of poor personal choices. Those who, like me, rebelled against God's commands and despised the plans of the Most High. It speaks to people making choices, leaving them at the mercy of their enemy— people wandering, troubled, and distressed. But it also speaks of God's goodness: His enduring love, how He satisfies the thirsty and hungry, and how He hears the cries of those who made choices to rebel against Him. Then He delivers, redeems, and restores them. He responds to the cry of regret with loving redemption. Oh, the "loving deeds of the Lord."

That's what He does for you and me if we cry out to Him. He swallows up the choices you have made (which have led to your deepest regrets) with His redeeming, enduring love.

We are the redeemed of the Lord, and we should say so.

He Never Lets Go

Here we were, living years outside of God's design in a defaulted state, which made me heartsick. Deferred intentions, little follow-through, and little follow-up within our home nearly destroyed my family. There was so much lack. But God, He was turning it all around. He just wouldn't let go of us. He never lets go.

You do not have to resign yourself to living outside of God's design in a defaulted mode. You can choose to pursue His design for your life and your family.

LOVE FILLS LACK

One of the first things God began to deal with me on, as I surrendered to Him and set my face to pursue His design for my family, was my understanding of lack in my life. From the moment a person is born, they enter a world of lack. Some are unwanted, abandoned, and at the mercy of unchosen circumstances. Others enter the world where those who should love and appreciate them most view them as an obligation, meeting their needs but neglecting their hearts. Others are born to material poverty with a heavenly hope, while others to riches with no eternal hope. Some are celebrated, yet without knowledge of the Creator. But one thing all have in common —ALL lack.

Because of lack, I felt unequipped to raise Godly offspring. My heart soared when I thought about it, and I wanted to accomplish this. But how? I had no idea how to have a Godly healthy marriage, family, or home, and I could not find a person to teach me.

I prayerfully considered how to go about this as I strategized how to make changes in our family. I told the Lord I had a long list of what not to do but so little on what to do, I could not even compile a list. Ever feel like you have more knowledge of what not to do than what to do?

I kept praying and seeking. I read books, mainly the Bible. At one point, I went to a pastor and asked him to recommend someone for me to learn from, such as an older woman in the church, any older woman with Godly children who loved God. Sadly, he could only think of one person, and they were unavailable to mentor anyone at the time.

I felt alone and defeated. In my mind, I had come to grips with the fact that no one loved me enough to take time to invest in me. There was some self-pity but also a hefty dose of reality; it was my reality. One day as I fixated on the lack of available Godly people in my life to invest in me, the Lord whispered to me, "The more lack you have, the more room you have for Me to fill up." He reminded me He is able and willing to fill my lack. His Word would be my guiding light. My parental/marital example would be Father God Himself through the countless examples we see in His Word!

Please understand, I believe in discipleship. I regularly invest in people. I try my best to love others who have lack because I know from personal experience how sucky it feels to walk alone. Titus 2:3-5 instructs me to do this. In Titus older women are advised to "teach what is good, and so train the young women to love their husbands and children, to be self-controlled, pure, working at home, kind, submissive to their own husbands" (ESV).

My family lives its life openly for others to glean. In no way am I dismissing the biblical endorsement of elders investing in the younger generation. If you can find someone Godly who is willing to pour their life into you: Glean. Everything. You. Can.

I did not have this. If you do not have this yet, know this: God is always approachable and available.

When you are in Christ, all things become new. When you become a believer (a son or daughter of God) a new line of inheritance and heritage establishes through the blood of Christ. You become grafted into the family of God. All His people written about in the Word become your people. He is your example. They are your example.

God fills lack because He overcomes it with love—His love.

God can fill the voids in your life, giving form to the formless and creating new things through His Word. Maybe you are starting with little knowledge and understanding as to what to do. Ask God for wisdom. He has the know-how!

Maybe you do not have children yet but are excited for the day to come. What a great season! What a great time to gather all the insight you can and prepare for the future. Maybe you are like I was, married, already have a couple of kids, and God is breathing on you again. He is whispering that you and your family are more—destined for His glory. Yet there is chaos. Remember, He is the God who brings order to chaos. And you, you are created in His image with His Spirit in you. In Christ, you have the same capability to bring order to crisis and chaos. No home is beyond Him.

You do not have to come from a Godly family to raise a Godly family. We are proof of that. You do not even have to have a living human being example. You just need to trust and apply God's Word to your life. Your past lack does not define your family's future. God does! God offers heritage and Hope. He is our Hope! You just must come into agreement with Him. Love will overcome lack.

With me God began by having me acknowledge and confess to Him the lack in my life. Then He asked me to let go of the lack and trust Him to fill it with His love—my lack from childhood; my lack of someone to invest in me, mentor, or disciple me; my lack of personal spiritual disciplines; my lack of making wiser choices; my lack of love for myself; my lack of love for my husband. Lack. Deficiency. In need. That's where I began—confessing and letting go of not having and not being *enough*.

You Are Not Enough

I often hear "you are enough" stated by well-meaning people in leadership. Guess what, you (alone) are NOT enough. If you were enough, then you could satisfy everyone and be everything everyone needs or wants you to be. You cannot do this! You cannot even be everything you need for yourself. God did not create you this way.

This truth is liberating to me. Not only does it mean I am not enough, but it also suggests I do not have to try and be enough. The pressure from others and myself is gone! God created me with inadequacies and weaknesses. I am a creature who learns. I am not perfect, nor does God expect me to be. He has not created me to be enough on my own, but He calls me good—very good.

Think of it from this perspective: If we are enough, then Christ died in vain. It is in Christ we are more than enough. We become more than conquerors. It is me plus Christ that equips me to be enough for whatever He brings my way.

When we come to the moment of accepting this and let go and let God do His thing, He will infuse Himself into every aspect of our lives. Marriage and parenting other humans will not be so intimidating. Loving your spouse and preferring your spouse will not seem so impossible. You'll gain the understanding that your lack is just more space for God to move in and through. You'll realize God is enough, and you are not God.

I am great with being good; I don't need to be enough.

2.6

LORD AND LOVER

As I restarted this journey toward raising a family filled with heritage and hope, the struggle was real. God had a mess on His hands. Our marriage was not just rocky; it had mountainous boulders at every turn. My husband was even more unengaged and unkind. I was exhausted and untrusting, even though I did not want to be. Do you ever feel or act like you do not want to?

My children were well-behaved kids. They did know God, but I was at a crossroads with them. At this point in our story, we were beginning to just go about life in all the typical routines and daily muck. The dream God had reawakened in me revealed just how much we had lost a Kingdom perspective in our home. I just looked at our children as *my kids*. I did not view them in the light in which God does. I thought I did, but I did not. (I'll share more on this in another chapter.)

In some ways, I also remember these days fondly. As I mentioned earlier (Section 1.20 *A Blue and White Checkered Couch*) during my pregnancy with Linzee, God turned my whole heart and mind back to Him. I was full of revelations. Hope was springing forth as joy randomly flooded my heart through the day. I could sense His presence and feel His love for me. I sighted hormones as the reason, but I knew God was doing deep work. I was finding joy in Life despite my messy marriage and home life. I found joy in Jesus.

I was falling even more in love with Him.

Lord of All

It was in this season God reminded me He is Lord of all. All things. All.

I became grateful I always knew God existed. My earliest childhood memories consist of me talking to Jesus and feeling the presence of God. How cool is that?! I was thankful during my teenage years I was reawakened to the truth that He is Lord and Savior. I was grateful for the journey, even the stumbling around on wobbly legs as we all do as we begin to learn to walk as a Christ-follower. I appreciated that Shawn and I started our marriage as people who knew we needed Jesus. Grace and mercy reminded me we could just get lost along the way, but God knows exactly where we are.

God always finds lost things. We were not too far gone, nor are you. God revived me, and I knew He could revive my husband. Joy, hope, and hormones marked my pregnancy with Linzee Joy.

Lordship

Psalm 24:1 says, "The earth is the Lord's, and everything in it, the world, and all who live in it." Everything belongs to God. He is Lord, whether you recognize it or not. God challenged me to remember this, reflect on it, and respond to it by allowing Him to take our family and work as He saw fit. All I had to do was trust and do what He asked when He asked me to do it. It was that simple.

Sounds simple, yet it was hard to hand everything over to God. It was very hard. I'm not sure why; I could not fix things on my own. Yet it was hard to obey and trust Him. Why do we "fight Him for something we do not really want, then take what He gives that we need?"[1]

Surrendering to His Lordship meant some things I did not want to change would have to change. When God instructed me to stop working outside the home during this season, I did not want to stop. I enjoyed working, and I doubted our marriage could survive another year. I was worried about how time off would look on my resume and affect my future income.

Even as I write this, I realize how ridiculous it all sounds. Positioned in a place where God reawakened me to pursue a Godly family, I pondered how to cope with an inevitable divorce. I had random joy flood my heart because of Christ's love for me, yet it yearned for love from my husband. It was discouraging. I did not know what to do or what I had done that was so bad to make Shawn so discontent with me.

God reminded me He is Lord, and I must stop fighting and surrender it all to Him. Surrender my husband, myself and all my misery, and my children. Would I do this? Yes, I would—out of obedience which is trust. And, sadly, I would surrender because I viewed Him as my last option for my marriage to have a chance.

Let Go, Let God

Why is it we choose Jesus as our last option instead of our first? It's like we do everything we can think to do and what others suggest before going to Him. I wonder how much of my situation would have been different if I handed it all over to God first and then just did what He instructed. Not everything would have changed because other people still made their choices, but I would have been different. I know this because the moment I "let go" and "let God," everything began to change. If I could go back in time, I would tell my younger self, "Nichole, what you left with Jesus at the Cross when you were young, never pick it back up. Trust Him completely and live in WOW! He got you, girl!"

Oh, How He Loves Me

Just as God reawakened surrender to His Lordship in me, He began the process of displaying to me how much He loves me. It's one thing to obey God out of fear, or a sense of doing what you believe is the right thing to do, or out of desperation reaching for the last thing there is. It's another thing to trust in Him. Sometimes when we approach God as *Lord* our minds begin to think about rules and regulations—restrictions created to limit or propel us. And that's good because God's commands are best. But His Lordship flows simultaneously with His love.

As I meditated on the love God has for me, my trust began to grow. (Today, as I dive more and more into the depths of His steadfast love, my faith continues to increase.) Knowing how much God loves me is precious to me. God wanted me to obey Him because He's God, He knows best, and what the Lord says goes, but He took the time to reveal His love for my family and me. He showed me His ways are not primarily to limit me but to give me true liberty.

He desires my obedience, but He wants me to obey out of trust in Him. He desires my love and your love. Even His desire for our surrender to His Lordship is reflective of His love. He knows His ways benefit us the best and thereby glorify Him the most. The truth is I did trust Him (a little). After all, He is the Creator and created everything, so He should know how things work best. This makes logical sense to me, but I had also grown angry with Him.

2.7

WHY ARE YOU DRIVING LIKE THAT, JESUS?

I felt like God did not have my back. I had such high hopes and expectations for my marriage, ministry, and family. None of my circumstances seemed what I hoped for, except for my beautiful children. I was angry with God for my husband's behavior. I blamed God. It is sad how many things God gets blamed for that people do. I blamed Him for a long time. I knew God is God and had the highest wisdom; I just did not think He was all that kind to me. I was a pitiful self-pitying thing.

God is gracious and did not chastise me when I vented on Him. He is big enough for my heartbrokenness and wrath.

Today I know God has my back and front. Moses told Joshua in Deuteronomy 31:8, "The Lord Himself goes before you and will be with you; He will never leave you nor forsake you. Do not be afraid; do not be discouraged." I know God is with me and guiding me, as He is with you.

I surrendered my lack to Him. I began diverting blame from God to the appropriate offenders. In return, my Lover filled all the lack in my life with His love.

God Gets All the Blame

We should all stop blaming God for people's failures. People let us down: they disappoint, betray us, and say horrid things. People can be downright nasty! People fail, but God does not fail!

By blaming God for so much, I hindered my personal growth and transformation. I did not take responsibility for what was in my hands to do and within my life to control. Also, I avoided necessary confrontation with other people I should have had much earlier in life. Blaming God created a giant smokescreen that kept me from seeing the true culprits: Satan and selfishness.

Surrendering Shawn

During this time of my revival, you may be wondering what was going on with Shawn. Well, Shawn behaved worse. He continued to lie and not be a good husband. Things got worse relationally with him, but other areas in our lives got better.

The job opportunity he took after leaving the shelter was financially advantageous for us. He was the Vice President of Marketing for an oilfield company. I was able to quit my job and stay home with our three children, which was terrific. It was a new season, yet Shawn was still doing his own thing—he was selfish and barely available. His marketplace success brought to the surface many undesirable qualities.

When Jesus Takes the Wheel

When you hand everything over to God in your marriage/parenting, it does not mean it will get better right away. I've often seen just the opposite occur. It's like the moment you say, "Jesus, take the wheel," four cars come and crash into you from every direction. And you wonder, "Why are You driving like that, Jesus?!"

It may not seem like a good sign, but it is. When all of hell seems to unleash, take it as a good sign. Forces are fighting hard for a reason. They wouldn't fight so hard if there was not something spectacular about to shake through. Just hold on tight to Jesus through the crashes. You will survive and live!

· · ·

More

I wanted more for myself and my kids. I wanted all that God had for us. The more I knew God, the more I loved Him. In knowing Him, I knew myself better and loved myself more. I did not do anything to deserve better than I had, but God desired me to have it. He had more for me; I wanted it and was becoming bolder in asking for it and seeking it.

I could define more clearly what it was I wanted. I wanted my husband to love Jesus and know His love for him. I wanted a man I could minister side by side with to others. I wanted a man who would spiritually strengthen and encourage me. I wanted a man to live life with and explore this incredible world. I wanted someone who wanted me.

I was following Christ to the best of my ability. I had become His disciple. The difference between being a follower of Christ and a disciple is disciples do what Jesus did and does. Followers of Jesus experience many of the same things that disciples do. In the Bible, followers witnessed miracles. They heard Jesus teach, and they walked with Him for days at a time. He healed them. Their encounters with Jesus impacted them. The disciples received more profound revelations, and they did what He did. They did not just receive from Jesus; they treated others like Jesus did.

Through God's grace and guidance, I developed into quite a momma and leader in our home. I was trying to be a better wife. I was becoming *more*.

IMAGINARY ARROWS IN HAND

One day, while sitting at our white dining room table, I read a book about breaking generational curses. The author highlighted how the sins of a parent can visit their children to the third and fourth generations (Exodus 20:5). It's not children who are responsible for their parents' choices, but oh how they often are the recipient of the blessing and cursing of these choices.

After I read, I prayed for God to break generational curses in our family. During prayer, the Lord led me to a peculiar passage found in 2 Kings 13:14-19.

 "Elisha had become sick with the illness of which he would die. Then Joash the king of Israel came down to him, and wept over his face, and said, 'O my father, my father, the chariots of Israel and their horsemen!' And Elisha said to him, 'Take a bow and some arrows.' So he took himself a bow and some arrows. Then he said to the king of Israel, 'Put your hand on the bow.' So he put his hand on it, and Elisha put his hands on the king's hands. And he said, 'Open the east window'; and he opened it. Then Elisha said, 'Shoot,' and he shot. And he said, 'The arrow of the Lord's deliverance and the arrow of deliverance from Syria; for you must strike the

Syrians at Aphek till you have destroyed them.' Then he said, 'Take the arrows'; so he took them. And he said to the king of Israel, 'Strike the ground'; so he struck three times and stopped. And the man of God was angry with him and said, 'You should have struck five or six times; then you would have struck Syria till you had destroyed it! But now you will strike Syria only three times.'"[1]

The Spirit guided me to a strange Scripture, right? I did not even understand it. I'm sure theologians could enlighten you with layers upon layers of significance and meaning regarding the nation of Israel specifically, so I will leave that to them and just share the insight I gained.

God told me to pretend I had an arrow in my hand and to beat the floor right there in my dining area. After debating what I heard, I took my imaginary, invisible arrow and acted as if I was striking the ceramic tile beneath my feet. I felt incredibly foolish. I did it about three times, and then I felt tired and embarrassed. Remembering what I just read in the Bible about the prophet being angry because King Joash only struck the ground three times, I continued to pound my imaginary arrow into the ground.

What was the purpose of this? What was the Holy Spirit showing me? As I began to strike the ground, I began to weep. I realized how exhausted I felt fighting the enemy. I told Jesus I knew He had already won the victory and asked Him to please take over for where I did not have the energy to fight anymore.

Shocked by my lack of zeal to keep fighting, I realized I needed more fervor for what lay ahead. God revealed to me that I could not be halfhearted or faint-hearted. I would say I needed the heart of a lion, but really, I just needed the heart of a woman surrendered to God. I was in a battle for the man and children I love.

Spiritual warfare on behalf of our family requires fervor and intentionality. What is needed is a warrior who is not ashamed to beat imaginary arrows into the ground and proclaim victory for the lives of their loved ones.

I began to pray to God to break generational curses in Shawn's life. I asked God to release him from the effects of his parents and their parents and their parents' choices. The Lord said something to me that shook me. He said, "Nichole, what do you want?" I said, "I want Shawn free." He said, "It will cause you great pain."

That statement puzzled me. I thought a while and prayed some more. I told the Lord that I still wanted him free. Then the Lord challenged me with something I think is key. He told me to love Shawn as my brother in the Lord first, even before loving him as my husband. I started thinking this did not make sense because a husband-wife relationship is a covenant, so that should be the prioritized relationship. However, if you think about it, in Heaven no one is given in marriage or married. We are brothers and sisters for eternity (Matthew 22:30). (I know this may not make complete sense, but I am just sharing my genuine processing here.)

I began to pray for Shawn as though he was simply my brother in Christ. Guess what! My prayers changed. Interestingly, my expectations also changed. I stopped praying about what I wanted from a husband and started praying about what Shawn needed and had rights to as a child of God. I did not look to Shawn for spiritual strength or leadership. I looked harder to see what I could do for him or give to him as a sister in Christ. I looked for ways to show him love and bless him. I stopped being disappointed *in* Shawn and became disappointed *for* Shawn (and all he was missing out on).

Studying Shawn

Also, the Lord instructed me to study my husband like I studied His Word. I thought it was a funny thing to recommend, but it makes sense. If you want to know someone, study them: watch and listen to what they say and do, how they respond to things, what they put effort into, what brings them joy, or what robs their happiness.

As I pursued God to serve my spouse better, God began to deal with and heal many of my hurts almost instantaneously. He broke generational curses in my life. He opened my eyes to the blessings of my childhood—the awareness of Him, the understanding I have that He never lets us go, and how God shared His heart with me when we talked by the roses. I was overwhelmed. I felt so loved and humbled. The more I prayed for Shawn's deliverance, the more freedom I found. It's quite amazing how that worked!

I began to ponder what I knew about Shawn's childhood—a family divided, divorce stemming from adultery, two houses but no feeling of home, terrible things done to him and his siblings, and he had done terrible things. Abuse tainted several of the good memories he possessed. I realized that as much as my childhood positively and negatively affected me, his affected him.

I began fervently praying God would break what needed breaking, stop what should cease, and do something inside Shawn. He needed healing. It was time it all ended so we, not just me, could be part of establishing a new line of heritage and hope in our family.

Time to end the cycle—enough.

2.9

DRAWING STRAWS

Weeks later, Shawn and I were sitting in Applebee's, a restaurant, with close friends discussing a mission trip to Romania. Our pastor wanted Shawn to go on the mission trip. (It may be important to mention here that no one knew what was really happening in our lives.)

I wanted to go on the mission trip. Shawn and I decided to handle the decision of who would go as all spiritual people do—we drew straws. So spiritual, right? Shawn won. I'm not going to lie; I was bitter. I thought to myself, "He isn't even serving God."

What I did not know was I was pregnant with my fourth child, Josiah. Linzee was only six months old when I found out I was pregnant with Josiah. I figured that is why God picked Shawn. It might have been dangerous to travel across the world mid-pregnancy.

(As I am writing this, I think that if I read this, I would wonder, "How in the world does she keep getting pregnant through this craziness?" It may be worth mentioning here, without giving too much information, Shawn and I maintained a good sex life throughout all this mess. There were seasons of ups and downs during sickness, pregnancy, and heart-hurt; but overall, it was and is great. People often say the most prominent problems couples deal with include sex and finances. But it's not always true. Overall, sex isn't an issue for us; we are quite compatible. It was individual internal issues that affected us the most.)

I tried to justify God's choice for picking Shawn over me. I just could not understand why He would even allow him to go on a mission trip. I had no idea how divine the draw of the straw was. This mission trip is where God tangibly started to do something in Shawn which would transform everything.

WHEN GOD MOVES THROUGH YOU TO
MOVE IN YOU (SHAWN)

I had drawn the lucky straw. I would go across the world to preach the Good News of Jesus Christ to the lost. Only God could have orchestrated this unexpected trip. It was the beginning of the end of something which needed to die. It was the awakening to something MORE.

For the majority of the first decade of our marriage, I was discontent and fostered the mentality of, "What am I missing?" When you think you are missing out on something, you will have a conversation, debating and negotiating with your unsurrendered nature. The result is discontentment leading to compromise.

Nurturing unhealthy appetites fueled my discontentment. I became increasingly selfish as I attempted to find what I was missing. I was selfish and bound by two cousins: shame and condemnation. I carried so much shame and condemnation for past sins and the sins I committed regularly. I was sinking further and further into myself. I think shame lies at the crossroads of condemnation and conviction. And the enemy, if you allow him, will manipulate you with shame and keep you entangled. I let him do this. My convicted spirit whispered, my conscience screamed, but I would not yield. I resisted healing and deliverance; therefore, condemnation became my close companion.

I needed healing from things done to me. I do not know if I wouldn't allow God to heal me or if I just did not know how to allow God to heal those things. Nevertheless, I did not want to deal with them. Also, I did not want to let people down. I was a slave to my selfishness and fake reputation, as well as other people's expectations.

Whether true or not, I felt the Church Institution I was affiliated with was not built or structured for expressed vulnerability. People assumed I was well because I graduated from discipleship school; this could not be further from the truth. Although I gained valuable knowledge and experiences, I did not deal with what I needed the most help with. (You do not graduate from discipleship.)

My life consisted of good things tainted by unhealthy appetites and childhood hurts that I would not confront. I just thought, "It is what it is. This is how life has always been and will be." It's all I had known. Consistent sin causes a severe depth of deception. Sin causes you to believe things about God, yourself, other people, and life in general that are not true.

For several years, I pursued what I wanted at my family's expense.

Going in Circles

Do some of the thoughts in these paragraphs sound familiar? Does it sound like I am repeating myself? It should because I am repeating what I mentioned earlier in the book: same thoughts and feelings.

That's what happens when you prolong your need for healing and repentance. You keep chasing your tail in circles, experiencing the same emotions, feelings, and pain you have been experiencing.

Someone once said, "The definition of insanity is doing the same thing over and over and expecting different results." I was living in insanity.

Hey, Hey, Romania

Living in an endless circle of dissatisfaction was the condition I found myself in as I boarded the plane for Romania. Why was I even going? I did not fully know, but God knew. He had a plan.

During the mission trip, God's presence overwhelmed me. God turned the tables on me in that tiny eastern European nation. He made me keenly aware I WAS missing out on something, on more than I could ever imagine.

He gave me gracious glimpses of what I was missing out on. I was missing out on God and His plan, the promises He wanted to fulfill in my life, marriage, family, and ministry. I was missing out on the peace and joy He wanted me to possess. I was missing out on freedom in Christ.

As I stepped out to minister to the Romanian people, I felt God's presence. He awakened me to my lack and revealed more of His greatness. He demonstrated there was so much more to Him that I did not know. I wanted God. Ironically, God moved through me to reach people, all the while reaching me.

I remember thinking, "How do I move forward from here? Were my best days behind me?"

I ached for God; I did not want to live without His presence. I decided I would pursue God no matter the cost. At this point, I honestly thought I would lose my family and definitely lose my reputation if I became real. It came down to this: Either I was going to be a man of God, or I was not.

God must be my over-mastering passion, even if it meant losing everything but Him. He is most important. It had nothing to do with anyone else, just me. I had to choose. God asked me to love Him with my whole heart and to surrender to Him as Lord.

People did not know the real me. I'm not even sure I knew the real me, but God knew. He knew all the bad I had ever done. Yet He still pursued me and wanted me to know Him and have the fullness of the life He has for me. As I fulfilled The Great Commission and preached the Good News to others, God compelled me to come home to Him.

I died to myself that day. I awakened with a new love for Christ. Forgiven by Christ, the circle broken. This was the man boarding the plane back to America.

2.11

CONTENTMENT (SHAWN)

Contentment is a state of happiness and satisfaction. Discontentment is dissatisfaction with one's circumstances.

Rarely is any of us satisfied in Christ alone. We sing about God being everything and the only One we need, but when people or things are not exactly like we want, we get cranky. Then we realize we are singing lies.

There are times when discontentment is a good thing. It can push you to reach for more when you need to. It can help drive development and change. But overall, discontentment with your God-given lot in life is dangerous. It opens you up, giving the enemy access and free reign.

Unhealthy discontentment leads to covetousness and compromise. You're always seeking to be filled by something or someone else, only to eat from the world's hollow troughs. Discontentment is the enemy of your soul and your family.

The enemy of discontentment is gratitude. If you are grateful for someone or something, you will cherish the blessing of who or what you have—and hopefully the One who gave you the blessing.

Discontentment divides. Gratitude multiplies and generates feelings of satisfaction. In Philippians 4:11b, the apostle Paul stated, "for I have learned to be content whatever the circumstance." Contentment is a learned behavior that we should practice.

AN APOLOGY AND A PRAYER

When Shawn returned from overseas, he sat on our coffee table and apologized to me for being an awful husband. He committed to being a better husband and changing his ways. Shawn promised to start attending church with us again. With tears in his eyes, He described God's presence he so strongly felt in Romania. He spoke about how God used this mission trip, His presence, the lost people, and the struggling Romanian church to rekindle a fire in him for Him.

I listened.

Wednesday night came; it was time to go to church. As we were getting ready to leave for evening service, the phone rang. His hockey team needed a player; Shawn decided to skip church and play. I was livid.

I loaded the car seat and kids in the van by myself. Then I got into our vehicle only to jump out; I decided to give Shawn a piece of my mind. Suddenly it felt as if someone yanked my shoulder from behind. Then the Lord said, "Leave him to Me."

Understand that you do not have to attend church every Wednesday night to do well with the Lord or be a Christian. That was not the issue. The point was that he promised to put my request over his friends' expectations and his sports in this season.

I got in the van. I was done.

Wresting (Shawn)

When Nichole and the kids left for church that night, I put on worship music. I wrestled inside, knowing she wanted me to go to church with her and the kids while I wanted to play hockey.

While I was getting ready and stretching, I suddenly felt God's presence as strong as I had in Romania. I thought and prayed, "God, no matter what it cost me, my life or my marriage, I want You more than anything. I want You more than anything else. I'm willing to lose everything else if I can have You."

More than wanting my family or my reputation to stay intact, I hungered for the presence of God and to be in His fullness. I desired to be the father and man of God I am created to be, yet I also knew the realities I must confront. It was just that simple. Not much more complicated than that.

I went to the hockey game. Within minutes I was lying on the ground with a broken femur.

2.13

YUCK

I checked all our children into nursery and kid service before entering Wednesday night service. As I sat down after worship, I quickly jumped back up and said to my friend beside me, "I have to go to the Hockey Plex." I went back to the nursery, checked all the kids out, and headed to the hockey arena. I was fuming. I knew the Lord wanted me to get to the hockey complex, but I was beside myself with anger. I just knew I had to get there. How did I know? I do not have an answer except for the Holy Spirit prompting me on the inside.

As we entered the parking lot of the hockey arena, I saw an ambulance. I knew it was for Shawn. An acquaintance exited the building and saw me. With a look of bewilderment, she said, "How did you get here so fast?" (This was the old days when most people did not have a cell phone.) I said, "I just knew to be here."

Shawn had broken his femur by hitting a wall. It was a usual hockey slam into the wall, but his leg snapped. The medics were taking care of him and prepping him to go to the hospital. I was so upset. I did not feel sorry for him; I felt resentful. His selfishness just kept affecting me, and I just did not want to deal with it anymore.

Shawn's brother Rocky graciously took my kids to his house. I went to the hospital, where friends and family arrived to pray for Shawn. For the next eight days, Shawn was in the hospital. For the first few days, he kept getting worse. His blood count continued to drop, and he was not able to do therapy. They could not figure out what was happening.

There I was, five months pregnant, sleeping on a hospital bed. Shawn did not want me to leave his side. He was a hot mess.

Several days into the hospital stay, I woke up to a man with tears in his eyes. He said, "Nichole, there is something I need to tell you." He proceeded to weep and confess to me what had been going on.

Honestly, it's hard to know what to write here, what's too much to mention or too little to mention. I've written and deleted it many times. The general summary of this conversation revealed more inappropriate relationships, selfishness, and lying. It also revealed his hurt, pain, and brokenness, as well as his regret, repentance, and desire for forgiveness from me. He proceeded to tell me He surrendered His whole life to the Lord and would do whatever it took to get well and restore our family.

I listened. I was relieved. I knew I was not crazy, and I felt a heavy burden lifted.

Too Much or Too Little

Ahh, but what did he do? What did she do? One evening, I sat in a service listening to people give testimonies about how they were in addiction but now living free. I kid you not; there was a good 45 minutes of a person listing, with way too much information, about all the sin he committed. Then a brief, "But Jesus saved me, and now I'm free." Forty-five minutes glory to Satan and self, then forty-five seconds glory to God. I wanted to hear more about what God is doing in his life now. That's the testimony, old to new.

The Bible says we overcome by the blood of the Lamb and the word of our testimony (Revelation 12:11). The story of God's transforming power in our life is powerful and should be shared. However, it seems in church culture, we may be more interested in a tantalizing testimony than the actual transformation Christ brings. We want to be wooed and wowed. We want all the juicy gossip. I know Jesus saved you, but I want the details of the sin He saved you from. We want what should remain in confidence shouted corporately to raise money for ministries by evoking strong emotion and proving we are doing something for God. It really makes me sick.

As I was expressing my frustration over this to some friends, one lady told me when people share their story it helps her see how God can move in her situation better. I agree. What God does in our life inspires others. So I looked to the Scriptures. In Acts 22, the Apostle Paul shares his past sins with a group of people. He mentioned he imprisoned and killed people. However, we do not get the nitty-gritty details of how they were put to death, how many stones were thrown, or how hard they hit. We do not know how many people Paul murdered. Paul acknowledged who he was, and then he stated who he is. Most importantly, he testifies to his life-changing encounter with Jesus.

Covering your brother and sister in the body of Christ is a lost art. When I set out to write this book, I had no intention of mentioning anything anyone did wrong. Through years—yes years—of prayer and a prophet telling Shawn and I straight up, "Hey, the book you're writing now—right now—all the *yuck* needs to be included. It is written for posterity's sake," we have arrived at what we have. I have prayed, sought counsel from others about what is TOO much or TOO little. It's a hard call.

We are including some of the yuck and the lessons we learned to give you hope in Jesus, not to glorify our foolish choices or out those who have hurt us. However, most of the yuck we reserve for Christ alone, where it will stay for an eternity. People do not need to know all your business or all of ours!

Yuck is Mostly Reserved for Jesus

One of the things Hebrews 10:24 instructs us to do is to "consider how we may spur one another on toward love and good deeds."

Our aim in writing this book is to do just that. We hope to spur, urge, prompt, encourage, motivate, and propel you toward love and good things in your personal discipleship, marriage, and parenting by sharing parts of our journey.

Our prayer is that you get a sense that Shawn and I were pretty messed up, but we hope you mostly see God's goodness, faithfulness, and restorative power. I pray when you finish reading this book, you do not think, "Well, Nichole did this and that. Shawn did this and that." I hope you say, "WOW! God did this and that!"

Everything good in my life is because of Jesus. He transformed me, us, and our family for His glory. I wish I could write every detail of His goodness in our lives, but I'd be writing literally for eternity.

2.14

CONFESSION

Confession, admission, and disclosure are freeing agents. I did not like what I heard in the hospital that day; however, at that moment, I felt a release and healing presence which is challenging to articulate. Hurt and healing joined hands in my heart as Shawn spoke each word. When he finished speaking, I went home to process and pray.

There was also a resolve in me. During Shawn's confession, I settled something in my mind and heart. No person would ever again define me or how I viewed myself. Only God's Word would do this. Shawn always appeared to be more spiritual than me, even though I did not like his behavior. I often assumed I must have done something to inspire and provoke how he acted toward me. I allowed the way he treated me to make me feel negative about myself.

After his confession, I concluded that Shawn and I were the same —both in need of a Savior. We both needed to daily surrender to God. We both allowed other people, their words, and their expectations too much place in our lives. We both needed to own our faith, our marriage, and our home.

Shawn and I were one; the Bible says so. His confession was an uncomfortable, vital part of the process of our restoration. His confession opened the door to healing. Healing others would witness on the outside but, more importantly, healing Shawn would know on the inside. It was an essential step in a long, winding staircase of living whole as individuals and as a couple.

God answered my fervent prayers for my brother in Christ. Truthfully, God was working in Shawn for years, moving him towards Him because He loves Him. I just had the privilege of joining Jesus in His passionate pursuit of Shawn's whole heart.

James 5:13-18 states,

> "Are you hurting? Pray. Do you feel great? Sing. Are you sick? Call the church leaders together to pray and anoint you with oil in the name of the Master. Believing-prayer will heal you, and Jesus will put you on your feet. And if you have sinned, you'll be forgiven—healed inside and out. Make this your common practice: Confess your sins to each other and pray for each other so that you can live together whole and healed. The prayer of a person living right with God is something powerful to be reckoned with" (MSG).

If we all followed the wisdom found in James chapter five, we would all live more peacefully and whole. Since Shawn's confession, we have!

What Do I Do?

I prayed about what I was to do next. God led me to a specific pastor friend, David. When I met with David, I opened the conversation up by pointing out I would sue him and the church if he did not keep our talk confidential. I was concerned with protecting Shawn. Why? Because he is my brother in the Lord. I knew people aren't always as gracious as God. I knew this was not who Shawn would be in Christ. I knew God was changing him. I wanted Shawn to live on without looks or gossiping tongues pulling him back.

My goal was not to dishonor or shame Shawn. He lived with enough shame; his health and healing were my goals. I told David what transpired and what I believed Shawn needed to confront. Our pastor friend was shocked because he had no idea what was happening in our lives.

He asked me, "What do you want? How are you doing?" It was the first time anyone in church leadership ever asked me how I was doing. A few tears fell. It's astonishing how one question could affect me so much. I told him I wanted Shawn saved and not to go to hell. I wanted him to live in freedom. I wanted him healed and whole. I then asked the pastor if he thought I had biblical grounds to divorce. (Shawn had crossed lines but not all lines.) He said, "Yes. Absolutely." I requested for him to meet with Shawn as soon as possible. He agreed to meet with Shawn that day and have a conversation with him.

I was quiet as I drove home. I felt a sober peace and strength I cannot explain. I breathed better than I did in years.

After I arrived home, I stood in my kitchen by our phone (a land-line). I just talked to Jesus. I said, "Jesus, our pastor says I can divorce Shawn biblically. Is this Your *acceptable* will?" Jesus said, "Yes."

I thought about Autumn, Tyler, Linzee, and the baby to come, Josiah. I knew my choice would impact them. I did not want them to think God was powerless because He could not fix their dad's issues or to believe God's love isn't enough to teach their mom to forgive. I wanted them to know God, His love, His peace, His stability, and His power. I considered how God forgave and loved me.

Interestingly, the faulty perception I had as a young girl about God's powerlessness became the agent God used to propel me to make my choice. I did not want my kids to think God was powerless to save and restore. I knew He was powerful to save. I cared very much about the image of God I presented to my kids. My redeemed past lack and understanding fueled my determination to love and live a life of faith before my children.

I was thankful there was a choice before me. It was my freedom to choose. I told Jesus, "I do not want just to do Your acceptable will; I want to do Your perfect will. What is your *perfect* will for this situation?"

Jesus said, "Nichole, I want you to send Shawn two white roses and one red rose. Have her (the florist) put on the card: "Shawn, it's the Red One that makes all the difference."

So that's what I did.

REDEMPTION IS A BROKEN LEG (SHAWN)

There are moments when the Divine and a human being intersect and align in purpose causing something powerful to occur. When those three roses entered the hospital room that day, I knew there was hope for my family. I began to cry. Well, I wept.

I knew God forgave me and loved me, but I did not expect Nichole to forgive me. When I saw the Red One, relief flooded my soul.

There was hope because Nichole yielded to Hope. She made a choice to trust God and invest in me. She chose to believe the best and to trust God with the rest. I discovered not only did God love me more than I understood, but she loved me more than I understood. She believes I am worth investing in even when I prove to be unworthy.

God's divine love manifested Himself to me through Nichole. She had no guarantee what the outcome would be. She demonstrated perseverance. She trusted God, knowing that He would hold on to her no matter what the future held for us.

When the Divine and a human love you well, you change. I cannot explain what all happened to me, but the anointing broke things in me. With the roses beside my bedside, I knew there was a path onward for me, for us, and for us to create a home full of heritage and Hope.

There may be mountains of disappointment and disillusionment within your marriage you must face to move forward. Your family may lack the foundation of *a Godly start, but your home can become a God-loving, God-honoring environment. Today, at this moment, it can all change.*

It's the Red One who makes all the difference.

Jesus Christ makes all the difference and will continue to do so throughout your whole life. He will even work through you to make a difference in the lives of others. He will break through and tear down the walls of disappointment, shame, hurt, lust, discouragement, selfishness, and lack, even if they are invisible to you. He does not want you to remain in slavery to anything; He wants you to be His free son, His free daughter.

He wants you to love Him, yourself, and others well. He wants you to raise children who love Him, themselves, and others well.

In God's Kingdom, it is never too late to start again.

We were starting over. Nichole forgave me; I forgave myself. I recommitted myself to God, my marriage, and my kids. It was a difficult season in many ways, yet it was a refreshing season as well. There were encouraging moments and tough ones, but God was faithful, and His presence lingered in our home through it—through countless conversations, moving three steps forward, one step back, He was present, teaching us to put things right.

Weeping and Wonder

In this season, I experienced a personal revival—great healing and growth began in me. However, my relationship with Nichole was broken, and there was sadness and disappointment in the reality of what I had done to her.

I really cannot explain what happened in words, but I'll try. It was like God downloaded a blueprint into my heart and mind. He gave me vision for an abundant life marked by the Red One: a vision for my family and our future, an image of our home filled with heritage and Hope, a global desire for blessing others and utilizing my marketplace success for advancing God's Kingdom.

I began dealing with the enemy within. Because of the broken leg, I was stationary more than I had ever been since birth. I would listen to worship music for hours at night and pray. As the Spirit led me to explore the avenues of my heart, there was struggle, and there was pain. As I trusted and rested in Christ and His redeeming power and grace, there was healing, and there was Hope.

Sighs and praises, weeping and wonder—all in the same breath.

Weirdly, two of the things I'm most thankful for in my life are that mission trip to Romania, where I felt God's presence again, and a broken femur that happened during a hockey game. For me, redemption looks a lot like a broken leg.

Deal with It

You may have heard part of the passage in Philippians 3:13-14 cited in church to help people get over their past. The apostle Paul states, "But one thing I do: Forgetting what is behind and straining toward what is ahead, I press on toward the goal to win the prize for which God has called me heavenward in Christ Jesus." Then maybe the sermon continued with something like, "It does not matter what you have done or what's been done to you, it's about what Christ has done for you. Look to the future. Focus on the new."

This interpretation of Scripture is valid in many applications, but our past does matter to some extent. We do not get over our past; we surrender our past, embrace the healing God provides, and learn from it as God teaches us.

The Apostle Paul wrote Philippians years after His conversion experience with Christ on the road to Damascus. He had some things to deal with and relearn in God's Word. He was zealous for wrong things, and he had done some damage to the followers of Jesus.

The point is, Paul became a witness for Jesus almost immediately after he encountered Him. Still, it took years for Paul to re-examine and learn God's Word within the context of the arrival of the Messiah. God established truth where Paul had developed distorted views over time. It also took years for people to stop viewing Paul as a murderer. Even the Apostle Paul, who had a stunning salvation experience, dealt with the weed growth from his past life.

In His timing, Jesus made the difference in Paul's life. After Jesus chose Paul, Paul surrendered, he relearned, and he was made new. But things existed that Paul had to challenge, confront, and change. He did not just magically fulfill the apostle calling on his life well, nor did people around him allow him to.

I have learned that you must deal with your past or you and your descendants will dwell in it.

I'm so thankful God walked me through dealing with what I needed to deal with, but it was a process.

2.16

HEALING TAKES TIME

It would be a lie to tell you forgiving Shawn also meant I trusted him; I did not. Forgiveness and trust are not the same things. It would be years before there was trust between us. That's how it works sometimes.

His confession was the beginning of our healing, his and mine. It opened wounds that needed to be opened, assessed, and cleaned out. At times the damage is deeper than you realize, and healing takes longer than expected.

Physical wounds must be cleaned, treated with ointment, covered with a clean dressing, and changed regularly for healthy healing to occur. It is necessary to find the root cause of the infection. Is it from bacteria within, or is an outside contaminant contributing? What symptoms does the infection present? Also, you must understand what risk factors will contribute to slowing down the healing process and eliminate them.

Next you must press on for complete healing. It's a process. You can do everything correctly and healing still takes time. There is itching, oozing, stinging, stretching, and new growth. Then, depending on how severe the wound is, a scar will form. When you have deep wounds, you are often left marked. What that scar signifies to you and the story it tells remains your choice!

. . .

Scars Do not Define You

You can stand upon your scar and use it as a platform to tell others about healing, or you can hide it away and pretend it does not exist; but it's still there. Scars do not define you, but they are part of your story. And all God's people have scars. Every single one of us has a story to tell.

Shawn and I addressed the wounds. We discussed and decided upon clear expectations and boundaries for each other that we felt comfortable with regarding media outlets, relationships, and where and with whom we spent time. Shawn committed to weekly meetings with an awesome accountability group of three other men. (It was not wise for me to be his only form of accountability and encouragement.)

No more secrets were allowed, even if it meant I would have to hear stuff I did not like or want to hear. (I would rather live in the reality of where I am than the imagination of where I want to be.)

During this time, I again reached out to a pastor, asking if he could think of anyone who could walk with me through this. He could not think of one woman in the church able and available. It was frustrating. Also, we did not have the finances to spend on counseling and pay someone to help navigate me.

The lack of someone to walk with me is one of the main motivations for being vulnerable and open with my inner processing in this book. I hope that if you lack someone, our story helps you. You are important. God sees you. When no human seems to see value in you or is willing to walk with you, God will walk with you. He is the Great Physician and Wonderful Counselor.

God was faithful and present, but it was a hard time emotionally and physically for me. During the six months following Shawn's broken leg experience, I was diagnosed with a tumor on my kidney, possibly cancerous. Testing to evaluate the tumor (that the doctor wanted to do) could potentially cause damage to our baby in my womb. So I opted to wait until our fourth child, Josiah, was born before testing.

Because of the broken femur, Shawn could not walk independently for weeks, so I assisted him around the house: bathing, using the restroom, getting his meals. Linzee was still waking up at night for a bottle. I had an eight-year-old, a four-year-old, a one-year-old, a husband who needed spiritual, emotional, and physical assistance, and

I was dealing with a difficult pregnancy and a possible cancer diagnosis. Life was hard. Really hard.

I was extremely thankful for what God was doing in Shawn's life, but I was exhausted. My brother in the Lord was experiencing God's grace at its finest; that was my joy and hope. There was such hope, but it was so hard.

A LITTLE SPARROW

Finally, Josiah was born in December 2001. He was a ten-pound, two-ounce bouncing baby boy. The doctor induced him around two weeks early. Long story short, I had an emergency cesarean section as I was bleeding internally for various reasons. The next day my gynecologist informed me I indeed would have died (as well as Josiah) if they had not operated.

Within weeks, Josiah was in ICU for RSV.

A couple of days into this challenge, I left Josiah, my baby, in the ICU to go home and shower. I sat in our Honda Odyssey in the hospital parking lot for a few moments trying to catch my breath before getting on the road. The toll the difficulty of the previous months had taken on me was getting harder to avoid. Every single part of me felt drained. I whispered to the Lord, "I know You love me, but it sure does not feel like it."

You may or may not believe what happened next, and sometimes I even wonder if my sleep-deprived mind played tricks on me. I saw numbers in my mind and felt the Lord suggest that I put my CD player on and change it to the numbers I visualized. So I did. The song "More" by Matthew West was the song in queue. The lyrics were like water to my soul. They reminded me that God sees me, His daughter. He loves me and desires me just to be in Him—shining for Him in dark places.

Just then a little bird landed on the wing mirror of my van. "I see you," God emphasized. I remembered Matthew 10:29-31. "Are not two sparrows sold for a penny? Yet not one of them will fall to the ground outside your Father's care. And even the very hairs of your head are all numbered. So do not be afraid; you are worth more than many sparrows."

I was comforted, yet I was undone.
Sigh—sometimes all you can do is sigh.

How was I to shine through all this? I wouldn't understand what this meant until years later. I just needed to absorb God's love, trust Him, be who He designed me to be, and He would shine through me —one step, one day at a time.

Blessed in this season, I was aware that God sees all and knows all and that He loved me even if I did not feel it. He went out of His way to prove this with that little bird. Some people do not realize God is with them in trouble. Some people even think God purposefully causes their problems. I knew God did not give Josiah RSV; but I wondered if He could make numbers and a little bird appear, why did He not just heal Josiah. Why not stop Josiah from getting sick at all? Give Momma a break!

I questioned. It is normal to question. This season taught me that I can just *be* in Christ, no matter my circumstance. There was not any expectation for me to do anything. There was not anything I was doing wrong in this circumstance. It was not some great test to pass; it was just life on this planet.

Josiah recovered, then just a couple of weeks later he contracted the Rotavirus and needed medical care daily for a week until he was better. Back and forth to the doctor I drove each day to make sure Josiah was not dehydrated and was progressing in healing.

Sigh.

During this time, the doctor told me the tumor on my kidney was gone—unexplainably gone. The doctor had no medical explanation. I was healed. Wow!

Praise!

A few weeks later, I required the removal of my gallbladder. During surgery the surgeon nicked my liver, which formed an incredibly painful blood clot. I was hospitalized again and given blood transfusions because my blood count was too low. My internist said I had the second worst infection he had ever seen.

Sigh.

During this ordeal two pastors came and prayed for my healing. I barely even looked at them. Shawn was at work. Shawn was transforming by the day to be more Christlike, but he still did not get that I also needed help. I was angry and so done with putting on a happy face in front of people. As psychotic as it sounds (I know it sounds crazy), I also thought maybe God was allowing me to die. Shawn was on a course toward God, and I might just get in the way. I may distract him again. How our mind works, especially when we are low on blood and what words and thoughts stay in our brain, is baffling at times!

Sigh.

What is amazing is God divinely healed me. The internist came in the next day and said he did not understand what happened. My levels were normal, and the test showed I was fine. It did not make sense. He had me retested the next day before he discharged me from the hospital. Still fine! It was a miracle despite my bad attitude. This was the second divine healing I experienced—the tumor on my kidney and this nicked liver issue. Miracles!

Praise!

More Than I Could Handle

Why God allowed all of this to happen to my family and me during this short span is beyond my understanding; it was a lot to handle. God told me I would "have great pain" during Shawn's deliverance. But man, it was hard to handle. And I still do not fully understand it all. However, at that time, we financially did better than ever. Shawn made more money in that season than he ever had. Our marriage was on the road to recovery and restoration. I, however, felt like I was falling apart.

Hindsight! I can see some truth, even though I still do not fully understand "why." Satan (evil forces, spirits of selfishness and division, sickness, the effects of living in a fallen world) had attacked my spirit, my soul, my emotions, our marriage, and our home, and this evil was losing. Now this force seemed to be at work attacking my physical body and my child's physical body. God allowed it, but God also engaged, healed, and was present.

For clarity purposes, I want to state that I do not think God created or orchestrated the "great pain" He spoke to me about. I believe God foresees, and He chooses to reveal certain things by describing what will happen. To me, this is His grace. I'm not sure *why* He allowed so much at once, but it created a dependence on Him I would not have developed otherwise.

In 2 Corinthians 1:8-10a, Paul and Timothy describe a circumstance they endured that was more than they could handle within themselves.

 "We do not want you in the dark, friends, about how hard it was when all this came down on us in Asia province. It was so bad we did not think we were going to make it. We felt like we'd been sent to death row, that it was all over for us. As it turned out, it was the best thing that could have happened. Instead of trusting in our strength or wits to get out of it, we were forced to trust God totally—not a bad idea since He's the God who raises the dead! And He did it, rescued us from certain doom. He'll do it again, rescuing us as many times as we need rescuing" (MSG).

People say God will not give them more than they can handle. Maybe He does not, but He does allow things to come our way that are more than we can take. I do not believe God creates it, but this world will surely press down on you until you are desperate and from the depths of your being you cry out to God Himself. At least, this is my experience.

It was a hard season! But the Red One made all the difference to me.

Maybe you read our story and think, "Girl, you did not have it bad. You should watch the tragedy called my life." Truthfully, there is so much worse happening in homes all around us. Maybe your life is like what Paul and Timothy stated, "It was so bad we did not think we were going to make it. We felt like we'd been sent to death row, that it was all over for us." People have different causes of despair. Your story is not nullified because others have more pain than you.

Or maybe you read our story and are filled with gratitude because you recognize the blessing of God, and the choices you have made have given you a *better* life than we had. People experience different blessings and joy. Your story is not void because your life is better. What a testimony!

Maybe you are in a season where you have both—pain and blessings.

Cry or celebrate or do both. Do whatever is for you today to do. Because tomorrow your story will continue, and who but God knows what is coming.

One thing is the same no matter your story. God sees all, and He knows all! He does not miss a thing! Healing can come. It may take time and be full of sighs and praises at the same moment, but it will come. The Red One can make all the difference for you! Learn to let Him!

2.18

DISAPPOINTED AND HEARTSICK

Unlike the example God gives of the first family in Genesis, most families begin with little intentionality and with the Word of God virtually absent from daily application. We marry someone with whom we want to share our whole lives. We dream of what it will be. Anticipating a lifetime of love that includes a few little ones to tote around, we envision a day where we will be old and gray, still holding hands, rocking beside our forever soulmate. (Committed and deeply devoted.) Our children, how awesome they will be: cute as buttons and well behaved, bold but not boisterous, ambitious but not too aggressive, confident but humble, and God fearing.

We believe this will all come to pass. After all, we are Christians. We love God.

While there should always be feelings of favor and an expectancy to flourish for the Christ-follower, we must do more than just dream and long for someone to do our somethings with. We must plan how we will obtain our life's deepest desires or, chances are, we will forfeit them.

Sometimes life does go smoothly. We experience and receive things that simply originate from God's good grace and mercy, with no effort on our part. Our relationship with our spouse is terrific, and our kids are wonderful. Thanks be for this! More than often, however, marriage relationships and parenting turn out to be a whole lot tougher than we have bargained for. Our dearest desires are drowned out by real-as-hell life fueled by our lack of effort, intentionality, and follow-through.

On reflection, I've never met a person who has a perfect life with no misfortune or misunderstandings, especially if the person is married or has children. Relationships, this world, and life are hard. Life and people throw random, unwanted stuff at us. Things, trappings, cheap talk, and tragedy leave us feeling tainted and jaded.

For many of us, even Christ-followers, we live in places of slothful inaction, neglecting the very ones God has given us the privilege of doing and living life with. Not because we necessarily want to, but because all the junk this world hurls at us leaves us feeling exhausted, defeated, and robbed. Life just keeps moving on, and it's hard even to catch our breath.

Our families exist, but they live in a deficient, undeveloped state partly because we cannot control everything, but mostly because we do not choose to control what we can. Sometimes we are fearful, sometimes we are ignorant of our power, and other times we simply slack. We live more of a zombielike, worried, survival-mode life than the abundant life Jesus speaks about. We put *living* on hold while pressing on to survive our personal apocalypse, aka our home, all the while knowing there is more!

Proverbs gives us insight into why this may be occurring. Proverbs 13:12 says, "Hope deferred makes the heart sick, but a longing fulfilled is a tree of life." Another translation of that verse begins with, "Unrelenting disappointment leaves you heartsick" (MSG). That is not a fun state. When we do not get what we desire, we become disappointed, distracted, and discouraged. This makes for a sick heart that permeates every area of our lives, including marriage and parenting. Nobody gets everything they want from life or another person, so disappointment is a force to be reckoned with for everyone.

God does not want disappointments or unmet expectations to become chains hindering Godly change in us or our families. He desires all families to display His glory for all the world to see: to be Godly, to be alive, to dive into His goodness, and live beyond disappointments and unmet expectations with grateful hearts. He wants us to love each other with deep affection and to encourage one another with the assurance of Christ to be all He has called each of us to be in commissioned community. Together, growing and becoming more and more like Jesus every day while standing side by side through times of rejoicing and times of difficulty. As one people, unified and praising God.

Maybe you're thinking, "This Good News sounds wonderful, but my family sounds more like one with deferred hope." Perhaps you find yourself in a similar situation to ours.

Maybe you do not even like each other. Maybe you're a parent and you do not like your child. Your family does not encourage one another; you criticize each other. Maybe you think your child is the spawn of Satan. All you know is that your spouse disappoints you often; there are so many unmet expectations between you; you do not see a future together. I do not know what season you are in or the discouragement you deal with, but I know it's not God's desire or design for you.

Control

Sometimes it is difficult to discern what is within our control in the madness of our life. During this part of our journey, I often prayed to discern what was to be trusted entirely to God's sovereignty and what was within our human responsibility to exercise authority and control.

Oh, how we need discernment! We need the ability to distinguish what is our responsibility to control and what is not. We need His wisdom to know the difference.

Recognizing there is much not in my control has been a liberating force in my life—that is after I got over not being "in control." We do like to control, do we not?

When I recognized I could not control everything, it eventually brought me a sigh of relief. I began to learn to let go of what was beyond my control; it became God's responsibility. I applied Philippians 4:6, which states, "do not be anxious about anything, but in everything by prayer and supplication let your requests be known to God."

Breathe in. Happy sigh out!

But when I recognized there was much within my control, that was a different story. That revelation became a transforming agent in our family.

Knowing God entrusted us to exercise control over certain things within our family was alarming at first. Still, if you want more for your family, then you must grab the bull by the horns and be intentional about what God entrusts to you.

As Shawn and I began to recognize some things were not in our control, we also realized many things within our marriage and family were and are under our authority and power. Then we began to grab the bull horns!

HOPE IS NOT LOST

Even though each of our stories originated in a Garden, we are not all starting from the same place. Today, you may be married, separated from your spouse, divorced, remarried, a single parent, a widow or widower, adoptive parent, not yet a parent, serving as a spiritual parent, a foster parent, or in some other relational capacity. That's okay. God works in whatever situation we find ourselves. He is God, and God can do that!

One thing many people have in common is wanting to do things differently from what they (as children) witnessed adults doing, yet they grow up and replicate the things they do not want to. Maybe that's you. Perhaps you are struggling in your marriage and barely hanging on. You are in a relationship filled with selfishness and sin. Maybe you are a widow because of uncontrollable circumstances. Perhaps you are divorced, and you feel it's too late and have messed it all up. Maybe you are a single parent and feel like you are in it alone. Wherever you are, you're probably bewildered how you ended up where you are.

Listen up: Hope is not lost!

I have never met a person who wanted to grow up and be divorced. I've never met anyone who dreamed of being a source of conflict and tension as a leader in their own home. Most people do not dream dreams like that.

You may be responsible for some of the ways your life has turned out. Others may have contributed, or your circumstances changed because of things completely out of your control. You feel stuck because of a lack of control over custody issues or the poor decisions your ex-spouse is making. You feel paralyzed because of a crisis in your faith journey and the sin you have allowed to run rampant in your life.

I have Good News. Hope is not lost!

He Does Not Condemn

I want to remind you of a beautiful Scripture passage found in the Gospel of John as paraphrased in The Message: "

> This is how much God loved the world: He gave His Son, His one and only Son. And this is why: so that no one need be destroyed; by believing in Him, anyone can have a whole and lasting life. God did not go to all the trouble of sending His Son merely to point an accusing finger (to condemn it), telling the world how bad it was. He came to help, to put the world right again. Anyone who trusts in Him is acquitted" (John 3:16-18a).

Maybe the choices you have made caused most of the chaos and pain in your home. I want to encourage you today to make another choice. Trust in Jesus and His power to change you and your home. He does not condemn you. He offers love, forgiveness, and a new beginning. He desires to put things right in you and your family.

If you have a pulse, it's not too late. If you are breathing, you can begin again. Wherever you are, with who you have or do not have by your side, God will make a way. It will not be easy, but God can step in and restore your home.

. . .

One Decision

You can do something about the condition of your soul and home. You do not have to remain heartsick. You may have no idea how to make this happen, but you can decide today to create a Godly home and refuse to live in a defaulted state. Won't you choose today to have the home God designed for you and your family? It starts with just one decision.

Hope Hears Your Cry

If there is still air in your lungs, you can pray. If you have lost hope regarding your family, simply pour out your words to Jesus. Let the very air inside you become words of honesty and a cry for help. That is where hope begins.

Yet do not fear. If your sorrow is too great and you cannot find the words to speak, Hope Himself hears the heart.

Just start where you are today—no shame, no condemnation; only Hope and a choice! If you yield to Him, He will position you to establish and nurture your family from a place of

design rather than default,
love rather than lack,
promise rather than potential,
and thriving rather than surviving.

You Decide

Here is some of what one of the patriarchs of the Bible, Joshua, said "So now: Fear God. Worship Him in total commitment... If you decide that it's a bad thing to worship God, then choose a god you'd rather serve—and do it today...As for me and my family, we'll worship God" (Joshua 24:14-15 MSG).

It's a choice. Who will your family serve?

THE CALL OF THE SURRENDERED

By March of 2002, the future looked bright. Shawn and I fervently pursued Jesus and our family. Shawn transformed by the day. I remember Tyler making a statement that encouraged me and attested that the change in Shawn was real. He said, "Mom, I know my daddy loves me now. He spends time with me." If changes occur on the inside, others will see the fruit of those changes on the outside. God was turning Shawn's heart even more toward his children.

There was progress but not perfection. We had habits to break. We both had to learn new ways of communicating and living. With four littles to care for, work and school, we were busy people. We also decided to homeschool our children that year.

Homeschooling, Say What?

Early in the summer of 2002, Tyler asked us to homeschool him. (He attended K-4 at private school with his big sister Autumn the previous year.) I told him we would certainly not be homeschooling. The only previous experiences I had with homeschooled children were not good ones. They were socially awkward, naïve, disrespectful, and a little weird. I assumed this was because they were homeschooled. When I told Shawn about Tyler's request, he surprised me by asking, "Why wouldn't we homeschool them?"

What?! What?! What?! Shawn's response was so strange because he did not hold the best opinion of homeschoolers either. So I talked with Jesus about it. To my utter shock, God instructed us to do this task. This. Daunting. Task.

I did not know the first thing about homeschooling, so I did my research, ordered a curriculum, and began another new thing. God was at work restructuring our whole family for His purposes, even how we educated our children.

In August of 2002, Shawn attended another mission trip to Romania. This time Autumn, who was about nine years old, participated as well. She *felt* called to go. She worked hard to earn and fundraise finances. God stirred in her a desire to fulfill His commission to reach people globally for His glory.

Jesus made quite the changes in our home. He was and is always for you and your family. Now that Shawn and I aligned ourselves with Him and His desires, our entire family steered even more toward God, His ways, and His purposes.

Doing Laundry

While Shawn and Autumn were in Romania, something unexpected happened to me. I was doing daily chores and carrying a laundry basket in my bedroom. I sensed a transition in my spirit, and then God spoke to me and called our family to the nation of Romania.

When people say God called them to this or that, one can wonder how this happens. It happens differently for everyone. Some people have indescribable God-given passion for something. Some read a phrase in the Word illuminating their whole heart and world. Others see a need, are moved with compassion, and meet the need. And yet others hear a still small voice, sensing a stirring to go somewhere for something and be someone for somebody.

When God spoke to me about moving to Romania on that ordinary day filled with ordinary tasks, I asked Him, "Do we really have to go?" He said, "Why wouldn't you go?" I sat down on the side of our garden tub as a flood of emotions overtook my soul. I vented to the Lord for minutes which turned to hours. Complete. Word. Vomit. I highlighted why Shawn and I were utterly unqualified as if God did not know. It had only been a year since Shawn broke his leg and became honest and recommitted his life to God and his family. Things were better, but I did not feel whole and complete. And um, hello! We had four young American kids with American expectations.

I questioned God regarding how many people He asked to go before us that were simply unwilling and wouldn't go, suggesting He should maybe prod them to go. I explained I was uninterested in going when I could not seem to manage my family as I wanted. I needed more time. I needed more from Shawn. We were getting along as people. He was an outstanding dad; however, I wanted and needed more as a spouse. We were just beginning to make some headway in our home, but I still wanted a bit more time.

During my venting session, I realized something was unwell in me. I had been caring and concentrating on Shawn's health and wholeness for about a year, not to mention caring for our young children. Yet I hadn't been caring for myself and my well-being. I did not realize how frustrated I was. Now God requested I add more stress to the equation by following Shawn overseas to another nation. Just us?! "WHAT ARE YOU THINKING, GOD?" I bellowed.

All the Lord said was, "Your brothers and sisters have a need and have asked you to come." It was that simple. Someone had a need, and they asked us to fill it. The Lord later reminded me He never called me to follow a man but to follow Him. *He* was asking me to go.

Sometimes God Does Not Make Sense

If I were counseling someone like me in my circumstance, I would have told them they had done lost their mind. There is no way God would call them to go when they weren't even whole and healthy. It just does not make sense. We must put God first, then family, then ministry. That's the order of how it's supposed to be. Right?

What I have learned is God is a clever one. He knows how to bring you to the place you need to be to receive what you need from Him.

The ancient words of Isaiah 55:8-9 say, "For My thoughts are not your thoughts, neither are your ways My ways, declares the Lord. As the heavens are higher than the earth, so are My ways higher than your ways and My thoughts than your thoughts."

We did not have our stuff entirely together. We had two yielding hearts, children who loved God, and we were willing to embrace His desire for His people both at home and around the world—including Romanians across the Atlantic.

I responded to God, "Okay then. I'll go." Then I went about finishing my chores for the day and taking care of our children, our little disciples.

2.21

SOMETIMES YOU ARE THE ANSWER
(SHAWN)

While Autumn and I were in Romania, nothing else mattered but Jesus, His call, and His working on earth. A strong sense intensified in me to be Kingdom-minded. It's like God gave me a vision of His hope and plans to reach each person in this world. My life seemed so small and insignificant in comparison to God's plan for the world.

One night, while one of the Romanian pastors and I had a conversation over coffee, he shared with me about how many foreigners visited and told them how to do things differently, but no one came to live among them and show them. They offered lots of advice, lots of finances, but little help with practical action. He said they needed someone to teach them and show them.

Later, outside The People's House (the Palace of the Parliament), our group prayed with our Romanian brothers and sisters. I prayed for God to raise up people to reach the nation of Romania. As I prayed, the Holy Spirit interrupted me asking, "Why not you? Why don't you be the answer to your prayer?"

I explained to the Lord that I had just put my wife through a hell of a season, and though we were finally making great money, we were still in the middle of a hard transition. It was the worst time He could ask such a thing. I told Him He would have to speak to Nichole if He wanted us to be the answer to my prayer. I was not about to ask her to come across the world with me, so if it were Him asking, He'd have to talk with her. Then I asked Him how we would even do such a thing. How do you launch something like this and survive long term? If He were calling us, He would have to provide and speak to my wife.

When I returned home from the trip and walked through the door, Nichole asked me, "When are we going?" God had spoken to her.

PART III

CROSSING BRIDGES AND BUILDING

[THE MAKING OF TWO DISCIPLES]

"For there is one God and one Mediator who can reconcile God and
humanity—the man Christ Jesus."
~1 Timothy 2:5 (NLT)

Before we continue with our story, I want to pause and touch on the
significance and centrality of Jesus and the discipleship journey we
embraced during the first year and a half of healing and restoration
after the Red One made His appearance in that hospital room (before
we went to Romania).

I cannot express enough how vital our discipleship journey has
been and still is. Being a disciple of Jesus transformed our hearts
toward each other and our children, impacting our kids more than
anything. Being in God's presence and praying to Him compelled us to
want to join Him in a co-mission of building a Godly home filled with
heritage and Hope.

Discipleship is the bridge to the fourth part of this book, which
focuses on core things that changed in Shawn and me. The changes
that occurred in us through discipleship paved the path for Christ-
centered parenting we write about in Part Five.

3.1

BRIDGES

When I first set out to write this book, I aimed to share lessons in parenting which Shawn and I have learned over the years. However, each time I sat down to write, there was a compulsion inside of me to include the first half of this book, our journeys of becoming disciples of Jesus Christ. I just could not shake it.

Honestly, there is no joy digging through the garbage of the past. It's not fun writing about embarrassing things you have done or sharing your most painful moments. To my surprise, as I prayerfully wrote and rewrote and rewrote and edited and re-edited, there was way, way, way more good than bad. Darkness and feelings of loneliness lingered at times, but there was always a dawn and God's relentless presence. God is always working more than we know.

Nothing is wasted. God redeemed and utilized everything—good and bad—in our past lives to build bridges for our family: a bridge to Himself, a bridge between Shawn and I, and a bridge for our family to cross over into the fullness of His Kingdom. And now, hopefully, a bridge to help you cross into Hope for your marriage and family. This is what Spirit-built bridges do; they reconcile and form connections allowing you to cross over.

Bible Crossings

Throughout the Bible, there are many *crossing-over* moments. It is the way of the people of God. We cross over from unbelief to trust, from offense to forgiveness, from hate to love, from an orphan to a son or daughter, from worry to worship, from apathy to awe, from bondage to freedom, and from death to life. The life of a disciple of Jesus Christ is marked with crossing-overs—over and over and over again.

Throughout the Old Testament, people crossed over to other lands and crossed over in their belief systems. "The Parting of the Red Sea" is probably one of the more known crossing-overs (Exodus 14). One of the reasons this crossing-over stands out more than others is because there was no going back (geographically) for those who crossed over. God brought His people across a sea on dry land, but the water walls came down and filled the space after they crossed. God destined the people of Israel for freedom, worship, and learning what it means to be His people and His priests.

Jesus

Jesus, God's Word manifest, often *crossed over and to the other side.* When He crossed over waters and land, miracles occurred. Crowds heard the Good News preached. People were touched by Him, forgiven, and healed. He commanded the wind and the water. People glorified God. Peter, one of His challenging disciples, even walked across the water with Him. And His followers were given more profound revelation into who He is and who they are in Him with each crossing (Matthew 9, 14-17).

Jesus is responsible for the most crucial crossing over in all human history. The Message paraphrase describes it this way in Philippians 2:5-11,

"Think of yourselves the way Christ Jesus thought of Himself. He had equal status with God but did not think so much of Himself that He had to cling to the advantages of that status no matter what. Not at all. When the time came, He set aside the privileges of deity and took on the status of a slave, became *human!* Having become human, He stayed human. It was an incredibly humbling process. He did not claim special privileges. Instead, He lived a selfless, obedient life and then died a selfless, obedient death—and the worst kind of death at that—a crucifixion. Because of His obedience, God lifted Him high and honored Him far beyond anyone or anything, ever, so that all created beings in heaven and on earth— even those long ago dead and buried—will bow in worship before this Jesus Christ and call out in praise that He is the Master of all, to the glorious honor of God the Father."

Did you get that? Jesus crossed over from Heaven to Earth, then from Earth to Heaven through a literal *cross*-over. He is the Bridge who reconciles God and humanity. God crossed from the invisible to the visible. Humans brutalized Him, and He took it! God died on a cross and redeemed us.

Jesus showed us another way to live—to free others, to heal, to love, to give, to forgive, to not retaliate, to invest, to do justice, be merciful, be gracious, to share with those in need, to bless, to bring good news, and so much more. He showed us how to transform our world as we obey God's design and ways.

2 Corinthians 5:16-20 puts it this way,

"So from now on we regard no one from a worldly point of view. Though we once regarded Christ in this way, we do so no longer. Therefore, if anyone is in Christ, the new creation has come: The old has gone, the new is here! All this is from God, who reconciled us to Himself through Christ and gave us the ministry of reconciliation: that God was reconciling the world to Himself in Christ, not counting people's sins against them. And He has committed to us the message of reconciliation. We are therefore Christ's ambassadors, as though God were making His appeal through us. We implore you on Christ's behalf: Be reconciled to God."

Old is now new. Brokenness is made whole. The oppressed are set free. Sinners become saints. And not only are the lost found, but they learn Who and for what they are found.

After reconciling to God, you are given the ministry of reconciliation. You become a bridge for others to encounter Jesus, the One who is the Bridge of God. He is the most significant One in our family's story of heritage and Hope.

I Do not Know Jesus

Maybe the Jesus you have been reading about in this book is a stranger to you. Well, you are no stranger to Him. But allow me to make a more formal introduction:

He is God; He is good, beautiful, and loving. Jesus came to earth and lived a life for you and me, so we can see who God is and how we should live. We deduce from His life that He is willing to do what it takes to have a relationship with humans.

We all have had bad things done to us, and we all have done some awful things. Jesus died because humans did some terrible things to Him. Even though they beat, mocked, rejected, and ultimately murdered Him, He demonstrated forgiveness and a longing for a relationship with them. God desires goodness, peace, and unity with and within His creation.

He created you on purpose with purpose. You are loved lavishly. You were His dream before you were ever in your mother's womb.

Do you want to know Him? He already knows you, and He is calling you home. All you have to do is respond to His grace and surrender.

Lift your heart to Him and call out to Him and then respond to Him. You can pray in your mind, you can whisper, or you can shout! Just respond. Tell Him you want to know Him and surrender all your life to Him. Ask Him to teach you to love Him.

God will not disappoint you. Open up your Holy Bible (get one if you do not have one) and start to read it. You can start in the book of Genesis, Matthew, Mark, or anywhere. Ask Him to help you understand it; He will. Then find a Jesus-loving, people-loving, Bible studying, Word preaching and teaching church, and get involved. It may be a little uncomfortable at first, but you are so wanted and needed in God's family.

I cannot wait to hear what God does in you and your family's life. Jesus makes all the difference. God will lead the way as you cross into a new life in Him.

GROWING AS A DISCIPLE

I t is one thing to believe God exists; it is another to believe in God and become His disciple, trusting His Word and patterning your life after His. Maybe "being a disciple of Jesus" is unfamiliar terminology to you or a foreign concept. No worries. Let me share four ways through which I approach this concept.

Communion
Community
Communication
Creation

When I intentionally engage in these areas, I see personal growth in my spiritual life and direct outflow to others I disciple. (My marriage and parenting are different and better because I invest in these four actions.)

Maybe you have responded to God and asked Him to teach you how to love and live for Him and you are wondering what's next. Let me share how I practically walk out being a disciple of Jesus.

First, I focus on communion, simply spending time with God. I pray; I talk to Jesus regularly and offer a listening ear. I study His Word, the Bible. Also, I read books others have written regarding their perspective on God. I meditate on their writings and talk to Jesus about them. If you want to know someone, you must spend time in his/her presence talking to him/her and listening; otherwise, you just know *about* that person. In communion, there is a sharing and exchange. I am in an ongoing conversation with God. I nurture my relationship with God; I intentionally invest in it. I then do my best to apply whatever He has shared with me in action in my life.

Secondly, I focus on community. Spending time with people will grow you in many ways. When our children were in the home, I made spending time with my family a top-of-the-list priority. They are the people God divinely put in a close relationship with me. We have giftings to offer each other. We benefit and learn from one another.

I also spend time with people outside my family. The diversity from one person to another, from one culture to another, will expand your understanding of God. Because God created us for community, people-time is necessary. Jesus called twelve, not just one disciple. I strongly encourage you to get involved and commit to a local church and small group if you are not. Grow with others. You are part of God's large family.

Communication is a third area I engage in. I write about what I've learned about God and His Word. Writing helps me process who God is and who I am in Him. When you need to articulate what is inside of you through verbal or written correspondence to communicate with another person, especially to teach something, it forces you to deal with questions. This process leads to a deeper study of what God says about something, usually leading to more questions. Questions, in my opinion, are the lifeblood to discipleship.

Also, I verbally communicate about God and my faith journey. I talk of God's goodness often.

And lastly, I engage in creation. I spend lots of time in nature. Psalm 19 begins by saying,

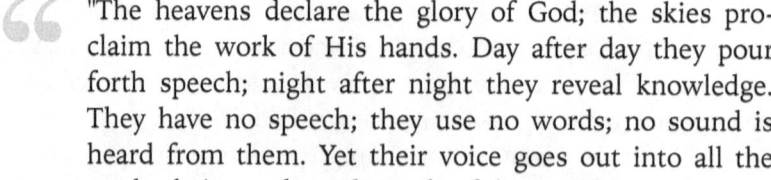

> "The heavens declare the glory of God; the skies proclaim the work of His hands. Day after day they pour forth speech; night after night they reveal knowledge. They have no speech; they use no words; no sound is heard from them. Yet their voice goes out into all the earth, their words to the ends of the world."

Breathtaking areas on this planet await you! Spending time

observing what God created and how He designed it to work will blow your mind. Evening and morning, you can rest, you can begin again. Tender mercies are new every day. Awe, humbleness, curiosity, empowerment, and gratitude fill your heart. Creation is good; God said so. It tells you something about Him.

The four ways I engage being a disciple of Jesus is not an exhaustive how-to list. They are just several of my intentional practices. There is no need to be scared if this is new to you. When you take one step toward Jesus, you discover He is already with you. It's not like you can mess up. He loves you and wants you to know Him.

If you do just these four things:

- Seek Jesus - spend time with Jesus, talk to Him, study His Word, and do His Word
- Spend time with people (those created in His image). Learn from others and love them well
- Share what you know of God with others; ask questions
- Spend time studying His creation and appreciating it

His fragrance will fill your life and flow out to all those around you. You will discover more of who God is, who you are in Him, and who your children are in Him.

Disciples discover deeper revelations about God and what it is to be human. To know God or yourself more, all you have to do is seek, knock, and ask.

3.3

RALPH LAUREN ROMANCE

About a year and a half into our journey of living our life as disciples of Jesus Christ, we continued to take our faith life seriously. Hand in hand, Shawn and I embraced Jesus and became intentional with personal disciplines of discipleship. The change was evident. It's incredible how a whole family becomes new when people actually walk out new life in Christ.

The more you seek God the more your heart will turn toward your children and to future generations. This marks a man or woman of God.

Disciples of Jesus Make Disciples

Disciples of Jesus Christ make disciples. Discipling our children became a core focus in our home. (Disciple is just a fancy word meaning a devoted follower and doer.) Developing a Christ-centered culture in our home began to rise to the top of our priorities; it was the natural effect of the cause of discipleship.

A cause is someone or something that makes something happen. *Effect* is what happens as a result of a cause.

The cause — Jesus
The effect — discipleship which made a difference

Jesus, the Red One, chose Shawn and me to fulfill Malachi 2:15 and the Cultural Mandate common to all humans found in Genesis 1:28 with our children. He desired Autumn Brook, Tyler, Linzee Joy, and Josiah to be His disciples long before He fashioned their lanky toes and big brown eyes in my womb. God wants to be the head and heart of the Marcell family, not just a part of it. He desires to be the source from which everything flows. It's the same desire He has for you and your family. God desires to be your Lord and Lover. He is deeply passionate about you and those you love. And I believe He will have His way as you say, "Yes," to Him and align to His ways.

I know I've already emphasized this, but say yes to Jesus. Saying yes to Jesus changes everything. Together in alignment with Jesus' yes, Shawn's yes and my yes, is a force to be reckoned with. "A cord of three" is not so easily broken. It is how you enter the co-mission of raising Godly offspring to know Him, be known by Him, and make Him known. Each day it begins with a yes. Building our family began, is centered in, and will end with our daily yes to Jesus.

Chosen Impact

1 Peter 2:9-12 describes who the chosen and called of God are. It states,

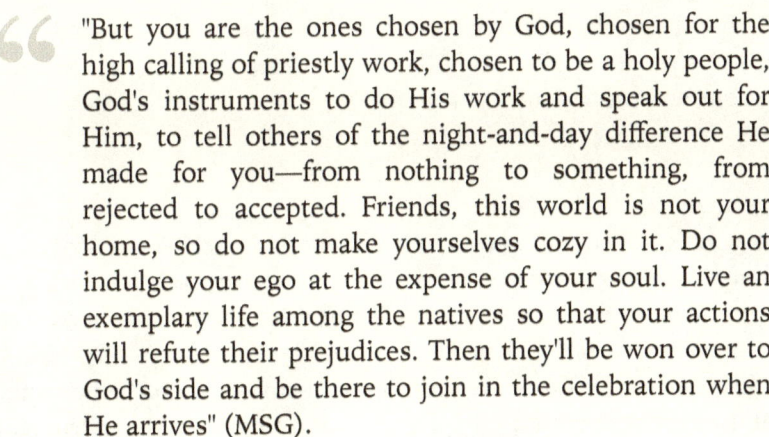

"But you are the ones chosen by God, chosen for the high calling of priestly work, chosen to be a holy people, God's instruments to do His work and speak out for Him, to tell others of the night-and-day difference He made for you—from nothing to something, from rejected to accepted. Friends, this world is not your home, so do not make yourselves cozy in it. Do not indulge your ego at the expense of your soul. Live an exemplary life among the natives so that your actions will refute their prejudices. Then they'll be won over to God's side and be there to join in the celebration when He arrives" (MSG).

You are God's chosen, called, conforming-to-Christ, commissioned son or daughter with no greater honor than to disciple the next generation. You have the privilege of doing priestly work in your home—to teach your children to love God and walk in His ways. You are blessed to be a witness before your loved ones of His goodness and mighty works. If you are a disciple of Jesus, you will not be content with sitting idly by while your kids embrace the world and all its corruption. The compassion of Christ in you will not allow you to continue to do this. You will be His witness in your home.

The impact He makes in you will overflow into and through your family because His transforming power is ever-expanding. It is uncontainable when there are yielding hearts.

All parents make an impact—bad parents, good parents, and absent parents. Most of the time, parents focus on making disciples of themselves. Anytime you train or teach someone to follow you (as many do with their children), you are making or hoping to make disciples—people who follow you and your way of life. Parents who are disciples of Jesus Christ primarily make disciples of Jesus.

If you are a disciple of Jesus Christ, you will spend time in God's presence and Word. As you do this, He *attaches* to you and impresses upon everyone and everything you touch and build. Disciples of Jesus make a difference in the world around them. His Word and ways influence your words, ways, and work. But you produce, in many ways, who you are. And you cannot produce Godly offspring if you are not a disciple of God.

To fulfill this commission, it required Shawn and me to spend time with Jesus, to learn Him and His ways. As we did this, we became infectious and contagious like a germ.

Fragrance

A germ's infectious spreading process is an excellent analogy for communicating my next concept, but it's gross; so, I'm using a perfume analogy instead. (If you are a guy, you can mentally choose to exchange perfume for cologne.)

I like to wear perfume. It's pleasant, and I'm not about being stinky at all. I squirt perfume on my hair, neck, and clothes in the morning. I just like smelling nice; it produces happy endorphins.

For years, Ralph Lauren's *Romance* fragrance has been my go-to for most occasions. It mixes well with my body's chemistry. Even after years of wearing this perfume, I am almost weekly told I smell nice and asked by someone what kind of perfume I wear. Random people have sniffed me, which is creepy yet complimentary.

My fragrance goes with me everywhere I go. If I touch and hug someone, my scent sticks to them. In each room I enter and walk out of, *Romance* lingers. However, our home is where my fragrance is experienced most potently. The aroma of *Romance* fills our house each time I spray. Starting from the bathroom, where I initially perfume myself, the sweet smell will travel to the kitchen. The aroma changes the atmosphere.

The people most affected by my scent are my family. If Shawn is near when I spray, his eyes will water up, and he will start gagging because his allergies kick in as my fragrance overtakes him. My spouse is affected the most. Then if my children are in the house, they will get a healthy dose of good smell.

2 Corinthians 2:14b-16 describes God and His effect on His disciples. The Message paraphrases it this way,

> "In the Messiah, in Christ, God leads us from place to place in one perpetual victory parade. Through us, He brings knowledge of Christ. Everywhere we go, people breathe in the exquisite fragrance."

Let's look at a portion of this passage a little more closely. It's written regarding everywhere we go and everyone we encounter, in our home and the world: our living room, riding in our car, our marketplace, school, grocery store, gym, field trip, vacation, church, and the many places the people of God travel.

Now let's personalize this Scripture (using the English Standard Version translation) and focus just a bit on what this scripture is communicating within the context of our home.

> "Through us (*you, Dad and Mom—follower of Christ*), He brings knowledge of Christ (*Jesus is made known*). Everywhere we go (*including within our home and beyond*), people (*our spouse and children*) breathe in (*inhale, receive life-giving force*) the exquisite fragrance. Because of Christ (*the difference Jesus makes*), we give off a sweet scent rising to God (*worship pleasing to God*), which is recognized by those on the way of salvation (*awareness of the Way, the*

Truth)—an aroma redolent *(strongly suggestive of)* with life."[1]

Get Out of the Way

Mom, Dad, if you are not spending time with Jesus, there will be no divine fragrance to linger or cling to your children. God wants your kids to smell of His scent. It's not about making *primary* disciples of yourself. God wants His offspring to bear His likeness—not Shawn or Nichole's likeness, not *your* likeness.

It is very cool when my children do something well that looks like Shawn or I do. We feel happy because we taught them something good like a helpful skill or behavior. It's fun to see your good mannerisms reflected in your kids. However, when our children do something which reminds me of Jesus, my heart smiles the most. I thank Jesus, then say, "Good job, Nichole. Good job, Shawn." We got out of the way, and Jesus came through.

The Fragrance of the Kingdom

Parent, as you live as a disciple of Jesus Christ, everywhere you go and everyone you touch, including those in your home, will experience Jesus and life. It is a natural order that takes place within Kingdom culture. As you seek the Lord, you become saturated in God's presence, and His fragrance permeates your home through you.

If Jesus is the center of your life, He becomes the center of your family; a Christ-centered culture will form in your family. Some instant transformation will occur, but other changes will come over time as you surrender daily to Christ. It takes prayer, intention, planning, patience, mercy, grace, trial and error, and a whole lot of follow-through and love. Mostly, it takes time spent in the presence of God for the fragrance of the Kingdom to saturate your family.

He Got on Us All

I love how God came down to earth in human form. Jesus lived and walked with people. His life and death impacted our world so much the earth shook, rocks split, and the veil of the temple ripped in two.

Tombs opened, and dead people rose and appeared (Matthew 27). His influence reached into the heart of man. Jesus brought sight, healing, freedom, and hope to everyone around Him. Synthetic perfume permeates for a time, but His incarnate fragrance is eternal and is still lingering on this earth, thousands of years later, passed on from person to person.

Redolent with His Spirit, we become instruments of Hope. Things shake and come loose; life breaks forth from dead places, beginning first in our homes. Our efforts have a lasting effect, leaving a lingering fragrance of legacy in and through our children.

This is the most crucial aspect of our home regarding raising our children as Godly offspring: We are disciples of Jesus who have not neglected to make disciples of Jesus with our children. The fragrance of Christ *got on* our kids because He *got on* us as we spent time with Him.

3.4

TODAY, LIFE ON THE OTHER SIDE

Early in our marriage, we raised our children *in God* as much as possible within the context of the choices we made and the circumstances we lived. Now, we crossed over. There was no more avoiding God, struggling with self, or fighting with each other. Things were not perfect at this point in our journey, and they are not perfect today. The difference is that we run toward God, acknowledge Him in all our ways, surrender ourselves, and fight FOR each other. And all of this positively impacts our parenting.

We are a couple of decades on the other side of those spiritual bridges we crossed over, and it is still just flat awesome on the other side! I hope the story of Jesus, His patience, His faithfulness, His mercy, His grace, and His gentle guiding of us encourages you to surrender every aspect of your life and family. I pray you take the steps needed to cross over into your promised land if you have not already.

Our crossing-over process was filled with chaos brought to order, denial of self, preferring others, trusting God and His ways, unfamiliar territory, unforeseen outcomes, forgiveness and letting go, and refocusing on our family. The vision God gave me for raising Godly offspring to His glory was not only mine but Shawn's now as well. As mentioned earlier, when a man or woman spends time with the Father, His heart for his children will ever expand.

All this is part of discipleship. All of it is so worth it! Life looks a lot different on the other side. It is filled with heritage and Hope.

Since our restoration over twenty years ago, our family has been doing well. As a family, we have presented and practiced the Gospel before thousands of people while working in vocational ministry and the marketplace. For fifteen of those twenty years, Shawn and I have served side-by-side in vocational ministry; we have served in the local church, in non-profits, and abroad as missionaries in Romania. Each member of our family is a disciple of Jesus Christ, making disciples. We love the Lord and are awed by His goodness.

We no longer live in a defaulted place but rather within His Design. Love replaced lack. We aren't just surviving; we thrive. The potential that once lay dormant within our family is alive and being fulfilled in His promises.

Since we crossed over together in 2001, we have not wavered in honoring God and our kids (to the best of our ability) or in raising our children to be God's offspring. Not only have we yielded to what the Lord says regarding them; we now embrace it passionately and engage it at every turn.

We have learned a lot and are still learning. Today, all our children are adults. Three of them are married, and we adore our "son and daughters-in-love." Our first grandchild, Hazey Grace, was born in 2020. And we are expecting our second granddaughter, Jubilee Mae. We are in a whole new season of life, and it is good. God is good. He is so good! I'm teary-eyed as I write this because He is so good to us, so good to me.

Transformation

All things transformed in our family because Jesus made us His disciples. Then God gave us more vision for what a Godly family is—what Godly offspring is. Then He called us to build what we saw in co-mission with Him. We became present, engaged, and intentional with our faith journey and family.

3.5

GOD SPEAKS, WE ECHO

What is Godly offspring? I want to define what I mean when I use *Godly offspring* or *a family of God*. A particular image may come to mind when people think of a Godly family or Godly children. I know I had a perception of how I thought we should look. Right after we *crossed over* and things started coming together, I had a certain way I thought everyone should act—a specific look, a certain vibe. How wrong I was! Not only do we put God in a box, sometimes we put His people in a box bordered by limitations we have imagined and constructed.

Why do we create images of how a Godly person or family must look in our minds? Like people projected an expectation of what I should look and be like as a pastor's wife in the 80s, I quickly developed an opinion of how my Godly family should look and be like— how they should best act to represent Christ.

I was wrong to form such a thing. We were on the right track at this point, but I was about to ruin it and limit my family by adding all kinds of fluff to the vision God gave me. I was about to conform them to what I desired. I can confidently state God is not about your family becoming what you think it should be; He is about conforming each member to Himself.

God quickly intervened and shut me down. He emphasized daily dependence on Him for myself and my children. He reminded me of the glimpse of a Godly family He gave me during my teenage years. It was not an image to obtain; it was life in Christ fulfilled within and with people divinely designed with different personalities and God-given desires who honor Him and each other. That simple.

I was instructed at every turn to be careful not to require my family to conform to any standard or system, but to point them to Jesus. 2 Timothy 3:5 refers to people who "will act religious but reject the power of God that could make them Godly" (NLT). Humans fall quickly into a particular way or system of doing things. That is not a Godly family; it is a religious one.

Maybe this seems like a minute thing, but it matters; God wrestled with me regarding this. It's best to follow God's leading. I think of it this way: God speaks, we echo, God does, we do what He does.

I encourage you if you have a picture-perfect image you have created in your mind of a family that would best reflect a family of God, dismiss it. Your vision, even on its best day, will fall dramatically short of the grandness of what God has in store.

A Godly Family

While writing this book, I struggled with something I found in Scripture or, rather, did not find. I could not find an example of a family which looked more like a Godly family than ours. Every single family I read about, like our family, consisted of profound failures or, at minimum, had or experienced division.

I prayed for God to reveal to me a Godly family (from my point of view) from His Word to write about that exemplified Him better than we did. I sought to use what I deemed a better Godly example: a family without massive dysfunction and junk. I mean, just one. I thought I could reference them instead of our family to give you a better example. Well, I still cannot find this family in the Word. (Please contact me and tell me where they are in Scripture if you know of one, but I do not think you will find one.)

After months of wrestling and chewing on this, I thought maybe there's a divine point in the lack of a perfect or better (according to me) family example. Perhaps it's not about being flawless but about the One who redeems us despite our failings. Aaaah, revelation!

So let me be clear, if you think a Godly family is a family with only good *things*, well, you'd be wrong. If you believe a Godly family consists of people who are always pleasant and in a good mood or people who always make the right choices, then you are in for a rude awakening. If you think they all look clean-cut, have friendly smiles, drive great cars, and wear cute dresses to Sunday church, wrong again! Having a Godly family does not mean you will not deal with disappointing ungodly things. It does not mean your children will not sin or bad things will not happen to you.

Having a Godly family is simply being a family of God's. It is a scandalous, beautiful realization to discover that the families that God labels as His in the Bible are far from perfect. Some of the family circumstances I read about in the Word make my skin crawl and give me a sick stomach. But God still claims them as His. It's shocking the families written about are still God's family even when they do not act Godly. Scandalous!

Bible families, the families the Father built and used for His glory, divinely created to bear His image, were scarred by the infliction and embracement of sin. To mention a few sins, they dealt with disobedience, distrust, deception, discontentment, sibling rivalry, murder, estranged relationships, and not taking responsibility for personal actions. If you continue reading past the second chapter of the Bible, you will discover the first family God created possessed all of these. Also, we must consider that Adam and Eve, the first parents of mankind, walked with God in the cool of the day. They experienced the Father like few ever have and still dealt with disobedience and these undesirable elements. Yikes!

If you think a family unit filled with disciples of Jesus will not deal with undesirable things, again, a rude awakening is coming your way. Just speed-read through the Gospel of Mark. Disciples of Jesus Christ, who walked with Jesus while He was on earth in human form, dealt with objectionable things. For example, they dealt with lack of understanding, lack of faith, hard hearts, competitiveness, arrogance, selfish ambition, a desire for violence, anger, fear of man, and being cliquish to the point of rejecting others. Yuck!

Also, being a Godly family does not mean sickness or natural disasters will not strike you. Three of my friends who love the Lord have children who are no longer on this planet but are Home with

Jesus. Their children died at very young ages. It does not make sense. During the writing of the last chapters of this book, three hurricanes hit Louisiana, our home state. Some of the Godliest people I know suffered loss over and over again. Blah!

Do not misunderstand; there are definite marks of God on His families. Godly families share many Godly attributes: love, patience, kindness, joy, endurance, goodness, faithfulness, not keeping a record of wrongs, gentleness, honor, and forgiveness. All these wonderful characteristics and more exist and are evident upon the people of God. But think about this: For patience to be displayed, there must be a moment where patience is needed. There must be an offense to forgive. There must be a lengthy list of wrongs if we choose not to keep a record.

The point I'm hoping to drive home is this: People make up a family of God, and people are not perfect. And God's people deal with everything everyone else does. What marks a Godly family is WHO and WHAT they honor above all, HOW they deal with what comes their way, WHO they run to, and HOW they demonstrate love for one another. God marks us as His, but it takes time for His Spirit to teach us His ways. Sometimes we struggle to adapt to His ways. God does not just snap His fingers and "BAM!" we are perfect. It is not His way.

After pondering my findings and lack thereof in the Bible, I define a *Godly family* like this:

- A family made up of humans God calls His own.
- A community that loves the Lord and loves each other (even when one does not deserve it or maybe even when they do not like each other for a time).
- People who reveal Jesus to the world because of their unity and love for one another.
- People who know, honor, and love God.
- Men and women who do not hide from God nor feel the need to hide from each other.
- People who understand they can run to Jesus no matter the failure or struggle.

- A group of disciples who delight in time with God and in His Word.
- People who stick together, forgive, and strengthen one another.
- People that support each other through the yikes, yuck, and blah of life, even if they result from poor choices they have made.
- A group of people very good at responding to grace and surrendering to God even when things do not make sense.
- Fellow journeyers who believe in the restorative power of God.
- A family who loves mercy and display that love in word and action to each other.
- They are a people entrusted to one another who are full of heritage and Hope because of the difference Jesus makes in their lives.

I pray you allow the Father to build this with your family. This is what we are still building.

BUILD WITH GOD

As a reminder, I want to restate what I wrote at the beginning of the book: Godly children and building a God-honoring home is a cooperative effort. It is a joint mission. An exploit between God and man. As a parent, you possess the privilege of partnership with God in raising part of humanity. You have an opportunity to influence your child's life and impact people beyond your reach through the life of your child. Parents have the opportunity to disciple a person for Jesus. From the moment a child arrives on Earth, a parent is the one with a chance to affect nations by raising the person God entrusts to him and her.

Only with God by our side do we successfully build Godly homes. We create something significant and beautiful as we align with His design, purpose, and will.

Psalm 127 gives us some remarkable insight into building. It states,

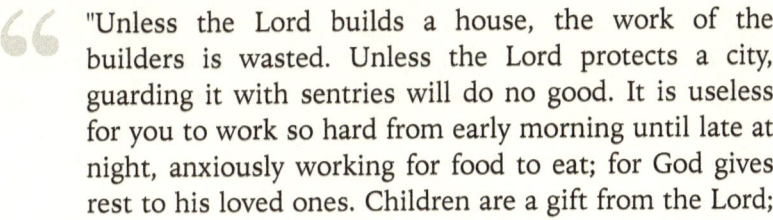 "Unless the Lord builds a house, the work of the builders is wasted. Unless the Lord protects a city, guarding it with sentries will do no good. It is useless for you to work so hard from early morning until late at night, anxiously working for food to eat; for God gives rest to his loved ones. Children are a gift from the Lord;

they are a reward from Him. Children born to a young man are like arrows in a warrior's hands. How joyful is the man whose quiver is full of them! He will not be put to shame when he confronts his accusers at the city gates" (NLT).

The first verse in this Psalm testifies that if God is not in the mission of building with us, then we work in vain. As parents, we may raise healthy, civil, confident, and joy-bringing children. Some families do not serve the Lord yet raise *good* kids. Some non-Christians love and nurture their children (to the best of their ability), making significant impacts in their communities. However, we miss the mark when a family omits God from the equation. God designed the family unit for His purposes. If we do not acknowledge our partnership with Him, how will we know His purposes or who we truly are? Who our children are? How would we live in our fullest promise?

One of the things I appreciate about Psalm 127:1 is it speaks of a partnership between God and man in building a house. The Lord establishes the house, but He partners with "those." The word *those* refers to humans. God and humanity building something that is not futile. In other words, God must be involved, engaged, and active in what we create for our endeavors to hold eternal value.

Let's acknowledge this fact: You will build something. We can construct by design with the Great Designer or by default, where division and dysfunction run rampant. It is frustrating to do or make something that is irrelevant and insignificant. Why would a person exert blood, sweat, tears, and time into an effort which has no eternal effect or gain, yielding little if any value? Why would we spend our lives doing the best we can, without God, when our family can have much more with God?

Marriage and parenting are hard work! Can I get an "Amen"? I want the best return for my efforts for my family and myself. I believe you want this also. I do not wish for the efforts I execute to be wasted. I believe you do not want your efforts squandered either. Therefore, considering God's design and ways is absolute to building something worth building, like a Godly home!

Our story is evidence of the grace, mercy, and faithfulness of God at work building our family, even while Shawn and I fostered division and dysfunction—divisively tearing down our home. God did His part, no matter our lack of cooperation or opposition.

I'm sure you can identify areas within your own life where you have received grace, getting more than you deserve, and mercy, getting less than you deserve. A time God showed up and out for you when you did nothing to earn it. Remember when He preserved, protected, and provided for you simply because He is who He is? We all have at least one moment we can identify. However, when we acknowledge Him and our partnership with Him and come into alignment with Him, we can build some things and somebodies of eternal effect. Something simply wonderful!

As stated earlier, nothing is wasted from either Shawn's or my childhood or early years of marriage. God took the good and bad we experienced, using each experience and lesson to teach us what to do and not do with our kids. As we go forward in the next part of this book, you will see the connection between *how and why* we do things.

Imagine it this way: Every good experience is a trampoline, you know, the individual-sized ones. Now imagine running with all your force and jumping on the trampoline and flying forward. God uses the good experiences and lessons of our lives like this. They are launching pads to propel us further for His glory.

In contrast, each lousy lacking experience is a vessel. It's a sweet-tea pitcher in my mind. I'm from South Louisiana, so I think sweet tea thoughts. Okay, picture this sweet-tea pitcher sitting empty and isolated on the dry dirt—empty, lacking, not serving its purpose. Suddenly, two giant hands pour the liquid into the pitcher. Refreshing sweet tea fills the pitcher and continues to overflow until it soaks the ground around it. Then, BAM! Green shoots break soil, emerging from the ground. Before long, you have a beautiful sweet life-giving garden hydrated by the sweet tea nectar of Heaven. (Yes, I know water would better illustrate, but sweet tea is what I see.) You get the point! God uses your bad experiences and lessons learned from lack to produce a life-giving substance for others to drink—He does not waste a thing! Some of your past deficits may become the strongest foundational stones and pillars of your home.

3.7

ASK FOR WHAT YOU WANT

Can you *see* the differences occurring in our lives as you read? No longer was it about just me or us, but our kids and God's desire for us all. The more we grew closer to Jesus, Shawn and I grew closer to each other and how our hearts grew for our children. (It was also increasing for those beyond our home.)

It's hard to write it out in categorized order because it is all connected. Because you are connected to others, how you live for God affects them. That's why in this part of the book, I write about discipleship practicalities, about God's fragrance permeating our home, then about what a Godly family is, then about building a Godly home —it is all connected.

The more we practiced living out our faith, the more answers we received, but more questions surfaced. Maybe you too have more and more questions. Who is God? What is He like? Who are we as a married couple? Who are we as parents? Who are our children? What is the role of a parent? What is the role of a child? What's the best parenting style? Are there absolutes to follow? How do I gauge success in this venture? Let's ponder these questions for a moment.

Well, God is absolute to answer all these questions. He is the Author of Life. Jesus, the Word manifest, is the Bridge of understanding into who God is and who He desires us to be. You will spend a lifetime plus learning who He is. We can partially answer the questions, but we will discover the more complete answers throughout eternity.

Regarding parenting, we know several things contribute to our perception: our upbringing, how our parents did or did not do something, our culture, the community we are part of, what society tells us, and what statistics report, to mention a few. All of these affect our thoughts more than we realize.

Who are our children? How we view our children is also affected by the things mentioned in the above paragraph. Sometimes what we hope to gain in having children may make a difference in how we perceive them. So who are we? Who are they?

These are questions that will not get answered at once. They take time to discover and grab hold of. There are many books to read and people to receive counsel from on marriage and parenting. I believe they are helpful to uncovering marriage and parenting nuggets of wisdom, or I wouldn't be writing this book.

Early in my parenting journey, I read a few books, joined several groups focused on parenting, and watched a few families from a distance. I gleaned knowledge and wisdom. However, learning about being a Godly parent has been a prayer-pondering process for me. Most of the wisdom we gained—the revelations we know are essential to the fruit people witness in our family—came straight from the throne of God and His Word. We simply applied the instruction.

When you seek out God and the Word regarding your family, He will begin to give you divine viewpoints regarding who you are, who your children are, and what your roles entail and do not involve. All those other resources complemented and encouraged me like I hope this book does for you, but they were and are not a substitute for God's sovereign knowledge about our families or us.

As you continue to read this book, I encourage you to pray that the Holy Spirit will speak to you specifically about your family. Make personal notes, lots of them. Then apply those divine discoveries to your home and build something good.

A Giant Elephant

There's a giant elephant in the room I want to acknowledge at this point. What if only one of you in the marriage/parenting relationship says yes to Jesus? What if only one of you lives as a disciple of Jesus Christ?

While writing this book, I walked with two people through divorce, another person through separation who is currently filing for divorce and another woman who is separated, still in hopes of reconciliation. All four of these women are daughters of God. (Not perfect people, but daughters of God who live in God's ways.) It is devastating to watch as their families are breaking apart.

Sins like lust, lying, and primarily selfishness are satanic. They rob peace, kill unity, and destroy people in their wake.

The reality is you can do everything you can do and your family may still fail to be reconciled to wholeness if the other person does not say yes to surrendering to Jesus and laying down selfishness. Even as I write this, I know how sad this sounds. Sin is horrid. Selfishness is at an all-time high. However, with Jesus, you can still produce Godly offspring with God and *your* yes. Things will be more difficult without the partner who promised to walk with you forever working alongside you; however, God is faithful. God does not lie. God does not abandon His responsibilities toward you.

Maybe your spouse decided to say no to Jesus and broke your heart. I wish I could sit with you, hug you, and cry with you. This is hard. But I also wish I could grab you by the shoulders, pick your chin up and say, "There is hope if you say yes! Just watch what God does in you and with you. Just watch how the spiritual seed you plant and nourish in your children will grow."

I know you can produce Godly offspring because the Bible is full of broken families, yet each generation yields Godly offspring; God is faithful. When one person chooses righteousness, amazing things happen. Two Godly parents did not raise Moses and Timothy, but they served God well! Moses led a nation out of physical and spiritual slavery. Timothy became Apostle Paul's right-hand man and ministered to the early churches. And let's not forget Mary. Most Bible translations do not mention her parents. She carried and birthed the Savior of the world.

I cannot hug you now, but you can run into the arms of Jesus. Right now, He is with you. He sees all and knows all—nothing escapes His notice.

I also want to acknowledge that it's not just men that are selfish. Women cause permanent brokenness to family units as well. Sin is not limited to just one gender, and it sucks no matter who does it.

You may be thinking, "What's the point then?" I did think that at moments. My rationale led me to accept that I can only control myself. There were moments when I thought, "What if I invest even more into Shawn and it does not work out." For me, the point was God's desire for Autumn, Tyler, Linzee, and Josiah. The point was His desire for Shawn. They are worth my investment. My thought was that at the end of it all, if Shawn did not surrender to God, I would trust God for myself and my kids. For me, it all became about trusting God with it all, whatever the outcome.

God Loves Your People

Remember: God loves your family more than you do. You may feel good emotions or regret as you ponder your faith journey, marriage, and parenting. You may see some places you have missed the mark and are feeling guilty and ashamed. All this can stop today. Just give your whole life journey, the successes and failures, the abundantly good and the lack, over to Jesus. Ask Him to make up for the past lack in your life and failures. Ask for wisdom to not repeat those mistakes.

If you ask, He will answer with revelation and guidance. Matthew 7:7-8 reminds us,

"Keep on asking, and you will receive what you ask for. Keep on seeking, and you will find. Keep on knocking, and the door will be opened to you. For everyone who asks receives. Everyone who seeks finds. And to everyone who knocks, the door will be opened" (NLT).

Also, James 1:5 states, "If you need wisdom, ask our generous God, and He will give it to you" (NLT). What an encouraging Scripture! It authorizes me to believe that whatever God asks me to be or do He will tell me how to fulfill it. My responsibility is to ask and listen, seek and find. Just knock and walk through the open door He provides.

The sacred Scriptures are plentiful with wisdom. They are alive and help you gain understanding. What a comfort, encouragement, and empowerment the Word is to me during trying days of life. I encourage you to dig deep into the Word of God for your counsel. You will not be disappointed. I never am.

PART IV

TRANSFORMATION

[DEVELOPING NEW EVERYTHING]

"By this everyone will know that you are My disciples,
if you love one another."
~John 13:35, Jesus

There were major changes to the Marcell home because of the life-changing transformation in Shawn and me. Everything was becoming new.

Through our discipleship process, our hearts were turned home. But individual changes were required in each of us to carry out the vision God gave us. In the first few sections of this part, Shawn will share some core changes that transformed our family in tremendous ways. Then I will share several ways in which the transformations in me fashioned the foundation of how we moved forward in our marriage and raised our children to be disciples of Jesus.

This divine transformation ushered in the understanding of who we, Shawn and I, have been entrusted with and gave us the heart and insight to pass down spiritual heritage and center our whole family around Hope Himself.

4.1

SON OF GOD/A NEW MAN

When we become new in Christ, there is an instantaneous rebirth. In that very first moment of surrender to Christ, you begin again like a newborn baby entering the world—a clean slate. However, when God creates a new person from an old one, He must tear down old ways of thinking, bad habits, and false idols to continue transforming and building a person in conformity to Christ. Saying yes to God means saying yes to a new life and new ways of looking at things and living life out. A new life in Christ means making new choices according to God's Word and will for your life.

When a person truly surrenders to Jesus, you will not have to ask if he/she knows Jesus. You will see and hear that he/she knows Him. His/her life will look different than it was. How he/she lives, treats his/her spouse, raises his/her kids, loves others, and how he/she functions in the workplace will change.

When you cross over to the other side and say yes to the God of the journey, you must trust in the transition process. Next, you must trust Him in the demolition, reconstruction, and the growth process as all things become different.

Romania

I could write a whole book just on our missionary adventures in

Romania and the lessons learned. I am still in awe of how God used this time in our lives to teach us to live in new ways. That missionary assignment was like a big object lesson for our family.

We said yes to the call to go to Romania. Our whole family hopped on a plane in 2003 and crossed over the Atlantic Ocean. Just closing down our lives in the States and taking this trip with four little children was quite the undertaking.

When our feet hit the ground on Romanian soil, I realized my surroundings were different. Of course there were similarities to my life in the States, but even similar things had differences. For example, people greeted and welcomed us at the airport with bouquets of flowers and kisses on the cheek. Obviously, there are humans in Romania just like in America, yet they sounded, looked, and welcomed us a bit differently than Cajuns back home. In Louisiana, greetings come with hugs, a cup of Community Coffee, and some yummy Cajun food waiting on the kitchen stove.

When we left the airport, I noticed tall buildings lined the city streets of Bucharest just like a city in the States, yet the beautiful architecture of the buildings played down by lack of color felt cold. It seemed tan and gray were the only paints on a palette to choose from in this post-Communist country.

Dogs. So many dogs roamed the streets. "Where is animal control?" I thought.

The sky still hung over our heads, and the ground was below our feet. But even that was different. Snow was up to my thighs. Being from south Louisiana, I had never seen so much snow.

And the potholes. We hit pothole after pothole after pothole as we drove in an overloaded microbus for two and a half hours to our new home. Well, truthfully, that was not much different than Louisiana roads.

The most startling observation I made within the first hour in this country regarded the signs on the sides of the road. The traffic signs, billboards, and posters on buildings were not in English. I could not read a thing. I do not know why it never crossed my mind that the signs would be in Romanian and not English, but it did not. The moment this clicked in my brain, a sober awareness I was not in crawfish country anymore hit me like a tidal wave. I thought to myself, "I'm gonna have to relearn everything."

. . .

Just Different

Romania's culture is very different from the culture I grew up in. When our family resided in Targoviste, the western mentality which we possessed clashed in extreme contrast with the mentality of the Romanians we worked alongside. To function in this new territory, we needed to understand how and why they thought a certain way. We had to change how we approached aspects of everyday life: sleep patterns, grocery shopping, work schedules, and language.

In the states, my kids had a bedtime. At this time, they were all under nine years old. When they attended private school, the standard bedtime was around 8:00 pm. When we homeschooled, it was around 9:00 pm. In this new culture, people showed up at our home to visit around 11:00 pm. Once, people showed up at 12:30 am. Most of the people we knew started their day mid-morning instead of early morning. We thought this schedule was crazy.

Grocery shopping was different. In the States, I usually grocery shopped once a week. I would load down my basket with everything I needed and hoped I wouldn't have to return to the store again until the following week. The first year we domiciled in Romania, we shopped for one to two days at a time. The stores did not have grocery baskets to load. We visited markets and several corner stores to locate items we needed and wanted. The American items we enjoyed were unavailable; the grocers did not even sell packaged meat in our new town. We adapted and altered what we ate.

We were accustomed to working eight-hour to twelve-hour days in the States. Most of the people we worked alongside in Romania worked maybe four hours per day doing one specific job. We were accustomed to starting the workday around 8:00 am. We were multi-taskers, but most of our team liked to focus on one task at a time. We would hear the phrase, "It is impossible," several times throughout the day. We were not used to this mentality. It did not mean our way was better or worse; people just accomplished things differently in their culture.

And obviously, the language was foreign to us. We instantly understood the necessity to hire translators at least five days a week. We did our best to learn the language, but we quickly realized that language is more than knowing what word to use. Even if you know the words spoken, you do not always understand the slang, tones, tense, emotion, and concept of what someone says.

Things were different.

We built a new life through change, adaptation, altering what needed altering, transformation, learning new things, and creating new habits. As aliens, we learned valuable and priceless life lessons by embracing the Romanian culture and functioning in a new way.

We also came bearing good gifts for this new-to-us country. We carried over the good things God fashioned and placed in us. God called us to this new place to work with Him alongside His Romanian people. God put valuable gifts for the Romanian team to glean from each of our family members. The fruit they picked off our lives, embraced, and applied helped to build the body of Christ in Romania.

Embracing New Life

When you become a disciple of Christ, life may seem foreign to you at times. You must relearn, change, alter some things, think differently, create new things, and stop other things. Disciples of Jesus live different.

As disciples of Jesus, Shawn and I took on a *foreign spiritual* culture: The Kingdom Culture—Christ's culture. Everything became different: Shawn, me, our marriage, how we raise our kids, and the team ministry concept we function in.

When our daughters read the first draft of this book, they said the man I wrote about in the first part of the book is not at all like their dad. Linzee said, "It does not sound like him, Mom. That's not who he is." After assuring her I agreed with her, I remarked, "That's the difference Jesus makes. You do not know that man because he does not exists anymore." What a powerful testimony to God's transforming power—our kids do not even recognize the person in the first part of this book.

Son of God

A wife sees the good and bad. We hear the real deal behind the scenes. Today I testify that my husband isn't the same man I spent the first decade of my marriage with. Shawn loves Jesus and is a bold, God-confident man of God.

Shawn is an articulate communicator. There is an awesome spirit of counsel within Him; many seek him out for counsel.

He is such a forgiving person. I've watched him not only forgive people who have wronged him but truly forgive them; he does not hold grudges. He inspires and challenges me in this area.

Shawn is more compassionate toward people than ever. He helps people in need.

He can cast vision, form, and rally a team like few can. He is an amazing minister and businessman. His peers highly respect him, but even more importantly, his family respects him. He is the husband I always wanted. He is faithful to God and me. He is the best dad I know. He loves his family well.

Shawn is who he is when he is at home and when he is not at home, with me and when he is not with me. What you see is what you get. He lives in liberty. I do not admire or trust another man more. He is my brother in Christ and my best friend, and I love living life with him.

How do I fully describe my husband? So much goodness and awesomeness exist within him! I see Jesus in him. We cannot write about every noteworthy thing, but there are four things I see in him that I believe are God's design for every one of His sons who are married and a father. These are powerful things Shawn lives out which impact our family for good and eternity.

Husband, Dad, if you are a man of God, the old made new in Christ, do what Shawn does.

Remember.
Be present.
Cling to your wife.
Love well.

4.2

REMEMBER (SHAWN)

*Z*akar[1] *is a Hebrew word meaning to remember and "to be male." God designed His sons to remember Him and His Word. (I read this quote somewhere, "To remember is to be male.") As Nichole cited earlier in this book, to remember, in Hebrew thought, is to act on what one is meditating and recalling. It is to recognize and fulfill the responsibility of what you remember. In other words, what you remember should lead to applied action in your life.*

Zakar distinguishes the man of God.

Zakar is not just about recollection: it is recalling parallel results. It is to remember God and others and act on their behalf—to honor and love Him above all and prefer others, not just in your headspace as you think about them but also through your actions.

For example, Genesis 8:1 says,

> "But God remembered Noah and all the wild animals and all the livestock that were with him in the ark, and He sent a wind over the earth, and the waters receded."

When God remembered, it resulted in making wind to make waters subside. He did not just think, "Oh, yeah. I have a zoo roaming the earth with nowhere to go," and did nothing. That's not the end of the story.

In Psalm 25:6-7, David prays, asking God to remember.

> *"Remember Your mercy, O Lord, and Your steadfast love, for they have been from of old. Remember not the sins of my youth or my transgressions; according to Your steadfast love remember me, for the sake of Your goodness, O Lord!" (ESV)*

David is not asking the Lord only to recall and think about how merciful and loving He is. He asks Him to remember who He is to pardon him for his transgressions. David wants action produced by remembering.

Another example is Psalm 143:5-6. We observe the psalmist's desperation through his proclamation and action,

> *"I remember the days of old; I meditate on all that You have done; I ponder the work of Your hands. I stretch out my hands to You; my soul thirsts for You like a parched land" (ESV).*

In remembering his past and the days of old, the psalmist took the action of pursuing God. His recalling caused him to seek out God and allow Him to quench his thirst.

I Remember

When faced with choices and challenges, I remember who God is, who I am in Him, what God has done, and what God's Word says. I trust in God's Word and take the action His Word instructs. I make choices based on His counsel. I do not fulfill my appetite with the things of the world; I find fulfillment in Christ. I do not forget who God is or that I belong to Him.

Whereas I used to worry about my reputation, now my hope is that people see Jesus in me. I pray the evidence of God's lordship and love is in each step I take (Proverbs 3:5-6).

I strive for my children to know me as a man who remembers God and His ways. I want them to have an example of a dad who does not deny God's goodness, faithfulness, and power. I live my life to honor Him. When my kids look upon me, I want them to see the reflection of the Father and the evidence of what God has done in me.

Dad, do you remember who God is and that you are His son? Do you remember His ways and counsel when you are faced with challenges and must make choices reflecting Who and what you honor? Whom and what satisfies your thirst?

I pray your kids see the Father in their father. They are watching you.

HERE I AM (SHAWN)

One of the most powerful privileges God gives a man is to be present with his family. I am present in each member of my family's life. You can tell when a man of God is immersed in the presence of God by how present he is with his family. When a man walks with God, he awakens to his ability to pass down heritage to the next generation, starting with his children.

In God's presence, a man recognizes the importance of his presence in the life of his kids. He understands God's Kingdom is built through him and his family first; the Father does not call you to abandon or neglect your family to build His.

I'm going to share what I've learned about God's presence in the life of His kids from three stories which may seem strange in this context, but stick with me: The story of Adam and Eve, the story of Cain and Abel, and the story of Abraham and Isaac. These scenarios drive home what it means to be present.

I share these stories because I believe a man of God learns to be present from God Himself. Because of how the Father treats me, I sought to develop and nurture the attributes and actions I found in God for my kids.

Hide and Seek

In Genesis chapter three, there is an account commonly referred to as The Fall of Man. Adam and Eve partake of the forbidden fruit and forever alter the course of every person who lives on this planet. Distrust, lack of discernment, distortion of God's Word, faulty rationalization and justification, eye-opening vulnerability, shame, blaming, and lack of personal responsibility enter the narrative. And hiding—hiding enters.

In Genesis 3:8, Adam and Eve hear God walking in the Garden after they partook of the forbidden. Upon sensing His presence, they hide among the trees. They hide from the presence of the Lord. God did not hide; man hid.

Verse nine reveals that God plays a version of Hide and Seek that day. He calls to them and says, "Where are you?" God knows where Adam is; it seems that He desires for Adam to acknowledge he hears Him and to admit where he is.

We cannot escape the voice of God or His presence even if we try. Even if we have disobeyed, distrusted, lacked discernment, blamed others for our actions, or tried to rationalize and justify our sin. We may try to cut ourselves off from His presence, but we cannot. He is present.

No Need to Hide

Because of how the Father has treated me, one of the aspects of Kingdom Culture we have formed within our home is how we propel our children to run to us instead of hiding from us, especially when they struggle or fail. There is no need to hide from me; I love them and am for them.

This came easily for some of our children; for some, it took time to develop. Each deals with their feelings and trust issues which have nothing to do with me. Think about it, Adam and Eve hid from God, who is love and good. They hid because of what they felt, not because of anything God did. Notice, God sought them out; He did not wait for them to come to Him. A father shows up, seeks his children out, and engages in communion through conversation and counsel—especially when our child is foolish.

The Father continued to seek me out even at my worst because God seeks out His kids even when we mess up.

Think about this: God called to Adam first and opened the dialogue.

How do you react when your children do something wrong and are hiding? Do you come in throwing a temper tantrum, slamming your fists, shouting about what they did wrong? Or do you call to your child in love, seeking communion and giving them time to explain what's in their hearts and mind?

God brought Adam and Eve into account through conversation—by asking questions and listening.

Or do you give your children the silent treatment and avoid them? If you do this, I want to encourage you not to do this. In my opinion, it is one of the worst things you can do. It is anti-God. It may give your children the perspective that *when the Father is not pleased with them, He will shun them. And this is far from true.*

Initiating and keeping the lines of communication open is vital to a relationship with your children and developing a culture in your family reflective of His Kingdom.

After the Father gathered Adam and Eve's perceived personal accounts of their failure, He held to account all parties involved. He then described to Adam and Eve what would happen because they ate of the forbidden.

Next, in a beautiful merciful display, God clothed them. Adam and Eve hid because they were naked; God's response: He covered their nakedness. God did this in my life. He did not expose me; instead, He covered me. From the Father, I learned that dads are present to cover their children when they are vulnerable; dads do not exploit their child's vulnerabilities or shame them in them.

Present. God is present with Adam and Eve through this mess. You may be wondering, "But did not God banish Adam and Eve from the Garden?" Yes, He put them outside the Garden, but He did not abandon them. In the very next chapter in Genesis, God is found outside the Garden with mankind.

It is of utmost importance for you, Dad, to nurture a relationship with your children in which they know even when they mess up and fail and must face the consequences of their failure, you will still seek them out and be present when they deal with the results of their actions. They need to know they do not need to earn their relationship with you; the relationship is unconditional.

It's not about your performance but your presence in their life. You will not always get everything right, but if they know you are present with them in good and bad times, they will see reflections of the Father in their father.

Do not Tell Dad (Nichole)

I, Nichole, remember when one of our children would confide in me then say, "But do not tell Dad." I would then reply something to the effect of, "I do not keep things from your father, and you shouldn't either. You should speak to him. He loves you, and he is for you. Run to your father." Usually, she would say something like, "He's going to be mad." I'd say, "He probably will be upset or angry, but it does not mean he does not love you. You needn't hide anything from him. He may not like what you have done or may disagree with you, but he will give you good counsel and be there for you. If you are going to hide, hide in him."

Many wives keep secrets (with their kids) from their husbands—

hiding things from Dad (or vice versa). This is disgusting and undermining. Although timing and presentation may need consideration when informing Dad of something, there should always be openness and honesty. When you, as Mom, hide things from your husband, you usurp the role he has in the life of his children. It is anti-Kingdom Culture. You damage and weaken the position he has in the life of his kids. His voice is vital in their lives. It's just as important as yours. When you do this, you deem yourself and your role in your children's lives superior to his. It's arrogance.

When we hide things from a child's earthly father, what do we teach kids about God the Father? Mom, if you do this, ask yourself that question and pray about it. You may be thinking, "Well, you do not know my husband. You do not know how he acts." That is true. Unless he becomes abusive when he hears things he does not like, I cannot think of why he shouldn't know what is going on in his household. (If abuse is an issue, you probably shouldn't be in the home with him at this time.) You may disagree with how he reacts or what he says, but it does not necessarily mean it is wrong or that your way is right or better.

My oldest daughter states it this way, "Parent, God has given you permission to be present in the life of your child." That means Mom AND Dad have God-given permission.

Parent, you do not have to be perfect to be present. Just be there. Get all up in your child's life.

4.4

HERE I AM: CONTINUAL COUNSEL (SHAWN)

For a second example of how God demonstrates His presence in His family, we will travel a little further along in the Bible. In Genesis chapter four, we dive deep into the gracious presence of the Lord. At this point in the narrative, the first couple, Adam and Eve, procreate two sons, Cain and Abel.

When the sons are older, they individually present gifts to God. God shows favor toward Abel's offering but not toward Cain's. Cain becomes extremely angry. In verses six and seven, we find God present, offering counsel to Cain. Cain does not heed the counsel and ends up murdering his brother in verse eight.

Did you get that? The first human son murdered his brother.

Where is God? IN THE VERY NEXT VERSE, Genesis 4:9, God is present speaking to Cain. God converses with Cain, giving him a description of the consequences inevitable because of his poor choice. Then God mercifully puts a form of protection on Cain in Genesis 4:15. Sadly, in verse sixteen, Cain decides to leave the presence of the Lord. God did not walk away; Cain left.

What an astounding account of God's presence in His creation's life! God is present as Cain is upset; God offers counsel and warning. God, who did not favor Cain's intention or effort in his worship, is still present with this son of Adam. Cain did nothing to earn God's attention, counsel, or presence; as a matter of fact, Cain did everything not to deserve grace or mercy.

What I do not like about this story is that Cain does not heed the Father's counsel. He continues in his emotional turmoil until he kills his brother. What I think is fascinating is that God continues conversing and is present with Cain through it all. God does not leave Cain. Cain wanders from the presence of God.

In the Good Times and Bad

As God was present with Cain (and me) in my life when I made poor choices, I am present with our children in good and bad times. Obviously, none of our children have murdered the other. What an extreme example we find in the first family of God! However, there are times our children have done things that do not warrant our favor. I still engage and love them when I do not approve of their attitude or efforts. I do not shut off my relationship with my child because I do not like what he/she is doing or his/her choices. I am still in his/her life.

I've seen families where brokenness exists because kids will not do it the parents' way. Now, I'm not talking about when kids are younger in the home. Everyone must follow rules and practices to live in peace and health in a community. I mainly refer to when our kids reach teenage times or young adulthood. Often, they simply do not yield to the wisdom we have shared for years. They'll do and say things that make us think, "Who raised them? Where did that come from?"

Your kids will not always do things how you think they should. They will not always make the choices you would have them make. But a man of God will not hide away or force his child to go away. He will not stop talking to his child and being present.

Cain killed Abel. What a tragedy! Yet God still showed up. He intervened when he saw Cain was despondent, and He continued to be there even when Cain defied His counsel. When Cain ushered in the first recorded physical human death in Genesis, God was present. God did not put a wedge in the relationship; Cain did by walking away, but God still pursued His creation.

Men of God do not abandon their children when they do not do what they want them to do. They continue walking with them outside of the Garden as long as their children will walk with them.

Where's Adam

Some men grow up without fathers present in their lives. Interestingly, we do not see Adam present in the account of Abel's murder and Cain's sin. Sometimes earthly fathers are not present. The lack of a father's presence is especially difficult in times of crisis for a son.

If you lacked an attentive father as a child, it might lead you to feel inadequate—lacking the resources and abilities to be the father you desire for your children. But Cain's story offers us hope by giving us a glimpse into the Father of all—and that all includes you.

Even when our earthly fathers lack, God does not. He shows up in the crisis. He is present. Maybe you feel overwhelmed because your earthly father is not present. Perhaps you desire to raise Godly offspring but have had no example in your life. Fret and fear not! The Bible provides stories of the most incredible Father; study how He loves His children and use Him as your living example. You will be an outstanding dad if you pattern your life after Him. You will be a dad the next generation can learn from.

I DO NOT KNOW (SHAWN)

The third story, which highlights the presence of God, is narrated in Genesis 22. It's a crazy account of a dad willing to walk up a mountain and offer his son as a sacrifice. There are onion layers to this story, including the fact that people engaged in child sacrifice during this period in history to satisfy the gods. But I want to focus on one thing: the presence of God and Abraham in the story. At the beginning of the story, God calls Abraham, and Abraham answers, "Here, I am." God is present; Abraham is present.

God tells Abraham to go up a mountain and offer his only son, Isaac, whom he loves, as a burnt offering. Abraham loads up a donkey with wood he chopped and takes a couple of guys and the son he loves and heads out to obey what he believes God is instructing him to do. Three days later, Isaac realizes they have wood and fire but no offering. He calls out to Abraham, "My father!" And Abraham states, "Son, here, I am." "Where is the lamb for the burnt offering?" he asks his dad. Abraham assures him God will provide Himself an offering. Abraham is present, Isaac is present.

As the story unfolds, we discover Isaac bound upon an altar, and Abraham has knife in hand ready to offer his child as a sacrifice. Divine intervention stops Abraham from slaughtering his son, and he lifts his eyes to find a ram caught in some bushes. Why? Because God does not desire child sacrifice (like the gods of the world at that time). (As history confirms, Jesus becomes the sacrifice.) God is present. Abraham is present. Isaac is present.

Honestly, I sometimes wonder why God did not just say, "Hey Abraham, just so that you know, I do not want you to sacrifice your kids on an altar for Me nor in the fire like other gods and religions demand. I do not require that." But instead, we are given an account of an intimate moment in this family's life where they learned an aspect of what it is to serve this God and what it is not. As dysfunctional as this seems, I want to point out that Abraham is present in this challenging time for Isaac.

Can you imagine this in real life, in real-time? You believe God is asking you to sacrifice your son after He's told you that your promised offspring, counted in the number of the stars, will come forth from him. You are walking the most difficult walk of your life up that mountain. Your son is questioning you about what is happening. You do not want to answer that question, but you must because it's a great question. You respond with hope, "God will provide for Himself the lamb for a burnt offering, my son" (ESV).

Abraham knew what God promised to come through Isaac, so this whole thing had to leave him wondering and questioning. Did he think God would allow him to kill his son then raise him from the dead? Did Abraham know God would stop him? Did he just lose all sense and start to believe this God was like other gods he had learned of growing up? We do not know. It does not say. What we do know is that this was a harrowing journey. But God did not leave, and Abraham walked it entirely out with Isaac.

Where's the Lamb?

What a profound question Isaac asked Abraham. "Where's the lamb?" Well, okay, it was not profound; it is an obvious question for a boy walking up a mountain to sacrifice without an offering in hand. But it does have a weightier significance to us as generations-far-removed readers.

Where's the Lamb? There are times when God asks you to do something that just does not make sense—things you do not understand. Clearly, He will not ask us to kill our kids as a kind of a test. However, within the faith journey, He sometimes asks us to do things we do not understand. At a minimum, He allows things to enter our life we do not understand.

A dad is needed most when a child is walking up a mountain of worship with questions. Abraham did not have the complete answer for Isaac. How could he tell him what was happening? He did not know how God would show up in this situation; he just knew He would. Abraham was walking the walk of trust. When Isaac called out and questioned, Abraham responded with what he knew —God will provide His offering.

There are moments when I do not know what to do or what will be the result of what God is doing. When our children deal with moments like these, I am present, walking alongside them, pointing them to God and His provision in all things. I do not avoid the hard questions. I also do not make up things to suffice; I tell them "I do not know" when I do not know while pointing to the truth I do know.

Dad, do your children see a man filled with panic or confusion when you or they struggle for answers, or do they see a man walking stably beside them pointing to Jesus (the Lamb) for answers?

Physically Present but Not There

We come from an oilfield community. Men sometimes leave their families for two to four weeks (or longer) at a time for work. At times, I have traveled extensively for work. Today all my children are adults and live outside of our home.

Physical presence in your child's life is essential. Kids need to touch you and see you. However, you can be physically in a home every night and not be present. Yet you can be away and be present.

Today if you asked our children if I am present in their life, they'd probably say I am present as much as possible with adult children. Three of our kids live a state over from us. We do not see them daily or even weekly, yet they feel their dad is present. Being present is about being intentional and engaged.

I consistently reach out to my kids via phone calls, facetime, text messaging, using audio apps, and social media. We also regularly visit our kids; we do not have the mentality of "If they want to see us, they will come to see us." We intentionally visit them.

While I do not want to diminish the need for physical presence, especially for young children and teenagers, I want to emphasize that you can be present even if you are not physically there because of work. Some people must work away from home because this is the job assignment the Lord has provided. Others cannot be physically present each day due to court rulings following a divorce. Just be intentional whether you are physically at home or away. Make continual contact with your kids. Let them know how much you think of them when you are away. Check on them. Figure out how they communicate and use those platforms to keep in contact. Seek them out. Be present in every way possible.

As the Father does, I choose to be in the lives of our children: through good times and bad, through correct choices and wrong choices, through times of certainty and times of uncertainty. This is what God does for me. I try my best to do the same for my children.

4.6

HOLD FAST TO HER (SHAWN)

The Kingdom Culture contrasts with the culture of the world in various ways. How most of us enter our marriage union differs from what Genesis describes. We generally witness a bride leaving her home and clinging to her husband in our Western culture. Husband and wife join as the bride takes his name.

The couple then exchanges similar vows as in many weddings I've attended. The couple often recites the pledge of submission to one another. It is a beautiful passage elevating preference of another over self—a characteristic of Kingdom Culture.

What is interesting is that in Genesis we gain another perspective. Genesis 2:24 states, "Therefore a man shall leave his father and his mother and hold fast to his wife, and they shall become one flesh" (ESV). The Hebrew thought suggests a man leave, forsake, cling, and loose. It implies a man becomes detached from his parents and clings, cleaves, and keeps close to his wife—sticking closer to her than even his parents.

For some men who do not hold solid relational ties to their parents, this does not appear to be a challenge at first glance. Yet pause and ponder this: The biological parent and a child share DNA. No one can deny who they are born to because of hereditary material. You cannot escape this reality or ever change it. According to Genesis, God desires and designed the union of the husband and wife to be deeper than even this unaltering biological relationship. And He established man's adherent movement toward his wife to establish this relationship.

This is where I stop and just sit in awe of the inspired writers of the Word of God. To point out the leaving of this relationship carries depth. Ponder it. We do not pick our parents, nor do they choose us; God decides. The choosing of your wife, even if you ask God to help select and yield to who you think He is suggesting, is still your choice. You decide to whom you say I do.

Choosing your spouse isn't always an option. Some cultures still arrange and force marriages. However, in our western culture, most men choose their wife. What's interesting is regardless of whether or not you have chosen your wife, you will decide on one thing no one can control but you. How you hold fast to your woman is up to you and only you.

Once you say I do, every morning you rise, you have a choice to cling to your wife or detach from her. You decide to shift everything to her—to stick to her, forsake others, and choose her.

Together, Apart, Together Again

In Genesis 2:20b-25, God splits mankind into two beings to bear His image as one.

> *"But for Adam there was not found a helper fit for him. So the Lord God caused a deep sleep to fall upon the man, and while he slept took one of his ribs and closed up its place with flesh. And the rib that the Lord God had taken from the man He made into a woman and brought her to the man. Then the man said, 'This at last is bone of my bones and flesh of my flesh; she shall be called Woman, because she was taken out of Man.' Therefore, a man shall leave his father and his mother and hold fast to his wife, and they shall become one flesh. And the man and his wife were both naked and were not ashamed"* (ESV).

This passage suggests man and woman were one, then split, and then one again. Adam verbally expresses equality and compatibility between himself and the woman. The two rejoin after Adam acknowledges her and moves toward her. In this order, we discover unity, harmony, and vulnerability without shame. There is the freedom to be true physical and soul lovers.

Husband, when you stick to your wife, you will find a good thing. Fidelity, loyalty, preference, honor, and love for your wife build a Godly marriage. Life-giving harmony enters the relationship through stick-to-it-ness. Sadly, some husbands do not experience the benefit of this type of union because of their personal choices.

You cannot experience the full blessing of union with another when breaking covenantal vows. Gazing upon another woman's nakedness in lust, such as through pornography or in-person in strip clubs, breaks your vows. Building emotional ties with a woman who is not your wife in which you seek their acknowledgment, admiration, wisdom, or touch breaks the union. Having physical interaction with another woman, in which your sexual appetite is stimulated or satisfied, rips the union apart. All of these hinder the harmony and health of your marriage. It also weakens the strength of your parenting. It affects your whole family.

How does the way you hold fast to your wife affect your parenting? Well, if you do not cling to your wife and you break your covenant with her, you rip your union apart and tear down your child's stable home life. Also, when you break trust with the one you promise to be trustworthy for, you become untrustworthy. Period. When you do not honor above all the one you have promised, you will lose honor. Period. People may trust you with particular things and they may respect you in specific areas, but those who know you well, your wife and children, will not respect you because you are untrustworthy.

The permission you give yourself to un-cling or cling to your wife sets a precedent for your descendants; how you treat your wife matters. It shapes how your son may act toward his wife, contributing to how he views and considers women. It demonstrates to your daughters how men should regard and act toward them. Many of the young girls we have counseled (while in student ministry) dealt with low self-worth attributed partly to how their father devalued their mother and other women.

Release

When I decided to detach from all inappropriate relationships and hold fast to Nichole, I released myself into experiencing the goodness found in our union. I moved toward a relationship where I could be vulnerable with my wife and find fulfillment in her and our relationship. I no longer hindered myself in experiencing one of God's greatest gifts—authentic communion with another human found only in a committed bond. We share a beautiful bond exclusive to each other.

I daily choose to cling to her and not another. I seek acknowledgment, respect, admiration, and wisdom from Nichole. I fulfill my physical desires with her. This intense bond forms a safe place for authenticity, vulnerability, and no shame.

There is the freedom to be who we are in Christ in our relationship. Because of God's faithfulness and grace and my surrender and response to God, our sons have learned well how they should love their wives and children. Our daughters have witnessed how men should treat them by watching their dad love his wife.

Husbands, something spiritual occurs when you fulfill God's relational design with your wife. You find your life-mate. You find companionship, accountability, and strength. As you hold fast to her, you construct a life in which you build up other humans for the Kingdom of God.

Think about it: Christ clings to the Church (His bride) and does not let go. Clinging to your wife is Christlike and critical to raising Godly offspring.

LOVE WELL

In the last several chapters, Shawn highlighted core changes in himself that occurred as he lived out being a disciple of Jesus Christ. Our family has directly benefited from these transformations. Jesus brought about numerous differences in his life, but these three stand out. When a man remembers, is present, and clings to his wife, he is the source of blessing for His whole household. His people are loved and feel loved well, positioning himself to lead well.

Growing up I heard abundant teaching regarding male leadership in the home. The passage often used for the basis of this teaching is in Ephesians 5:23. "For the husband is the head of the wife as Christ is the head of the church, His body, of which He is Savior." (In this Scripture, the head is the Greek word *kephale.)* Most teachers immersed within a patriarchal system validate their belief with this Scripture. Interestingly, there are hundreds of sermons, teaching, and books I have heard, seen, or read dealing with the topic of men leading, but few covering loving well. This lack perplexes and disturbs me.

Ephesians 5:23 is part of a passage of Scripture that speaks to how people should treat people within the context of different relationships. I suggest you read chapters five and six of Ephesians if you have never read it, paying close attention to relational context and all the action words present in the passage, and then study those words. In these chapters, you will find the passages promote nurture, love, cherishing, a giving spirit, and laying down one's life for another. The spirit of love, not lordship, is the principal focus. Verse twenty-three, however, is often used as a stand-alone, without the context of the surrounding scriptures, suggesting male leadership is the dominant point here.

When we read this Scripture in English, it sounds as if it indicates "the husband is the head" (has authority) over his wife. Interestingly, as I studied this word in Greek, I was astonished to learn *how* many theologians and Greek scholars define it. I've always heard it means "authority," but many scholars consider it to mean *source, origin, or starting point*. Other definitions include "cornerstone" and "uniting two walls."

Let's use *source* as the translation for the word *kephale* instead of "authority." Source suggests a point of origin, like the source of a river —where it all begins and flows.[1] Using source in the translated text gives a beautiful depiction of what Apostle Paul writes (which we miss in English). The man, who leaves his parents and clings to his wife, becomes the origin of the new family and from where the family will receive life. It all begins with this action; it flows from him.

Now, let's look at *kephale* as "a cornerstone." To be a cornerstone is to be a foundational element on which a thing depends. The man is foundational to the marriage and family unit. A cornerstone unites two walls. A man united to God and his wife is a solid cornerstone to build a family upon—he is stable and dependable.

My goal is not to take creative or artistic leeway here with Scripture. Neither is my aim to change your mind on theological thoughts you hold dear regarding this passage. I am sharing what changed in us, which led to us becoming a family filled with heritage and Hope. My view on certain theology changed as I engaged the text of the Word. As a husband, if you prioritize *loving* your family, your wife and children will gain. If you prefer to focus on *leading* your family more than how you love them, your family will miss out.

Leaders may lead through motivation, inspiration, enforcement of reward or punishment, respectableness, fearmongering, by example, and various other ways. But the leader who leads from love will arouse loyalty in their people like no other way. It is true what the writer proclaims in 1 Peter 4:8, "Above all, love each other deeply, because love covers over a multitude of sins." When a leader loves you well, it is easier to forgive their mistakes because you believe their intent toward you is good; when a *leader* makes mistakes and does not love well, it is harder to forgive. You will be conflicted about their intention behind the error, and doubt regarding their motive will permeate your mind. But if you know he or she loves you and is doing his/her best for you, it is easier to understand his/her mistakes and forgive, believing their intention toward you is good.

Popcorn

Shawn loves and leads well. It is because he loves well that he leads well. Even if he errs and makes a bad call, I know his intention toward his family is good, so the blunder or oversight is easily covered.

You may be wondering what Shawn does precisely that makes me feel loved well. There are many things he does. He speaks life-giving words to me. He tells me he loves me at least five times a day. When he is home, he sporadically touches me. I get random drive-by kisses each day. He works incredibly hard for me to live in abundance.

And popcorn, he makes me popcorn. What does popcorn have to do with love? Well, I like popcorn. But popcorn is like a sandwich; it just tastes better when someone else makes it. Shawn's popcorn tastes better than mine. He makes it in a Whirly Pop with just the proper heat, butter, and salt. Not only does he make me glorious popcorn when I ask, but he also serves it up with a coke with lots of ice. He demonstrates his love for me through the big things, like working and providing abundant provision, and small things like popping a popcorn kernel.

Some days when life is just taking over, Shawn will stop, look at me, and say something like, "Hey, I am being intentional to give you attention right now. I'm looking at you. How are you?" This may not sound romantic, but it's the best to me. I will take intentional engagement with follow-through any day over a romantic whim. Both are nice, but intention and follow-through are love in action even when a feeling may not be present. Love fills another's cup even when you do not necessarily feel like it. A romantic whim only comes when a person feels it. Therefore, it's also about that person and his/her mood in the moment. To consider that another person may need to feel connected and do something about it, well, that's love.

Shawn also loves our children exceptionally well. If you want to win my heart, then treat my children well. Be intentional with them. Honor, cover, provide for, and be present for them. Shawn loves them well.

The examples I've given are not necessarily the specifics you need to reproduce in your marriage and family. If you are a husband, your wife may receive love different from how I receive it. Your wife may hate popcorn and not be a touchy person. How you live out these ways in your family will manifest differently than ours. But today, as a husband, if you just embrace and live out ways as Shawn does: remembering, being present, and clinging to your wife, you will love well. As a husband does these, a Godly family is born and nurtured. Ephesians 5:23 is carried out—you become the source of flowing blessing and goodness. Your life is a solid cornerstone for your family to build upon. And you lead well because you love well.

DAUGHTER OF GOD/A NEW WOMAN

Life did not just look different for Shawn; it looked different for me. I may have thrown my hands up in surrender years before and became a disciple of Jesus before Shawn, but I also had habits to break and new ways of living I needed to embrace and engage within this Kingdom Culture God called us into.

God did so many things to get our marriage to the point of redemption and restoration; He even used a beautifully broken leg. To you, our story unfolds in just a few chapters; for us, it occurred in our tenth year of marriage, year thirteen as a couple. I changed in many ways before this pivotal moment in our lives, yet there were still things God had shown and taught me that I was not embracing and walking out. I'm not sure why I did not accept the truth and wisdom He gave me and apply it, but I think we all do this at times.

Work It Out

Why is it humans resist God's efforts so much? Why do we struggle to accept His truth and wisdom? Do you ever struggle in believing God's promises are for *you*?

Sometimes people believe in God's promises for others but not for themselves. However, God's truth, wisdom, and promises are for everyone. He does not pick and choose for whom He honors His

Word. He does not go, "Oh, I like you better than so-and-so; I am going to fulfill what I said. I do not like you as much as so-and-so; I am not going to honor what I said." That's not who God is.

My struggle was not necessarily about thinking God favored me or disliked me above another. I struggled to follow and obey His teachings because what I understood as I studied differed slightly from what I grew up learning. It's hard to let go of belief systems even if they are lies.

Because I believe so strongly in community learning and insight, I think you must be extremely careful when you veer from the teachings of the elders of faith who are more seasoned in life than you and have served God a long time. You must study, question, seek out others for thoughts, and do all those things again. This is where I struggled: I questioned what made my understanding more correct than what leaders in my life taught me.

Philippians 2:12 reminds us, "continue to work out your salvation with fear and trembling." This tells me I must own and live out *my* faith-walk with reverence and intensity, doing all the Lord has instructed me to do.

Understanding that I have personal responsibility in living out what I know and understand from the Word (even if it differs from the understanding of people I respect) was pivotal in my discipleship journey. Honoring God over honoring man allowed me to follow Him and His ways more closely.

Walking Out What Is Worked Out

I mentioned earlier that something happened to me while listening to Shawn's confession. I do not know how or why, but God undid some things and released other things in me in a blink of an eye. From that point forward, I walked differently. Burdens lifted, relief and clarity entered, and resolve formed. I decided to walk out what I (me, Nichole, not others) worked out with the Lord.

When a woman of God walks in her identity, anointing, and purpose, everything she touches will produce fruit that remains. She is a force to be reckoned with because the Spirit of God is alive, flowing in and through her. His fragrance attaches to her and lingers on everything she touches. She carries the image of God in a way no man can, just like a man carries God's image in a way no woman can.

My transformation emerged as I embraced being a daughter of the Most High God and all it entails (that I knew about). Also, I turned my attention even more to focus on my role in Shawn's life and my role within our home. To sum it up: I am God's daughter defined by His Word, I am Shawn's *'ezer kenedgo*, and I am a builder who embraces the Cultural Mandate and the Great Commission within my home and beyond.

DAUGHTER DEFINED

W hat does it mean to be a daughter of God? A woman of God? The world, the Church, culture, social media, your parents, your peers, and thousands of years of examples of "the way it's been" offer varying viewpoints. It can be quite confusing. How do you know who or what to believe?

Answer: Believe the Word of the Lord.

As a child, I learned men lead and women follow. Men are the head of the household, the protector and provider, and women help them. A woman is to submit to her husband. Period. Their voice does not matter.

When you have this mindset, it can be difficult—really hard—to navigate your marriage and to parent children. Living in this mindset, I always felt like I was steps behind or waiting on someone else to do what needed doing. I felt like I was in a war, having to wait for a man to come with weapons and fight on my behalf. The enemy used lies to deceive me for years. I allowed myself to be made weak by believing lies; therefore, my marriage and home were weak.

Whatever dawned on me that day in the hospital room awakened me. I believed God. In a moment, I let go of defective doctrine and chose to believe God's Word regarding who I am. Instantaneously, I received the truth that I am a daughter of God.

Being a daughter of God means I embrace the truth that I am an image-bearer of God (Genesis 1:26). Just like my daughters reflect an image of me in their mannerisms and how they live out their life, I reflect God. What an extraordinary privilege! Secondly, I am a child of God (John 1:12). God, a King, is my Father. I hold the honor and significance of a daughter of royalty and divinity. Thirdly, I am "God's handiwork" (Ephesians 2:10). I am an expression of The Artist upon this earth.

Within the community, I am a corner pillar in the house of God (Psalm 144:12). I am a strength and support to those around me. Within marriage, I am a good thing and an expression of favor from God to Shawn (Proverbs 18:22). As a parent, I am an entrusted recipient of a gift and reward from God (Psalm 127:3).

And woman, you are

a daughter of God,
an image-bearer of God,
His masterpiece,
a pillar in the house of God,
a gift and blessing to others,
—and so much more.

These are some of the changes of mind I adapted too. Believing lies did nothing good for my family or me. What did I have to lose in accepting and applying God's Word to my life?

When a person's belief system transforms, to some extent, they are re-created. When you believe the truth of God's Word about who you are—His image bearer, His child, His expression of art, a strength to His people, a good thing, a blessing to your spouse, and someone God entrusts with the gift of the next generation—you will not only know who you are, you will live out who you are. You will walk out the Truth that is alive in you.

Who are you, daughter? What do you allow to define you? Is it lies or God's Word? Are you walking out who you are in Christ? I pray you walk in your God-given glory, design, and destiny. Do not be intimidated. Do not back down. Your family and this world need the real you in Christ. You do not need a moment in a hospital to launch you in this new direction. Right now, wherever you are, you can have this moment. Choose to believe God—and damn the lies of the enemy to hell!

'Ezer What?[1]

Allowing God's Word to define me while condemning the enemy's lies freed me to operate in power in my marriage and my home. It released me to walk out being the 'ezer kenegdo in Shawn's life.

What is 'ezer kenegdo? For me, understanding what this is was key to transforming my marriage. Let's dive into the beginning of women to discover the meaning behind these two words. Genesis 2:18 states, "Then the Lord God said, 'It is not good for the man to be alone. I will make a helper who is just right for him'" (ESV). Some translations use *suitable* helper. The words "suitable helper" in this Scripture passage translates from the Hebrew wording 'ezer kenegdo.

Often when we use the word *help* in English, it suggests one who assists. For example, if you are baking a cake and your child is your helper, you may ask him to hand you the eggs or preheat the oven. They are helping with the little side things while you assemble the cake. Another example is an employer who has an employee as their assistant. The assistant will be assigned things such as general errands, tasks the employer does not want to do, the minutia, or things that make the employer's job easier.

This is not the case with 'ezer kenegdo; when studying the wording of 'ezer kenegdo, you discover "helper" is a poor translation. When studying a word phrase in the Bible, it is essential to investigate and analyze its use in other references. It is helpful to research the word's context in the different places within the Bible.

'Ezer Defined

First, I studied the word *helper* and the Hebrew word 'ezer. Surprisingly, I found that 'ezer did mean "help." However, not help in the way my Western mind thinks. 'Ezer is only used twenty-one times in the Bible (that I could find). In Genesis, 'ezer is part of the phrase used to define and describe the created woman. Yet, in almost every other reference, it is a masculine noun used to refer to God Himself as

"Help or the sender of help for the people of Israel." Below are some of the other references we view this wording in Scripture.

> "Blessed are you, O Israel! Who is like you, a people saved by the Lord? He is your shield and *helper* and your glorious sword" (Deuteronomy 33:29).

> "I lift up my eyes to the mountains—where does my *help* come from? My *help* comes from the Lord, the Maker of heaven and earth" (Psalm 121:1-2).

> "May the Lord answer you when you are in distress; may the name of the God of Jacob protect you. May He send you *help*" (Psalm 20:1-2a).

> "We wait in hope for the Lord, He is our *help* and our shield" (Psalm 33:20).

These Scripture references reveal God is bringing help: deliverance, strength, hope, and salvation to distressed, desperate people. God is not some sidelined little helper; He is a mighty force of help and hope.

'Ezer is a noun from the Hebrew verb *azar*, which means to rescue, surround, protect, or aid. Most of the time in the Word of God, it refers to military assistance or personal assistance.

Does this kind of help sound equivalent to handing someone some eggs to bake a cake? I think not! It sounds more like what I experienced several years back. I have a heart condition called S.V.T. One night during an episode, the emergency medical technician (EMT) timed my heart rate at 208+ bpm. The EMT immediately injected some medication straight into my chest. The doctor said I would have died if I was not helped at that moment. (At a minimum, I would have "stroked out.") This is more like the help mentioned in these verses. This help provided me with what I needed to live life out.

Being a helper is more than handling the things your husband does not want to deal with. It is aiding him in accomplishing what is impossible for him to achieve on his own.

Kenegdo

Now let's look at the Hebrew word *kenegdo*, the second part of this phrase. Genesis 2:18 (in the *New Living Translation*) translates *kenegdo* as "just right for him." Other translations chose "suitable" to best convey their interpretation. This Hebrew word group is found only within this passage in the Bible. The base of the word is *neged*, which means in front of, corresponding to, against, and opposite of. *Neged* comes from *nagad*, which means being conspicuous, telling, declare, and making known. It is prefixed and suffixed with the rest of the wording, making it like a prepositional phrase.

In summary, *kenegdo* is to stand in front of, equal, evenly matched, and oppose if need be. It suggested when the first man met the first woman, he saw someone who was his equal. Adam did not treat her like he did the animals. He did not name her or exercise authority over her.

A-Team Combination

When you combine *'ezer* with *kenedgo*, you quickly realize a woman, especially in the role of wife, is created to be much more than a little helper or subservient. God created her to reflect His image and fulfill the Culture Mandate with her male counterpart. He made her (if married) to be unto her husband like He is for the children of Israel. Deliverance, rescue, assistance, support, reinforcement, shielding, blessing, provision, trustworthiness, and hope are all found in her. The only way these things dim inside a woman is if she shrinks back because she allows the enemy's lies, intimidation, or insecurity to define her.

It took me a while to grab hold of this truth. But when I did, I began walking differently in my divinely designed identity. I embraced the truth that I am a gift and the favor of God upon Shawn's life. I am the one God designed to be a shield about him, to protect him, to bring hope, to reinforce the things of God in his life, to remind him to remember, to be present with him, to be trustworthy, to oppose him, or rescue him when needed.

In my mind, I picture a man and a woman facing each other, evenly matched. Both have strengths; both have weaknesses. Each has a God-designed role they play toward each other.

I see Shawn's blind spot and protect him through my perspective as we stand face to face—seeing what the other cannot. My voice is valuable, offering useful insight. It is protection in his life. If Shawn forgets and does not remember God, the position I hold of being "in his face" enables me to lovingly remind him who God is and of all He has done in our lives. When he needs confrontation, I confront him. When he needs a safe place, I am a trustworthy refuge. I am his intercessor and the one who blesses him. This is my designation in our relationship.

A woman is not under man's authority like the animals Adam named in the Garden; she is comparable to man.

A team of two is stronger and better together because they have a fuller scope. When a wife assumes the role of helper to mean a woman who only assists and follows as a man leads, the marriage weakens, and the strength of companionship is lost. If a couple adheres to the notion that only the man leads the home, the family loses out. As a wife, I must not allow this to happen. I must embrace who I am in my husband's life and home.

GOD DID NOT TELL ADAM TO NAME EVE

God created a community concept from the very beginning of time. When mankind disobeyed God in the Garden, consequences entered the world. Adam later named Eve like he named animals—a sign of him designating Eve to be under his authority. This Adam-given classification is not God's original design but the result of disobedience. Just because Adam declared it does not mean God did. God described what would happen because of the fall; He did not ordain it to be so. He told them not to partake of the forbidden.

Before Shawn came to a crossroads in that hospital room, I fought for him through what the ol' timers call spiritual warfare. In an earlier chapter, I shared the story of the invisible arrow I hit against my dining room floor as King Joash did. I fought for my husband and children, yet I was weak and lacked zeal.

When I grabbed onto the truth that I am *'ezer kenegdo*, I became the force in Shawn's life that I prayed for—I became my prayer's answer. I became a contributing factor in Shawn's deliverance, hope, and strength by God's grace. I am not just some side-lined follower who is not in the game; I am an equal player. The Divine touched this *'ezer kenegdo* and poured out His zeal and love for His son, Shawn, through me. And the rest is His-story.

It is awkward to write about myself in such a way, but this is my story. When you silence lies in your life, become bold about who you are as a wife and mom, fearing and fretting not, it's amazing what God will do in you and through you. You will take on the nature of a warrior as you walk in the Spirit of our Great Warrior God.

And woman, if you will just be who God made you to be, God will do amazing things in and through you!

Regrets Again

I regret not believing in God's Word sooner. I pray you study on your own and grab onto His Word as if your life depends on it. If I could go back in time, I would live my role of wife out differently the first decade of our marriage. But I cannot go back. But you, you can begin today, right now. Be the equal companion to your husband that God equipped you to be. Daughter of God, you are a capable warrior! Live like one!

MY BFF

I want to draw attention to another aspect of Genesis 2:18 which changed my life as God continued to construct us into a Godly family. The beginning of Genesis 2:18 states, "Then the Lord God said, "It is not good for the man to be alone." At first glance, it appears God wants Adam to have companionship. While a woman is a man's companion and vice versa, we gain more knowledge from this passage.

God created humanity with specific purposes. Some of those purposes are found in Genesis 1:26-28,

 "Then God said, 'Let Us make human beings in Our image, to be like Us. They will reign over the fish in the sea, the birds in the sky, the livestock, all the wild animals on the earth, and the small animals that scurry along the ground.' So God created human beings in His own image. In the image of God, He created them; male and female He created them. Then God blessed them and said, 'Be fruitful and multiply. Fill the earth and govern it. Reign over the fish in the sea, the birds in the sky, and all the animals that scurry along the ground'" (NLT).

God designed and commissioned people to reflect Him as they create and steward creation. According to God, man alone is not a good way to fulfill this. Immediately after declaring, "It is not good for man to be alone," God formed a community out of one. He created a man and woman, two to become one, to best carry His image.

As I surrendered more and more to Jesus, an acute awareness of how vital both voices and roles are in the Kingdom of God became evident. It became apparent that man and woman express the image of God best together.

Our marriage unions carry something special—the very image of God. Godly marriages are powerful because they support raising Godly offspring. I always wanted my marriage to work because I loved my husband and kids. But as I really grabbed hold of this, I desired my marriage to work well because I realized it is a testimony on display for the world. Our family shines beaming light in the darkness. Shawn and I represent God to the world in a way no other couple can, just like your marriage does. People can observe glimpses of God through us. We are His unfolding story.

Your marriage is more than two people in love and wanting to build a family. It's a spiritual endeavor with great significance: Godly marriages give people glimpses of God.

Brother and Friend

Our unions also provide companionship. As I mentioned in a previous section, I prioritized relationship aspects over others when Shawn and I reached the culmination of our crisis. I focused on Shawn as my brother in the Lord, then as my friend, and then my husband. I'm not saying this is the right way to do it, but it worked for us.

What's weird is, I think some of us treat brothers and sisters in Christ (friends) better than we treat our spouses. I began treating Shawn as my brother in the Lord and best friend. We focused on *living* life together—working hard to find things we both enjoyed doing. We are very different people, so we have had to work hard on this.

Today he is my best friend—my best everything. Companionship from God is a good gift. We do not take it for granted.

Do you treat your spouse worse than your friends? It's something to consider. I treat Shawn better than anyone else on this planet because I am his best friend.

CHANGE YOUR MIND, GIRL

Understanding what it is to be a daughter of God and an *'ezer kenegdo* led me to rule our home. What do I mean by "rule our home"? I led, exercised authority, was intentional, followed through, bound and loosed, and set the tone for the home. I did not wait around and look to Shawn for guidance; I brought what I wanted to do to the table. I became a leader in my home.

Does a woman leading in the home usurp a man's authority? Not necessarily. Someone must love well and lead well. And if you are married, strength is found if both spouses love and lead well. But when a woman steps back and does not fulfill the commission God gave all humanity, it's just as detrimental as when a man does not fulfill it.

A friend of mine struggled because her husband would not take leadership over *spiritual* things in the home. She told me she wouldn't do anything spiritual anymore with her kids because he is their father and is supposed to lead. I questioned her, pointing out she is a daughter of God and a parent who could lead her children spiritually. She said it was not her place and it was his role. I then asked her what would happen if her husband did not step up. She informed me that he would be to blame. (Sadly, this is what happens when we believe a faulty doctrine endorsing one's spiritual authority in the home over another.)

Someone told another friend of mine to quit working and allow her children to miss a few meals (if need be) because it would force her husband to find a job and provide for his children. It was on him if the child starved. She shouldn't be the only one working. This is simply ridiculous!! Who sits by and allows their child to starve to motivate a spouse to take responsibility?

The advice and actions I have shared in these examples are ludicrous and not wise. God blessed mankind—men and women—with the Cultural Mandate. Men and women are in this thing together. How this plays out will look different in each marriage, but it needs to play out. Both are blessed and commissioned with this divine undertaking. One's failure will not excuse another's.

Change Your Mind, Girl

I chose to believe God and changed my mind regarding my belief "the man is the head, and the woman submits." Yes, men lead and women submit. But women also lead and men also submit. That is the makings of a Godly marriage as found in Ephesians.

Sometimes Shawn and I met in the middle. When dealing with stuff in the home, I primarily ran the daily operations. However, if Shawn saw something happening that he had a different perspective on, we would discuss it. If we still disagreed, I would submit, because who am I to say my way is better. Other times, Shawn would yield. We would often combine our thoughts and develop a better strategy that reflected both of us.

Primarily what changed was that I sought my instruction from God regarding our home and our children, and then I ran with the strategy I gathered from God's Word. I did not wait on Shawn to tell me what to do or how to do it. I led. I discipled my kids. I exercised full authority in Kingdom Culture as a woman, wife, and mom. Fulfilling my role did not mean Shawn did not operate in the fullness of his authority. We both did as a team.

I took Titus 2:3-5 to heart. I loved and led in my home, engaging and being intentional. I preferred my family over myself. Then I invited others into our home to teach and disciple them with what I've learned and to see all God has done.

4.13

JESUS AND WOMEN

Jesus loves, values, includes, and empowers women. Over and over in the New Testament, we find stories of Jesus engaging women at water wells, on the streets, in their homes, and around the Temple.

Women traveled with Him. He taught, healed, liberated, forgave, and commissioned them.

Women ministered with Jesus and to Jesus (Luke 8:1-3, Mark 15:41). They were with Him at the cross (Luke 23:49). Women went to the tomb to prepare His body for burial (Luke 23:56). And a woman was the first to receive the Good News of Jesus' resurrection (Luke 24:1-8).

God is not the suppressor of women. It is a lie to say He is. He designed women to be equal contributors in the Kingdom of God.

Sometimes when we read stories in the Bible about what happened, we assume it is how it is supposed to be. We think God must have wanted it that way. We presume if something is allowed, permission must be granted; it is ordained. This is not true. For example, Cain murdered Abel. He did not have permission to do this. If you read that story and believe that because it was allowed, it is acceptable to murder your brother, you would be wrong. The story of Cain and Abel is an account of what happened, not what God desired to happen.

There are stories in the Bible regarding the poor treatment of women. These accounts are meant for our learning, not to suggest God endorses the people's actions in the story. Humanity is allowed to make choices—even ugly, ungodly ones. Often Bible stories show us what not to do.

I encourage you to open the Word and read what God speaks about women. Pay close attention to how Jesus treated and empowered them. Let His Word and actions show you who you are in Him. Do not settle for believing and living in what is allowed on this earth. Live in what God promotes and promises!

Busy Builder

Proverbs 14:1 imparts wisdom regarding The Cultural Mandate that we (as women) are empowered to fulfill. It says, "A wise woman builds her home, but a foolish woman tears it down with her own hands" (NLT). Homes are built. In section 3.6, I highlighted the blessing of building a home with God, contrasting the vanity in building without Him. Now let's look at what it means for a woman to be busy at home and build according to this proverb.

This passage spotlights the role of the woman in building a home. *Build* is from the Hebrew word *banah*.[1] It is used in this passage and in Genesis 2:22, where God made woman. It is an action word. What's powerful is when God fashioned woman, He established and created part of the equation needed to perpetuate mankind. In other words, a female could now connect with a male and produce and raise offspring. God built one who would now build others.

A wise woman establishes a Godly home, so God's name is glorified in the next generation. She actively works to produce heritage.

In the Bible, people *banah* such things as a temple, a city, walls, a defense, and an altar. There are many things we can build. According to Proverbs, a wise woman *banah* (builds) her house. "House" is translated from the Hebrew word *bayith*.[2] A wise woman builds her *bayith* (shelter, humans, descendants, home, household, and temple).

A daughter of God can build many things, including building her humans and home. She is a person of action regarding her family and home environment. She is busy loving her husband and children, creating an environment where heritage and Hope are passed down.

A foolish woman does the opposite. She invests her energy in tearing down her house "with her own hands." *Hands* come from the Hebrew word *yad*.[3] This word has multiple meanings, as "hand" does in English. In English, for example, you can hand someone something, you can clap and give someone a hand, you can take a handout, and there is the literal hand attached to your arm. In Judaism, *yad* also represents a traditional-shaped long arm with a pointing index finger used to point to the Torah during reading.

According to Proverbs 14:1, a foolish woman uses her own hands to destroy her home. She does the opposite of building. Instead, she prefers herself and is idle in her home. She does not establish and invest in the spiritual heritage of her children, thereby aborting Godly offspring from coming forth from her.

What I picture (I am taking artistic liberty here) is a foolish woman pointing the finger at others for the condition of her home. She accuses and is critical, not taking personal responsibility to build her own home. Instead of being a *pointer* to the Word like the instrument used in Judaism, she points to others. It reminds me of Revelation 12:10, where the Word refers to Satan as "the accuser of our brethren." He accuses; he blames others. A foolish woman points the finger, blaming others for her household condition instead of owning her home.

Wife, Mom, are you waiting on the sidelines for your husband to do it all? Do you blame him for the failure in your home? What is God speaking to you on behalf of your family? Are you incorporating God's instructions, or are you putting it all on your partner? I pray you rise to the commission to build your family and home.

If your husband is not living as he should, do not let it hinder you. If wrong mentalities are your obstacle, change them by believing the Word of God. You have authority in Christ to govern and reign in your home. Run it. God will equip you for that which He has entrusted to you!

November

To help me govern my home well, each year in November I would set aside a weekend, rent a room at a hotel and meet with God regarding my family.

First, I would typically get my hair done and a pedicure. Treat yo'self! Then I would take myself out to eat and spend the day with myself and the Lord, meditating, and praying about myself. I would seek God and ask if there was anything He wanted me to focus on or deal with regarding myself. It was a time of decompressing, emptying my mind and heart, and listening. Then I would meet with Him regarding my marriage and each child, writing down what He said. It was a little getaway to refresh and refocus. (I did similar things around May and August of each year. I just did not rent a hotel room because we did not have it in our budget.)

I believe in getting a strategy from the Most High God. Some years, God spoke concerning specific character issues to deal with in my children. Some years He would guide me in what they should learn in school. Sometimes He said just to play and rest with them.

I did not always do 100% of what He told me. I did my best. What is amazing is when I failed to hit the mark perfectly, God still did. What He wanted to work in them, He did. For example, one year, He led me to have Linzee read and study the Psalms. Well, I did tell her to read them, but I did not take as much time studying with her as I felt led. The Holy Spirit, however, guided Linzee to dive deep into them.

I share this to point out again—we are in partnership with God. He will fulfill what He desires, but we play an important (not perfect) part in building with Him.

The idea of getting a strategy from the Lord and writing it down came from a work practice I had. One day, I was praying and planning the schedule for our students and taking time to figure out each student's schedule and what they would be learning. (We ran a program, geared toward college students at a local church, centered around discipleship.) It dawned on me that this would be a good practice to do for my kids. I should seek God for specific wisdom regarding my children, write it down, then do it.

I took my *work skills* and employed them in my home. I think most of us give more of ourselves to work than our home. It ought not to be that way.

Daughter of God, Wife, Mom, I encourage you to allow God's Word to define who He is and who you are in Him, to embrace being an *'ezer kenegdo* for your husband, and to take seriously the Cultural Mandate given in Genesis within the context of your home. What you build will be spectacular, eternally significant, and shine Hope to the hopeless.

Embracing everything I have shared in the last few chapters was key for me in earnestly assuming all God entrusts me with.

And as Shawn and I transformed more and more as disciples of Jesus, God increased the vision we had for our children. The more we knew who He is and who we are, the more we began to understand who our kids are.

4.14

ENTRUSTED

"Nichole, you are not just having babies. You are birthing and raising spiritual beings with eternal significance." What a powerful statement the Spirit whispered to me many years ago! Even now, as an empty-nester, God often continues to breathe this into my spirit. Empty nesters are still parents, just with different seasonal responsibilities and privileges.

I bore four babies in eight years. Bottles, diapers, toddler tantrums, homework, not to mention my full-time job and rocky marriage, consumed me. This revelation from the Lord came sometime between being spit upon and cooking dinner or maybe doing the fifth load of laundry for the day. I do not remember; it's a blur. I just remember being stopped in my tracks at that moment and feeling like I was sitting right in front of Jesus with His full attention. This revelation not only marks our parenting but is foundational for it. It gives me insight into the mind of God, how He views the next generation, and how much He entrusts to us.

I understand my role in my children's life is a significant privilege. Parenting is not a burden or something small or just something people do as the world turns. When a Christ-follower (even one who wrestles in her walk) births a baby, she has the opportunity and privilege to build the Kingdom of God and raise offspring who will not only stand but dance on the heads of giants.

Chosen and Trusted

Parent, you are the chosen co-builder of God's family, you are the entrusted. You are the one God has ordained to care for another human being. You are anointed, appointed, authorized, and assigned with the responsibility and primary privilege of caring for the next generation.

Throughout the Bible, we read of humans entrusted with a wide range of missions. From people tasked with baking bread utilized in offerings (1 Chronicles 9:31) to restoring the Temple of God (2 Kings 22:5). Disciples are charged with passing on what they have learned from God to others (Matthew 28:18-20). Even Jesus, Himself, stated, "My Father has entrusted everything to Me" (Matthew 11:27 NLT). Through trust and entrusting, the Kingdom of God is built.

God is giving you His trust to work side by side with Him, a co-mission in raising His kids. Sounds a little intimidating, right? It is until you understand He is working within you and with you. Then it becomes a joy.

When I realized God entrusted us with "spiritual beings with eternal significance," the privilege of parenting overwhelmed my heart. I was not overwhelmed in a bad way but in a good way. I am so blessed. Whether your children are biologically born to you or not, every parent is blessed beyond measure. To have a part in raising God's offspring, I mean, who deserves this honor?

What an opportunity! Let's not take lightly the trust God places in us. Because of this precious privilege, I emphasized discipleship earlier in this book. It may sound like I'm beating the same drum here again, but the best way to honor the trust placed in you by God is to be a disciple of the God who gave you that trust. It's the only way you will get to know Him, His ways, and His will for your family. You must know Him to understand what He entrusts you with.

A scripture passage written to Timothy in 1 Timothy 6:20 both encourages and warns him of something we should all consider. "Timothy, guard what has been entrusted to your care." May this resound in our spirits by the Holy Spirit. We must not take this God-given guardianship of our children for granted; we must receive it soberly, guarding them.

As a Christ-follower, God entrusts us with the Good News of Jesus

Christ. 2 Corinthians 5:17 states, "This means that anyone who belongs to Christ has become a new person. The old life is gone; a new life has begun!" (NLT). In effect, this means we "Don't copy the behavior and customs of this world, but let God transform you into a new person by changing the way you think" (Romans 12:2a NLT). What transforming trust! It should produce an evident change in every aspect of our life, especially parenting. We must follow His ways and not the patterns of the world.

A Village

You are your child's parent. You are the one entrusted with the primary parenting of your child. An African proverb states, "It takes a village to raise a child." Well, we depend on others for *help*, but other people are not entrusted primarily with raising your child. This proverb leans more toward a worldly mentality which has become an excuse for many in relinquishing their God-given role and right as a parent.

Understand me; we are created for community and thrive in a healthy community. We should love each other's children and work to create loving, life-giving environments for everyone in our communities. We definitely help each other. Community is an essential foundational element of God's design; I do not want to downplay the significant role of community. However, God started this whole thing with a man and a woman who produced offspring that were their responsibility. He did not create a teacher, a youth pastor, government officials, or even grandparents as part of the primary care system to raise Cain, Abel, and Seth. He created Adam and Eve.

And for your child, He created you.

HIS ART EXHIBIT

When I state, "You are the one entrusted with the care of the child given to you," there is gravity to that statement because of *who* is in your charge. In this chapter, I hope to help you better perceive the privilege of parenting by giving you more insight into who your child actually is.

God's Dream

There's a passage of Scripture spoken to Jeremiah which suggests God knows the one created before He forms them in flesh and blood in their mother's womb. Jeremiah 1:5 states, "Before I formed you in the womb I knew you, before you were born I set you part; I appointed you as a prophet to the nations." This Scripture tells us that God imagined Jeremiah and his specific purpose before He created him.

Earlier I highlighted Psalm 139:13-18 (section 2.2), reminding us God is very engaged in the creation process of each person. He is in the secret place of the formation of each individual. We are His thoughts, dreams, purposes, and image, all housed in flesh and blood.

When you have a baby, you do not just birth a baby; you birth the very imagination, purposes, and image of God. That's who your child is. Wow!

Wonder and anticipation! That's what I feel when I look at my kids and grandchildren. I see glimpses of God's very nature, imagination, desire, and dreams.

A Gift

Your kids are a present from God. Psalm 127:3 reminds us, "Children are a gift from the Lord; they are a reward from Him" (NLT).

When we think of receiving and giving gifts, most of us think of Christmas time. Well, imagine it's Christmas and someone gives you a big red box wrapped with a gold bow. Inside the box exists a one-of-a-kind gift, something never seen by any other human in all eternity. Now imagine opening the gift and having the privilege of unwrapping it, holding it, seeing what it is up close. This is who your children are. They are gifts of blessing so elaborate they take years of careful unwrapping to see them for all their beauty and fullness.

How beautiful! Your children are unique gifts of grace for you and this whole world. They are gifts from the Lord. They are more precious than anything you will ever find under a Christmas tree.

Dad and Mom, we are graced by God to partner with Him in unveiling what is inside our children. You have the privilege of unwrapping the one God has placed in your family box. Not conforming the gift to what you like, but cherishing, nurturing, and caring for your given gift—treating them as God's valuable masterpieces (Ephesians 2:10). Spurring them on to be all they are to the glory of God.

His Masterpiece

Ephesians 2:10 says, "For we are God's masterpiece. He has created us anew in Christ Jesus, so we can do the good things He planned for us long ago" (NLT). This is who our children are: God's masterpiece, His handiwork, His workmanship created in Christ Jesus.

I love to paint. Sometimes when I paint, I quiet my soul, randomly pick colors, and start painting. I enjoy seeing the raw art emerge—it highlights what is in my soul at that moment. Other times I intentionally decide what I want to paint. Then I set out to try and paint that thing. Both endeavors display pieces of me.

I also enjoy writing. Occasionally I will sit and write random thoughts that pop into my mind. I've surprised myself while practicing this exercise. Other times I write with purpose, on purpose, regarding a specific subject. When people read what I write (through either efforts), they get a peek into who I am.

This is what your children are. They are the artwork and writing of God to this world. They are a part of the great mosaic of the universe created to give God glory. No one else can take their place in all creation, past, present, or future. No one can display God quite as they can.

One day as I was meditating on Ephesians 2:10, the Holy Spirit gave me a mental picture. I was entrusted with a canvas to keep in my home. The Artist instructed me to guard it and carefully care for it. Splashes of color and blobs filled the canvas. I could not exactly make out what the image was.

Each year I was visited by the Artist. When He visited, He added more color with brush strokes. Some years He removed certain things, covering them with white paint or water-washing them. The Artist visited for many years.

Throughout the years, I kept the painting in a safe place. I regularly dusted the painting off and kept it from elements that could damage or destroy it. I admired the image and tried to figure out what it would eventually portray.

The time finally arrived for the masterpiece to be displayed for all the world to see. It was time for His handiwork to leave my home. He was not finished with it yet, but He needed to take it outside the safety of my care and home into different lights and environments to add depth and texture.

I discovered the painting looked an awful lot like the Artist and a little like me, yet it was one-of-a-kind with its own composition and colors.

This is who our children are. They are a living script and an exhibit of who He is. We must cherish and care for them as the Author writes and the Artist splashes and brushes His color upon their lives, making His story come alive.

"Spiritual Being with Eternal Significance"

—This phrase is not just about the Marcell kids. It also is who your children are.

Dad, Mom, your child is a spiritual being with eternal significance.

I know some days it's hard to look beyond the temper tantrum, the teenage attitude, or the dismissive-of-you attitude young adults sometimes have. My advice: look beyond it. I cannot say look past it because, well, you've got to deal with those things. After all, it's part of the growing process in humans. But look beyond it.

Even when your kids do not behave or display a Godly image, honor them and treat them as if they are living in their fullness—remember who and whose they are.

They Are More

Your children are much more than the few things I've pointed out in this chapter; however, if you pray and ponder just those mentioned, you will develop a deeper understanding of the parenting privilege you possess. As we considered our parenting from this Kingdom Culture perspective of knowing who our kids are, we created a culture of honor within our home.

4.16

HONOR

Shawn and I engaged in creating an environment in which great respect for each family member, no matter the age or role of relationship, was fostered. We do not think our children are less than ourselves. We viewed them as equal to us (just with a little less knowledge and know-how). It may seem weird for me to point this out, but I have watched parents belittle their children for not knowing things or just being kids. They treat them with less regard than they do themselves.

But God never shames or belittles me. He always honors me, treats me with dignity (even when I do not deserve it), continually speaks life into me, and lavishes love upon me. I am not His equal, nor do I have the knowledge and know-how like Him. So if He loves and honors me, an unequal ignorant being, I can surely treat my children with honor.

Ephesians 6:1-4 states,

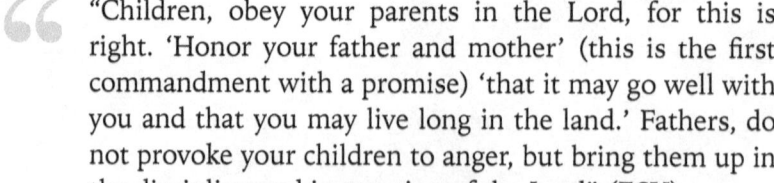 "Children, obey your parents in the Lord, for this is right. 'Honor your father and mother' (this is the first commandment with a promise) 'that it may go well with you and that you may live long in the land.' Fathers, do not provoke your children to anger, but bring them up in the discipline and instruction of the Lord" (ESV).

I've heard many sermons directed toward teaching children the importance of obedience, but very few focused on not provoking children to anger. To raise Godly offspring, these two go hand in hand. To cultivate a culture of honor requires obedient children and parents not provoking children to wrath.

There are various ways in which we can exasperate a child. Below are some of the things Shawn and I avoided to not provoke our children to anger. The following is not an extensive list but a list of our main avoidances: a critical spirit, hypocrisy, and name-calling.

A Critical Spirit

In my opinion, a critical spirit is one of the most destructive forces to the family unit. As a parent, we should tell our children the truth. Circumstances will arise in which we may have to critique something a child does or challenge a child in an area. We must remember that critiquing something a child does differs from criticizing a child. We can offer constructive suggestions without demeaning a child. At other times, we can allow the child to learn how better to do something for themselves.

Criticism is often negative. It is condemning, fault-finding, and judgmental. When it comes from a parent, it can produce resentment, anger, and low self-worth in a child. Constant criticism toward your child displays personal pride. It does not create a culture of honor in the home. It provokes children to anger, as well as other negative feelings.

The Bible gives clear warnings on being judgmental. Matthew 7:1-5 states,

"Do not judge, or you too will be judged. For in the same way you judge others, you will be judged, and with the measure you use, it will be measured to you. "Why do you look at the speck of sawdust in your brother's eye and pay no attention to the plank in your own eye? How can you say to your brother, 'Let me take the speck out of your eye,' when all the time there is a plank in your own eye? You hypocrite, first take the plank out of your own eye, and then you will see clearly to remove the speck from your brother's eye."

I am sure you have heard that verse quoted before. It seems like people who do not even read the Bible know part of that verse. But have you ever considered it with regards to your children?

James 4:11 says,

 "Do not speak evil against one another, brothers. The one who speaks against a brother or judges his brother, speaks evil against the law and judges the law. But if you judge the law, you are not a doer of the law but a judge" (ESV).

Our little ones may operate in the role of our child on earth, but they are our eternal brothers and sisters in Christ. Judging them is not acceptable.

Parents are charged with teaching (discipling) their children in God's Word, teaching what His acceptable way is and what it is not— what is right and wrong according to God. If a child lies, telling him it is wrong to lie is not a criticism. If a child forgets to use dish soap while washing dishes, it is not a criticism to remind him to use dish soap. Correction is not criticism.

A spirit of criticism manifests in the harshness of your tone and attitude toward your child when they fail to meet your expectations: not making the grades, not winning first place, not picking the parent-chosen career path, not getting into the in-crowd, not picking the right spouse, etc. Criticism also rears its ugly head when a parent feels embarrassed by their child. Oh, how we want our kids to behave! I watched a mother berate her teenager in a church parking lot because he acted unacceptably and embarrassed her. When a parent is embarrassed, often they will be over-critical of a child. Criticalness comes out when it's about you and not the child. Her son needed correction, but in this situation, because the mom made it about her and not what was in the teen's best interest, the teaching moment was lost. She embarrassed him because he embarrassed her. That's what she accomplished.

It comes out in phrases like, "Why are you doing it that way? That is stupid. You'd think you'd know better than that." "I am in awe of your stupidity." "Why don't you do it like your big brother? He does it better than you." "You're not good at that, obviously." "You shouldn't feel like that." Criticism is when you express your unmet personal expectation or disapproval. This critical-laced talk exasperates a child.

We had a funny, not-so-funny situation with one of our kids. One of my children asked me if they could sing. I said, "Yes." Then she asked if she could sing well enough to try out for American Idol. I immediately thought about all the people who tried out and were displayed on national television who could not sing well. I remembered saying to myself while watching these unfortunate souls, "Where are their parents? They should have told them the truth, so they did not embarrass themselves on national TV." I told my child the truth. While she can sing, she does not have the voice of a lead rock star. Singing is not her strength. She told me I was a dream killer.

Truth in love is not criticism.

The point is, sometimes parents offer their opinion, judgment, fault-finding, and pointing of the finger toward their child. They talk *at* them instead of *with* them when an issue arises in which they disapprove or are disappointed. But is it our right as a parent to do this? I think the texts in Ephesians and James suggest it is not.

Both Shawn and I are analytical people. We both strive to be better and do better. We regularly evaluate ourselves and all we do. We have raised our children to give one hundred percent to all that is in their hands to do. But oh how we have strived not to foster a critical spirit in the home. We have not done this perfectly, but we have tried to be truthful and encouraging while challenging and building them up. Yet we tried to do this without a critical spirit.

We honor our kids as people who are still growing and learning and are different than us—yes, different. They are not us, and we do not always know best. We must not judge our children, our younger brothers and sisters in the Lord. We do not always have to give an opinion or judgment. We can abandon criticism and provide truth in the spirit of love and honor them.

Hypocrisy

To develop a culture of honor and great respect in the home, you must live an authentic life. As you have read, we did not always live this way. But today and for most of our children's lives, what Shawn and I are in public is what we are everywhere. Our kids do not witness a difference in character or actions when people are around or when it's just us. I know without a doubt this is key to creating a home of honor.

Children know the real deal because they see what really goes on in the home. As youth pastors, we were privy to what was going on behind the scenes in many of our students' homes. Many of our students often expressed their lack of respect for their parents due to their hypocrisy; other students made covering for their parents a priority, hiding their parents' sin and dysfunction. This was hard and sad to deal with. Parents should cover their children; it should not have to be the other way around.

Parents who live a life of hypocrisy often expect children to live in a "do as I say, not as I do" way. Children do not respect this. Honor is lost when hypocrisy abounds in the home.

Do you live an authentic life in front of your children? Do your children see the same person in public (at church) as they do in private?

Name Calling

You cannot develop a culture of honor if you name call. I hate name-calling. It does not produce life. Over and over, throughout our years of ministry, I've listened as people recall the names their parents called them. So much sadness and bondage are linked to name-calling in the family.

When Tyler was young, I had trouble getting him to clean his room and do his other chores properly. I often found myself calling him lazy. I would say, "Tyler, you are lazy." One day, the Holy Spirit gripped me. It felt like the Lord was angry with me. I began to pray, and the Lord told me, "Tyler is not lazy." I thought to myself, "This cannot be the Lord. He would know Tyler is lazy." I questioned the Lord, "What do You mean, 'Tyler is not lazy'? He seems lazy to me." The Lord told me, "Tyler is behaving lazy in this area, but he is not lazy."

Again, perplexed, I asked the Lord what this even meant. God reminded me of many things Tyler was intentional and detailed in, even as a little boy. He asked me if I ever showed Tyler the Scripture about laziness in the Bible. I hadn't. God revealed to me I just wanted his room clean because I wanted it clean and organized. I was not looking at what was best for Tyler or at the possibility of a teaching scenario for Tyler.

I called Tyler over and showed him the Scripture about laziness. He got big-eyed and just took it all in. Then the Lord instructed me to write things out for him. I preceded to write out a list of actions for Tyler to organize his room. He did them all well.

The Lord reminded me that He created each person different. I needed to learn to teach my child in a way He could receive. When the Lord spoke this to me, my initial thoughts went to Tyler's future and how he would deal with a boss who just told him what to do if he could not even just go clean a room. But, again, I was reminded to just deal with today; the future will take care of itself. God makes people different; we learn differently. He speaks to each of us in different ways so we can understand Him. That day I learned to instruct my little boy so He could understand and do well.

The Lord emphatically impressed that negative name-calling does not mark a family of God or a house of honor. The people of God speak life over each other. How can your children truly respect you if you do not respect them? Shawn and I make it a practice not to call our children names.

I have messed up a few times. I called a few of my kids a moron once. They were stunned. I later apologized; they said, "We knew you'd apologize because that is not acceptable." And I have called my youngest a smart-ass. These were not proud parent moments; however, they are rare moments. They are so few that they stand out in my mind as I write.

Is it unusual in your home? Maybe another way to ponder this is to think about how you would react if your child called you what you call them? For example, if you call them stupid, how would you respond if they called you stupid? If you call them a loser, would it be okay if they call you that? What if they say, "I wish you were more like my friend's mother? She parents better than you."

You may think being a parent gives you the right to speak down to your child and call them names. It does not. If anything, it makes you look weak.

There is one form of name-calling that is acceptable. Shawn and I chose to name-call this way. We call our kids what God calls them: a masterpiece, a gift, God's image, His dream, His imagination, eternally significant, His child, our brother, our sister, wonderfully made, adored, and loved.

The Golden Rule

A critical spirit, hypocrisy, and name-calling are a few things we avoided to establish a home of honor. Encouragement and patience, authentic living, and speaking life are some of the ways we built it. If you want to develop a home of honor, I encourage you to fulfill Matthew 7:12, which states, "So whatever you wish that others would do to you, do also to them, for this is the Law and the Prophets" (ESV).

Treat people in your family like you want them to treat you as much as possible. Being a parent does not give you the right to treat your kids less than. Honor your child with the respect you desire from them. After all, God entrusts you with His kids. I do not think He takes too kindly to someone calling His kids names.

Summary

We are intentional not to have a critical spirit toward our children because God does not have one toward us. We do our best to live and be the same in the home as out of the house. We speak life to and over our children. We treat them as we want to be treated.

We immersed our children in a Christ-centered home through honor (respect). We lived out this Kingdom Culture attribute to the best of our ability. As God continued to show us who our kids were and how to honor them, we gained a fervency to teach what Christ taught us. We did not know everything, but what we did know, we could pass down.

PART V

PASSING IT ON

[DISCIPLES MAKE DISCIPLES]

"Then Jesus came to them and said, 'All authority in heaven and on
earth has been given to Me. Therefore go and make disciples of all
nations, baptizing them in the name of the Father and of the Son and
of the Holy Spirit, and teaching them to obey everything I have
commanded you. And surely I am with you always, to the very end of
the age.' "

~Matthew 28:18-20

Once we took hold of who we are in Christ and who our children are,
we unapologetically raised our kids to be disciples of Jesus Christ,
embracing conformity to Christ and not this world, which would
entail them being different. We taught them what we know. We
showed them how to be seekers of God and people of community—
hospitable, compassionate, on mission, generous, and a blessing. We
promoted trust in God and His Word above all else. Because in Him is
life, and in Him, we live and move and have our being (Acts 17:28).

We gave them heritage and Hope.

A, B, C—1, 2, 3

W hen a human enters the world, they are entirely dependent on another human being for continued life. They may live for a few hours or days, but eventually, death will come if no one intervenes. The role of a caretaker is one of life and death. Most parents embrace this role and immediately attend to their child's physical and emotional needs. This form of care continues as the child grows. Then educational requirements and more social development needs are engaged and nurtured as humans get older.

Shawn and I made a tremendous effort to meet all these needs of our tiny humans, even on our roughest days. Early in our marriage, (I would say) we prioritized the needs in this order: physical, emotional, spiritual, social, and educational.

When Jesus revived our family, nurturing our children's spiritual beings moved to the top of the list, side by side physical need. Feeding our children food and making sure they were nourished, had water, were clothed, and had shelter remained essential. But this shift in prioritizing spirituality made quite a difference.

A person's spiritual well-being, or lack of it, affects everything about him. Our spirit is so closely entangled to our soul that our souls are affected when it is out of alignment with God. This, in turn, affects everyone around us.

Our society often suggests faith is personal—a "you have your beliefs, I have mine" mentality. Keep it to yourself, or we will cancel and erase you. This is anti-biblical. The Kingdom of God is about sharing and passing on what you have learned. Our belief system matters. How we view God, ourselves, and others dramatically shape how we view life and transforms how we treat others.

As we surrendered our lives to Christ, He challenged me to prayer-fully consider and be intentional about my children's spiritual devel-opment and soul health. He empowered me by reminding me I am His disciple, equipped to make disciples. My children should not have to look past me for a living example of someone passionate for Jesus.

Your kids should not have to look past you. They do not need the children's pastor, youth pastor, or executive pastor to disciple them; they need you. Others in your community may complement and build upon the foundation and sturdy spiritual walls you partner with God to build in your child's life. Still, you are entrusted primarily with their discipleship.

A, B, C...

Do you feel up to the task of discipling your child? Do you feel up to teaching your little ones about who God is and what He can do? When God began to challenge me to be zealous in this area, I felt confident. Not confident in my knowledge or self, but confident in Him. Already, God had done so much and demonstrated He would make up for our lack. I trusted Him.

Discipling may sound like a frightening endeavor, but it isn't. It just means you teach and share what you know. Today, if all you know regarding spiritual matters is A, B, C you teach A, B, C to your chil-dren. You pass down what you have learned from the Lord.

Matthew 28:18-20 states,

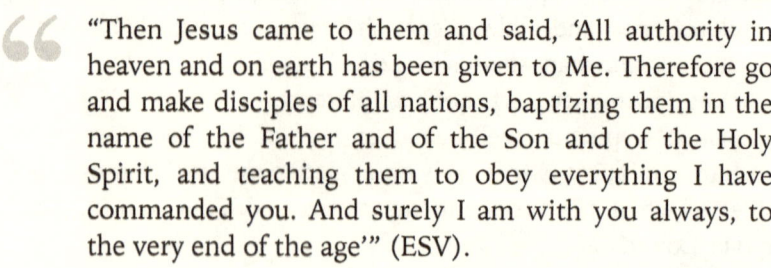

"Then Jesus came to them and said, 'All authority in heaven and on earth has been given to Me. Therefore go and make disciples of all nations, baptizing them in the name of the Father and of the Son and of the Holy Spirit, and teaching them to obey everything I have commanded you. And surely I am with you always, to the very end of the age'" (ESV).

There are several key aspects in this text, but I want to focus on the fact that He instructs disciples to teach other new disciples to obey all the commands He has given them. Jesus' disciples were and are assigned an awesome ongoing privilege and responsibility. God entrusts His disciples to pass it on. Powerful! So pass it on———

As a Christ-follower, you have a story. You have a story of what, how, why, and when God did something or some things in your life. You must tell your children the story. As a Christ-follower, you have learned *stuff* and are learning *stuff*. You must share as much as possible with your children.

1, 2, 3…

And you must continue to learn—numbers never cease. They go on and on and on. As a disciple of Jesus Christ, you, parent, must keep growing and learning. Then you must continue to teach what you are learning. We start with learning and passing down the A, B, Cs of faith, but we continue into the 1, 2, 3s. Deeper and deeper, we go into the endlessness of God. If you only pass down the A, B, Cs, your children may perceive that God and your faith have limitations. But growing by continuously trusting God and gaining new revelations to share reinforces the truth of a living engaged God. They are proof of vibrant faith.

Developed Passion

I had an intense passion to disciple my children because of the vision God gave me of who they are in Him. But I also knew what it was like to not have a human walk with you as you journeyed to know God, yourself, and to make Him known to others. I did not want my kids to think they were not worth my investment in this area. Again, God used my past lack to fill a future with purpose and love.

STORYTIME

A chapter in Deuteronomy offers beautiful, brilliant instruction regarding discipling our children. It all starts with the telling of a story.

Let's dive into Deuteronomy chapter eleven. Verses 1-7 of this chapter state,

 "You must love the Lord your God and always obey His requirements, decrees, regulations, and commands. Keep in mind that I am not talking now to your children, who have never experienced the discipline of the Lord your God or seen His greatness and His strong hand and powerful arm. They did not see the miraculous signs and wonders He performed in Egypt against Pharaoh and all His land. They did not see what the Lord did to the armies of Egypt and to their horses and chariots—how He drowned them in the Red Sea as they were chasing you. He destroyed them, and they have not recovered to this very day! Your children did not see how the Lord cared for you in the wilderness until you arrived here. They did not see what He did to Dathan and Abiram (the sons of Eliab, a descendant of Reuben) when the earth opened its mouth in the

Israelite camp and swallowed them, along with their households and tents and every living thing that belonged to them. But you have seen the Lord perform all these mighty deeds with your own eyes!" (NLT)

I love this passage. The author brings to remembrance what the people of Israel witnessed God doing. He reminds them of the miraculous deliverance power God demonstrated. He reminds them of their intimate knowledge of the caring, nurturing attribute of God they were recipients of in their wilderness experience. And for good measure, the author throws in a story suggesting God can even move the earth to accomplish an endeavor if He desires to.

Notice it is mentioned several times in this scripture that this is not what their children experienced or witnessed; it was the Israeli parents' experience. Astounding! He is drawing a distinction between the generations concerning their experience with God.

It's like God is shouting and clapping His hands, saying, "Come on, parents, this is your story. Your kids do not know Me this way. They have not seen Me move just yet. You have. So love Me and follow My ways. Tell them all about Me. Tell them the story." God is stirring up the older generation to remember and live in such a way that their lives testify to what they have experienced and known.

(It's interesting that we often look for revival to come with the next generation. Maybe it comes when fathers and mothers remember and pass it on! But I digress.)

Remember, your children were not present for your faith experiences. But sharing your experience with the living God with your kids can bring an awareness of God's existence, His greatness, His engagement with His creation, and give an accurate understanding of why you believe what you do.

Who have you witnessed God to be? What has God done in your life? Who do you say He is? What is your story?

Take time to write it down. Write down how you would describe God from what you have witnessed Him doing in your life. Have you shared any of it with your kids? Storytelling matters. Your kids do not know God as you do.

It matters how you portray God to your children. It did in my life. The image you create in their minds and hearts through your words and actions will propel them toward God or hinder them in coming to

Him. Do not just tell them who the preacher says He is. Tell them who He is according to His Word and what He has done in your life. If you are a disciple of Jesus, you know He is gracious, kind, a deliverer, a healer, loving, faithful, a forgiver, a seeker of the lost, intentional, and a life-changer. These are some of the things I have told my kids about God.

There were some things we waited to tell them until they were adults (mostly because they never asked certain things, but also because some things involve other people and confidence is required). We generally believe if your child asks you a question, you answer if appropriate. If they are curious, there is a reason they are asking you something. I tend to be open with my kids if they ask. But it is each person's prayerful decision to disclose certain parts of their story.

Description of Blessing and Cursing

Deuteronomy chapter eleven continues in verses 8-17, stating,

"Therefore, be careful to obey every command I am giving you today, so you may have strength to go in and take over the land you are about to enter. If you obey, you will enjoy a long life in the land the Lord swore to give to your ancestors and to you, their descendants—a land flowing with milk and honey! For the land you are about to enter and take over is not like the land of Egypt from which you came, where you planted your seed and made irrigation ditches with your foot as in a vegetable garden. Rather, the land you will soon take over is a land of hills and valleys with plenty of rain— a land that the Lord your God cares for. He watches over it through each season of the year! If you carefully obey the commands I am giving you today, and if you love the Lord your God and serve Him with all your heart and soul, then He will send the rains in their proper seasons—the early and late rains—so you can bring in your harvests of grain, new wine, and olive oil. He will give you lush pastureland for your livestock, and you yourselves will have all you want to eat. But be careful. Do not let your heart be deceived so that you turn away from the Lord and serve and worship other gods. If you do, the Lord's anger will burn against you. He will shut up the sky and hold back the rain, and the ground will fail to produce its harvests. Then you will quickly die in that good land the Lord is giving you" (NLT).

This part of the passage describes what it will be like if the generation of people who witnessed the Lord's characteristics, attributes, and power will remember and live accordingly. This passage speaks of possessing more ground, continued victories, growth, and expansion. It highlights divine promises fulfilled and more than enough provision to meet needs and wants. Also, it warns—if those who know forget what they know, then the future holds a wasteland of squandered opportunities for the next generation.

Dad and Mom, do not forget! It is so important to remember and live like you know Christ. Your remembrance not only affects you, but it also affects your kids. How you honor God builds or tears down your babies' futures. It demonstrates to your children Who life is worth living for.

Mom and Dad, do your actions suggest you have short-term memory regarding the things of God? What do they prove you know of God's reputation? What do your kids see in you and your life? Do continued growth and new victories mark your life? If someone asks your children to describe God using only what you have told them, how would they describe Him?

Teacher
Deuteronomy goes on in verses 18-21 to say,

"So commit yourselves wholeheartedly to these words of Mine. Tie them to your hands and wear them on your forehead as reminders. Teach them to your children. Talk about them when you are at home and when you are on the road, when you are going to bed and when you are getting up. Write them on the doorposts of your house and on your gates, so that as long as the sky remains above the earth, you and your children may flourish in the land the Lord swore to give your ancestors" (NLT).

If you are a disciple of Jesus Christ, you have witnessed and experienced the greatness and goodness of God. Your life should testify to the trust you place in God. Your children should see and experience the blessing of God in your life as you remember Him. Does His Word and Name continuously flow from your lips, or is it rare thing?

There is a saying, "Some things are caught, some things are taught." This is exceptionally true in discipleship. Our children will catch things from us through daily observation; our fragrance will get on them. Other things, we must intentionally choose to teach.

5.3

CHOICES

We, parents, have a choice to make. It's not good enough for only us to experience and know God; our children deserve to know Him and experience His greatness as well. I cannot make God do great things in my kid's life or make Him show Himself like I want Him to, but I can choose to testify to what I've witnessed to be true and the Word I trust.

I look at it this way: If I'm the only person who ever tells and demonstrates what God is like, then would my children feel like they have been with someone who knew Jesus once they encounter Him? Would they realize His goodness and faithful love are in me? Would they recognize God and I sound a lot alike because His Words are my words? Would the smell of the fire of His Spirit be familiar to them because they have sat in my presence and watched His fire burn within me? Or when they met Jesus, would they see my faith walk as cold religion?

Let's continue a little further into Deuteronomy 11. Verses 22-28 state,

 "Be careful to obey all these commands I am giving you. Show love to the Lord your God by walking in His ways and holding tightly to Him. Then the Lord will drive out all the nations ahead of you, though they are much

greater and stronger than you, and you will take over their land. Wherever you set foot, that land will be yours. Your frontiers will stretch from the wilderness in the south to Lebanon in the north, and from the Euphrates River in the east to the Mediterranean Sea in the west. No one will be able to stand against you, for the Lord your God will cause the people to fear and dread you, as He promised, wherever you go in the whole land. Look, today I am giving you the choice between a blessing and a curse! You will be blessed if you obey the commands of the Lord your God that I am giving you today. But you will be cursed if you reject the commands of the Lord your God and turn away from Him and worship gods you have not known before" (NLT).

Our choice to continue to pursue God and live His ways after He has done an amazing thing in our life is the difference between being one who has an encounter with God and one who is a follower of God. The choice to pass it on with the next generation moves us into the discipleship realm. It is moving from the A, B, Cs to the 1, 2, 3s. And, I believe, it is the difference between raising Godly offspring filled with heritage and Hope or just raising kids in the world with a form of godliness that denies the power of God. Our choice to seek God with all our hearts and keep moving forward, respond to His grace, and surrender amid our struggles and failures, opens the door of blessing for the next generation. God has done some mighty things; our kids should hear about them.

I Just Do Not Know

I acknowledge this passage of scripture in Deuteronomy has left me feeling excited yet sober at times. What blessings exist if you remember God! But "What if I mess up? What if I misrepresent God to my children? What if I teach them wrong about one of His ways?" This has weighed heavy on my heart several times while raising our children.

A distorted image of God so powerfully affected me; I did not want to do this to my kids. I found that when I felt this way, Jesus would simply ask me to tell Him who He is. I would then proceed to tell Him who I know Him to be from my experience and His Word: He is kind, the Truth, a healer, faithful, gracious, my lover, my King, beautiful, honest, present, my deliverer, forgiving, and so much more; He takes my breath away. This is what I need to tell our kids, along with the reason why I believe this.

I have messed up, though; hindsight reveals an awful lot! Once I instructed Autumn to read an old sermon, *Sinners in the Hands of an Angry God*.[1] It will put the fear of *God* into a person. Although I think it's a sermon beneficial for reading and dissecting, I wish I would have had her read *Sinners in the Hands of a Loving God*.[2] They offer differing and opposite perspectives and vary in interpretation of some Scripture. Reading both works would have made her dig into the Word of God to formulate thoughts on how God views sinners and what He does with them. By giving Autumn only one source, I planted a seed of how God views something that may very well be inaccurate or incomplete at minimum.

As I study the text of Scripture more, when I notice I may have taught our kids something wrong, I tell them I may have taught them something inaccurate. I say, "I am chewing on it." As I grow closer to Jesus and study His Word more and more, my views on a few things have changed. God never changes, but my understanding deepens. We are not God; we do not know everything, and we certainly do not know all about Him. If we misinterpret or misrepresent, let's acknowledge our miss to our kids and chew on it with them as we grow together. We get glimpses of God; therefore, we can only give glimpses of Him to our children. Let's be careful to make them good ones.

As parents, we are entrusted by God to pass on what we know to our kids. Pass it on! Let's just make sure we know as much truth as possible regarding God, not just trust what someone else tells us. But as parents, we do not just pass on an awareness of God through sharing our experience and knowledge; we must teach our kids to become seekers of God, studiers of His Word, and people who surrender. These are basic elements of discipleship.

REQUIRED READING

2 Kings 22-23 narrates the story of King Josiah. (We named our youngest son after this King.) I'll summarize the story before we dive into parts of the text.

Josiah became King of Judah when he was eight years old. He did what was right in the eyes of the Lord—not turning to the left or the right. When he was eighteen years of age, King Josiah sent one of his subjects, Shaphan, to the house of the Lord to count the money his people brought. Josiah designated the money as payment for honest workers who repaired the Lord's house.

As Shaphan followed through with the orders, the high priest found the Book of the Law given to Moses within the house's walls. Shaphan took the Book back and read it to King Josiah. Upon hearing the reading, Josiah ripped his clothing. He ordered the high priest and a team of people to inquire of the Lord because he recognized his sin, the sin of his people, and his ancestors' sin.

This troop set out to see prophetess Huldah. Huldah prophesied the destruction of the people because they forsook God, served other idols, and provoked God with the work of their hands. But because King Josiah had a penitent heart, humbled himself, and wept when he heard the Word, God heard him. The generation alive during Josiah's reign was granted peace and spared destruction.

In response, in 2 Kings 23:1-3,

"Then the king called together all the elders of Judah and Jerusalem. He went up to the temple of the Lord with the people of Judah, the inhabitants of Jerusalem, the priests and the prophets—all the people from the least to the greatest. He read in their hearing all the words of the Book of the Covenant, which had been found in the temple of the Lord. The king stood by the pillar and renewed the covenant in the presence of the Lord—to follow the Lord and keep His commands, statutes and decrees with all his heart and all his soul, thus confirming the words of the covenant written in this book. Then all the people pledged themselves to the covenant."

King Josiah read and responded to the Book, requiring those under his leadership to do the same. The Book became the core of his personal life and public function.

King Josiah ordered anything belonging to idols removed from the temple of the Lord. He burned ungodly emblems. He beat things to dust, and he tore down high places. In verse ten, King Josiah stopped child sacrifice. "He desecrated Topheth, which was in the Valley of Ben Hinnom, so no one could use it to sacrifice their son or daughter in the fire to Molek." Josiah, who prioritized the Book of God, brought reform to his nation.

He reinstituted keeping the Passover to the Lord. Verse twenty-five says, "Before him there was no king like him, who turned to the Lord with all his heart and with all his soul and with all his might, according to all the Law of Moses, nor did any like him arise after him."

Josiah

I hope you noticed in an earlier chapter when I wrote about the birth of our youngest child, Josiah, that it was right smack dab in the center of sickness, divine healing, hurt, honesty, confession, repentance, and rebirth. He was in my womb when we walked through the time of the Red One's redeeming and restorative power to our family. I experienced divine physical healing, and our marriage experienced rebirth and restoration. Josiah quite literally lived inside me through that pivotal time. Radical reformation surrounded his birth.

The Lord spoke to me concerning Josiah during this time: "No compromise." Those two words filled my mind and heart during this pregnancy. I saw a picture of black and white, no grey areas. (Right and wrong. Left and right.) Being brought up in the spiritual tones of the eighties, I imagined a hellfire and Heaven preacher, but that part did not quite sit right. As I pondered this, sincere and steady became the words encapsulating all I heard. *Genuineness, authenticity, firmly fixed, not faltering or wavering, sober*, and *established* are words echoing in my spirit. God was pushing our family into what old-timers call "glory to glory." We were moving into a new season, signified through the words God spoke over our son Josiah.

Several chapters ago, you read how the moments surrounding the red rose entering the hospital room freed me to believe God and allow His Word to define me. Well, from the moment Josiah entered the world, God's Word took center stage, not just in me but in my family. I do not know exactly how to explain it besides saying what God prophesied over Josiah, my baby boy, was a prophecy for our whole family: to be sincere, genuine, and authentic followers of Christ who will not falter or waver, firmly established in Christ, not veering to the left or right. We were to tear down what exalts itself against God and restore the ways of God in our family, and lead others to do the same.

Immersed in the Word

Being zealous for God's Word and ways brought reformation to our home.

We applied Deuteronomy 11:18-21 in our home. Shawn and I taught our children the Word of God (and still do when they have questions). We did this by intentionally initiating conversations about the Word. Often, we taught them the Word through our real-life day-to-day experiences. The Word of God is in our hearts and minds, so it flows out during a conversation with our children. We do not necessarily point out the book, chapter, or verse we are using. We speak His Word because it is part of our words. We lived out the Word in front of them and verbally taught them. We did not wait for the church leaders or others to teach our children God's Word.

A pastor's wife said one of the saddest things I ever heard said. We were discussing homeschooling, and she revealed they did not do Bible at home. Out of curiosity, I questioned why they made this choice. She stated, "They get enough of that at church." I was both alarmed and appalled. What the what?!

Let's break this down. Let's say you attend a church where the youth pastor preaches twenty minutes a week and a pastor about thirty minutes. Subtract about half the time for greetings, stories, and announcements; you come up with about twenty-five minutes a week of the Word coming forth. (And that's a generous estimate.) If a child makes every service the whole year, which is rare, they will hear the Word of God for a little over twenty-one hours total. That's not even one day out of 365 days. If this is your mentality, then the village of the world is nurturing your kid's spirituality.

Most children attend school more than 21 hours a week. Let's say children between the ages of eight and eighteen years view six and a half to seven and a half hours of media per day. In three days, this equals the amount of time they hear the Word of God in a church within a year if they make two services a week. What the what?!

I often incorporated Bible into our homeschool studies. At some point, each of my children complained about being forced to read the Word. They felt like Bible reading should be a choice to read, not a school requirement; I still made them read it.

In schools, we force our children to read literature, history books, science books, and other books that some random stranger in an office deemed necessary for them to read. Of all books they should read, a life-giving one should be the one they are required to read.

I wanted them to read the Bible so the Word of Life would get in their minds and heart. I knew this would help them recognize when people preach counterfeit Christianity. Now, as adults, overall, my children are happy with the knowledge they obtained when reading. One still says it should have been a choice. Whether I was correct or wrong, the Word still got in there. I'm okay with disagreeing about it.

The Struggle is Real

Also, when you read the Word of God, it reads you. You will be overwhelmed with love, but at other times you will struggle. I wanted my children to wrestle with the Word of God when they were in the home so we could discuss it. The goal was for our kids to learn what the Word of God says and form their belief system based upon their study (not just what Dad or Mom said).

For example, I required Autumn to read a book about modesty and how women should dress. The book is not biblically accurate; it consists of many opinions and lots of legalisms. As she read it, she became irritated. She said, "Mom, this cannot be what God expects. This is crazy." I asked how, why, and what she drew her conclusion from—how she knew it was not truth. Basically, in her opinion, it just could not be accurate. I told her to search the Scripture about what God says regarding women's clothing and appearance, then get back to me.

When she finally finished the book and searched the Scriptures, she questioned why I instructed her to read a book containing truth and lies. I explained to her that she needed to know the Word of God and be able to discern truth from man-made laws. I also informed her she could not just say something is not God's way because she does not like it. She must examine Scripture text to form conclusions.

Another time, Autumn struggled with the portrayal of slavery throughout the Scriptures. I encouraged her to pray, study the whole book of God, and scrutinize the context of passages. It's okay to wrestle with God and His Word. We do not always get immediate answers to our questions.

One of the coolest things I witnessed as a parent was when I entered Tyler's room. Tyler was a teenager at the time. On his desk was a notebook filled with notes and commentary he wrote on the book of 1 Timothy. Not only was Tyler reading the Bible, but he was also writing commentary. Beautiful.

13th Year

The one time I did not mandate for our kids to read the Bible was when they turned thirteen. We do a special ceremony when they enter their teenage years, which I will describe in an upcoming section. After that ceremony, I did not require them to read the Bible for a year. The way they handled the Word of God was entirely up to them.

I did ask what they were reading or what God was speaking to them through the Word during that year. Sometimes they had nothing to say; other times, they blew my mind. I still spoke the Word and shared what I learned when an opportunity arose. Their study time was left entirely up to them.

Through this process, each child found their bible reading rhythm. God's Word established a *pull* in their life by the time they were teenagers. The Holy Spirit prompted them to read, and they obeyed. Could they have read and studied more at times? Probably. But so can I as well. The point is they developed habits and became aware of deficits in their disciplines they needed to work on. Today they all engage the Word regularly.

Again I want to express that this is what we did, not necessarily what you should do. But you do need to do something to develop a zeal for the Word of God in your household.

5.5

HE DOES NOT HIDE HIS FACE

We taught our children that God is always present. He does not hide His face or look away no matter how we behave. God is in the shadows as much as He is in the sunrise. He is with us when we act as though we came straight out of Heaven or straight out of Hell.

We taught our kids that God is big enough for our questions, wrath, fears, and wandering. There is never a need to hide from the Father. Even if every impulse inside of you tells you to find some fig leaves and a tree and hide, we run to the Father.

The way Jesus responded to the cross proves He can handle it all. He is a living, loving God.

5.6

THE VOICE OF GOD

We taught our children that God speaks, and His Word is in His voice. He does not speak audibly, but He speaks.

There is a story found in 1 Samuel chapter three in which God calls three times to a young boy named Samuel. Samuel did not know it was God, so he ran to his guardian and priest Eli each time he heard the voice. After three times, Eli realized God was speaking to Samuel, so he instructed Samuel to respond to the Lord the next time He called. The Lord called to Samuel again, and this time Samuel answered. God established Samuel as a prophet.

A parent cannot make a child hear from God. We can only point them to recognize and respond to God's voice in their life. Shawn and I created an expectancy in our children to hear the voice of God. Practically, we did this by asking our children regularly what God was speaking to them. When they were very young, sometimes they did not say anything. They began to share what He spoke to them as they grew up. At times, when they would talk to us about stuff, we would recognize God was speaking and showing them something. We would point out to them when we felt God was speaking to them to help them acknowledge the voice of God. (But honestly, the Holy Spirit teaches us to know the voice of God. Sheep know the voice of their shepherd.)

We taught our kids that God speaks through His written Word and the inner voice. We also taught them about dreams. Sometimes you dream because of lousy pizza; other times, God uses dreams to speak to us.

Elmo

When Tyler was just a little tyke, he had a dream from God. One morning I woke up to find Tyler's giant stuffed Elmo in the hallway. "That's strange," I thought.

When Tyler woke up, he said, "Mommy, I had a dream. There was a man on the cross, and He was bleeding, and His blood came all over me and went on my head and flowed down all around me."

Tyler encountered the Man of the cross that night in a dream. We discussed it, and I pointed out to him that Jesus was speaking and revealing Himself to him. Astounding!

If you are wondering about Elmo, when I asked Tyler why Elmo was in the hallway, he said it was because Elmo kept staring at him with his big eyes and was freaking him out. So he put him in the hallway. I cannot remember exactly how old Tyler was at the time of this dream, but he was young enough to believe stuffed animals come to life.

The point is, God speaks to all His children no matter their age. I encourage you to teach your children to listen to the voice of God.

His Common Presence

Daily, Shawn and I treated God's presence in our lives as usual in front of our children. Why? Because His good presence is in our lives. Just like He is in yours.

He was, and is, central to how our family is fashioned and filled with heritage and Hope. How could an awareness of His presence not be treated as standard for a Christ-follower? We spoke of God, His Word, and what He was revealing to us on a very regular basis because, well, He is engaged in our individual lives regularly. Jesus' name was heard nearly every day from Shawn or my lips at home.

Let me be clear: God's presence is holy. He is a holy God. When I say it was "usual" or "common" regarding His presence, there is no disrespect. God created His creation to live in the Divine and flesh and blood of this world simultaneously. He desires to walk with His people.

When they were small, our children spoke about God often with us. They trusted in Whom we believed. But there comes a day in every human's life when who and what they will trust becomes their choice.

THEIR FAITH JOURNEY, NOT YOURS

W hen our children turned thirteen years of age, we held a ceremony and party. I was inspired to have this celebration during prayer over Autumn, who became our first teenager. I hoped to mark this new season of her life with something significant. I wanted a way to begin to teach her interdependent independence, especially regarding her faith. I aimed to teach Autumn that she is always part of a family community in which we have relational dependence, yet she is independent regarding her choices in whom she believes in and how she lives her life.

The Lord impressed upon me to commemorate this time in a significant way by giving Autumn ownership of her faith and declaring her responsible for her life choices and future actions. He also encouraged me to have her dream and write down some things she hoped to do in the future. I also felt led to encourage her to commit to not dating until she was eighteen. The primary goal was to teach her to be faithful to a commitment she made. Secondly, it was to protect her heart from unnecessary hurt that comes with childhood relationships.

As I prayed and researched, we adapted a few things from the Jewish coming of age ceremonies—the bar and bat mitzvah. This is a time when a boy or girl becomes accountable and responsible for their actions. They are also allowed to participate and lead in various ways during religious services.

. . .

Her Faith, Her Choice

Many young adults turn from faith because it is their parents' faith, not their own. By the time each of our kids turned thirteen, they had knowledge of God, had read all or most of the Bible, and had a relationship with Him. They were old enough to question what they believed and why. Shawn and I taught them the skills they needed to ask, seek, knock, and study the Word.

Shawn and I shared parts of our testimony. We spoke of how Jesus changed our lives. We pointed our kids to Jesus. We lived our faith in front of them. As Christ-following parents, we did all we knew to show them God's goodness, be authentic with our walk with the Lord, and raise them as His offspring. But there comes the point when each child must choose if, and how, they will follow the Lord.

During the ceremony our children would proclaim they would follow Christ (a decision they all said they had made by this time). They would read aloud and share a favorite passage of Scripture in front of those in attendance. Shawn and I, along with our family and friends and their peers, would anoint them with oil (symbolic of a season of "setting themselves apart"), pray for them, and commission them into their new season of life.

It was a lovely moment.

His Faith, His Choice

I want to pause here and address something: What do we do when our child tells us they do not even know if they believe in God?

All our children proclaimed they were Christ-followers and would follow Jesus by age thirteen. It made me happy (warm and fuzzy feelings) and grateful to hear our kids publicly proclaim they would follow God and His ways. But recognizing and allowing your child to own his faith precisely means that. Each human decides whom and what they trust.

During Tyler's teenage years (after he proclaimed to serve God at his 13th celebration), he began to question God's existence. It was a rough and dark time.

During my life I have questioned God about His way, His timing, and why He allows certain things to happen, but I have never doubted

His existence. To me, His perpetual presence is unquestionable. Therefore, Tyler's crisis regarding whether God existed or not just did not make sense to me.

I remember one conversation I had with Tyler. I said, "Tyler, when I tell you God speaks to me, do you believe that? Who do you think I'm talking to?" He said, "I believe you believe that. But He does not talk to me like that."

This troubled me. Tyler had made a proclamation he would follow Jesus, so what changed? I began seeking God regarding Tyler. I thought maybe I should stop talking (with Tyler) so specifically about my prayer life. Because Tyler was not relating to my faith walk, I thought I could perhaps alter how I shared my faith walk and testimony. Instantly I felt the rebuke of the Holy Spirit.

The Lord told me, "Nichole, I am big enough for Tyler's questions, or I am not God."

Wow! God is not afraid of our questions.

I asked Him what I should do as Tyler's parent at this time. He impressed upon me to continue to love Him fiercely and burn for Him. God shared with me that people do not come to watch a flame burn; they come to watch a fire burn. He encouraged me to allow Tyler to watch the fire for Jesus burn in my life.

He also encouraged me to love Tyler and just talk to him like I would talk to a believer. I should not shrink back or dumb down my faith walk, even if Tyler did not appear to understand it or believe it. I must authentically be who I am in Christ in front of him.

I was not responsible for making Tyler believe; only God could open his eyes, and He would.

I trusted God even when my child told me he was basically an atheist. I encouraged him to keep asking questions and seeking Truth. Both Shawn and I lived for Jesus with our whole hearts.

Questions

We taught our children to question their faith while pointing them to the text of God's Word. Questions are a valuable part of the process of discipleship. All through the Bible, we see people question and wonder at the ways of God and about God Himself. Questioning is part of the human experience. You will not find answers to questions you will not ask. Questioning is not a bad thing.

Questions lead you to more questions and more answers. They have always helped me to grow deeper in my understanding and trust in God. I read and study the English translations of the Bible. Then I study the Hebrew, Greek, or Aramaic text (through study resources) to gain greater insight into what the text says. Most of what I research originates from questions—they lead me.

When Tyler's questions led him to a hiatus in his belief in God's existence, it rattled me for a moment; but that season was part of Tyler's journey. Doubt and darkness can be components in the journey of a disciple.

Dream

Back to the 13th Celebration Party.

After reading and sharing their Scripture reference of choice during this celebration, our kids would share their dream-goal list: a monetary goal to obtain before eighteen years of age, spiritual devotional plans, a country they wanted to visit during their teenage years, and when they would start dating. It was fun to see what they hoped to accomplish.

The hope was to inspire our kids toward *yeses* during their teenage years. We allowed them to help define the yeses through this process. We did not want their adolescent years characterized by *no*. Of course, they were told "no" to things, but the aim was to focus on all they could do and achieve—teaching them to focus on the yeses in life and not the no.

Our children did not meet every dream or goal on their list; this was not the point. The point was to teach them to be people who dream, aspire, and believe they can live beyond what they can see. To plan big but know God will do even more! They plan their way, but the Lord will establish their steps (Proverbs 16:9).

They learned to dream and plan yet trust God for their steps daily. Sometimes life does not look like we thought it would; we may not do everything we want to do, or we may not arrive at our goals or dreams when or how we would like to. It's all okay if we trust God with our steps. But we can dream.

• • •

Dating

To some, our encouragement not to date may sound strange. (Especially after the drama we endured when Shawn was in the discipleship program.) Maybe it is. But it is how we felt led to lead our kids. We did not force them to do this; we strongly suggested it, but it was ultimately their choice. One of my boys asked me the rule regarding dating if he did not commit to this. I informed him that he could date when he could afford to take a girl out on a date with money he earned.

Three of our children decided not to date until they were eighteen. Our youngest decided to wait until he finished high school.

When our children decided not to date until a specific time, they did not completely understand their commitment. At some point during their mid-teenage years, each child made the statement, "Yeah, but I did not know what I was committing to when I committed."

Hormones raged. They became attracted to certain people. Like most teenagers, they wanted to be accepted and have a boyfriend or girlfriend.

As a parent, we encouraged them to be faithful to what they committed. I believe this is one of the most important lessons learned from this whole process. They learned to stay committed despite how they felt.

When they were troubled by their commitment, I would share with them that sometimes in marriage, you will have days or seasons you do not want to be married. There will be moments you did not sign up for. When you marry, you do not entirely understand what you sign up for with the other person. Some days, faithfulness to a commitment is an intentional choice of will.

And sometimes, it works that way with our relationship with God. We may not feel a thing, but we can trust He is faithful. And we can grow by being faithful in seasons we are not *feeling it*.

It also enforces the attribute of stick-to-it-ness, an essential quality for us to possess. You cannot just stop because things are hard. Push-through is often key to success. Not always, but often.

Through Jesus and our stick-to-it-ness, our family was spared the effects of divorce. We felt this was a practical way to teach our kids the skills needed to build a Godly family.

This commitment also offered our children protection. Being in youth ministry, we watched children hurt and damage other children in relationships. They dealt with each other as if they were children because they were children. They were not emotionally equipped to handle what a committed relationship requires. Damage was done to young minds and hearts that need not happen.

Well, you may wonder, how will our children learn to deal with romantic relationships if they do not have them during their teenage years? We taught our kids how to treat people according to God's Word. If a person treats another with love, respect, kindness, and as an equal independent counterpart, they will do well. If they follow God's Word regarding sexuality, they will do well. You do not have to be in a dating relationship as a child to learn how to deal with relationships.

You may also wonder how kids learn what type of person they want to have a relationship with without dating? People do not need to date and break up with ten people to know what they want. When our children liked someone, I did not shame them for liking them. That's normal, especially when hormones are raging. I asked them to tell me what they liked about them. Was it just a physical attraction? Was it a characteristic they possessed they were attracted to or appreciated? Did they make them feel good about themselves? What was it about the person they liked?

Walking them through the questions forced them to evaluate if they liked the whole person, or just a part of the person, or was it what the person offered them. Now, our kids did not always process out loud about what they were attracted to, but overall, I believe this helped them consider what they wanted and did not want.

Relationships are one of the most influential factors in each of our lives. Romantic relationships, specifically, have the potential to impact our mental health (soul) more than most things we encounter. This is another reason we guarded our children for their future romantic relationships, which hopefully will last for their lifetimes.

Ceremony Hindsight

After we did this ceremony for Autumn, each child looked forward to their 13th birthday. It was a fantastic time of celebration and commissioning. And Shawn and I believe this was pivotal in propelling each child to embrace their walk with Christ.

5.8

GOD-CONFIDENCE AND REJECTION

The 13th Year Birthday Ceremony launched each of our children toward teenage years in a unique way, setting the groundwork for how they would live life during their adolescent years. Because they outlined dreams, desires, and goals, we had a base to work from to support their vision as a family.

At this time, Shawn and I fiercely focused on teaching our kids to say *yes* to Jesus (to live a life of surrender). Why? Because saying yes to Jesus changed our lives. Saying yes to God and all His goodness left us little room to follow after the not-so-good things of this world. (The more in the *yes* areas, the less time in the *no* areas of life.)

Saying yes to Jesus makes you different from the world; it sets you apart. Just by *being* in Jesus, you change the world. How? You stand out, and it allows you the opportunity to tell people that God changed your life and helps you live differently (and He can transform them too). Saying yes to Jesus also empowers you to live a life of blessing toward others. You become a conduit of goodness upon this earth.

Shawn often reminded the kids, "You cannot change a world you are like." Disciples live differently.

Even though some of our kids decided to follow Christ many years before they were thirteen, there was something *magical* about the 13th celebration. There was an anointing that set them apart and helped them decide to stand apart: to unapologetically be who God created them to be, to say yes to God and yes to life, to be God-confident, not self-confident, and to be strong in surrender.

Wonder Woman Meme

There is an image of Wonder Woman holding a little girl's hand scattered across social media. "Here is to strong women. May we know them. May we be them. May we raise them," is written across the visual. I like this meme, so I posted it on my social media.

Later the Lord brought the picture to my mind with a slight change. The word *strong* was crossed out, and the word *surrendered* replaced it. I was like, "What? Wow!" The Lord reminded me that to be surrendered to God is to be positioned in strength.

It may seem like just a play on words, but in surrender to God I found the strength of God, strength in myself, and the understanding of the strength a family of God holds. Many people have told me I am a strong woman. Honestly, I am just a surrendered one.

We Do not Teach Self-Confidence

Shawn and I taught our children to be confident in God and who He is in them. We know that if they know God and who they are according to His Word, they will love themselves well. And when a person loves themselves well, they love others well.

God-confident people are surrendered humans who walk in boldness and strength because of Whom they serve.

Self-confidence is the trust in one's abilities, qualities, and judgments. Therefore, we did not teach this. In this world, we exercise judgment and our abilities each day. However, our abilities come from the Lord; it is Him who makes us capable. And His Word should inform and be the basis for our assessments.

God-confidence is trusting in the goodness of God and the goodness in which He created us. Possessing it offers a shield around our minds and heart. It helps guard us against the hurt the world will hurl at us.

Rejection

Being God-confident restrains the spirit rejection attempts to root in the heart of a child of God. When a person knows who they are and what they are capable of in Him, the ugly words of the world will not leave a devastating effect.

Rejection is a hard, hurtful thing for a person to deal with. It can leave a person feeling dismissed and depressed; it may damage self-esteem and cause all kinds of emotional turmoil.

All my children walked through situations where peers and church leadership rejected them. It is hard to watch your kids deal with rejection; however, it is a part of life on this planet. When rejection hurts our kids, we remind them they are loved and of who they are in God. The spirit of rejection sent a blow to their self-esteem. They were wounded but not destroyed because their confidence was in God and His Word.

They got knocked down, but they got back up confident and strong in Christ because He defines them. Their confidence and self-worth are not determined by others but by God Himself.

As a parent, you cannot prevent rejection from entering the life of your child. You cannot control how your child feels or how long they struggle with the feelings brought on from rejection. But you can interrupt and thwart it by reminding them of who they are and the acceptance they have in Christ and you.

You Are Not Pretty

One of my daughters was told by a friend that a girl said she did not like her and that she was not pretty. After hearing the scenario, I questioned why her "friend" even told her what the mean girl said. (Messy!) Seeing she was so upset that someone said she was not pretty made my heart hurt.

I initially wanted to tell my daughter that the girl was just jealous and mean and that her friend should not have told her what was said. But the Holy Spirit quickened me and instructed me to ask her if she thought she was pretty and if she liked herself.

She immediately responded, "Yes, I am beautiful." I asked her why she had so much respect for the girl who said this unkind thing. She said she did not respect her. "Then why do you give so much weight to what she said and allow it to affect you so much?" I questioned.

But then the Spirit prompted me again. I asked her, "What if the girl does not think you are pretty?"

She looked puzzled. I reminded her that there are people who she does not find attractive. It's a personal preference as to what each person finds attractive. I asked her to evaluate the value between what the girl said about her and what she knew to be true about herself; I asked her if what she said really mattered.

She said, "No."

I reminded her to believe what she knew to be true. She was beautiful to God, me, and herself.

My daughter had shaken confidence for a moment, but once she thought out the truth she knew, she stood in who she is.

Jesus is Rejected Every Day

The previous scenario was over some boy issue (if I remember correctly). The girl thought the guy she liked was interested in my daughter, so she was saying unkind things. This girl was dealing with her own rejection and lashing out. Therefore, my daughter was dealing with cruelty.

I also explained to my daughter something God revealed to me when He redefined my perceptions about rejection. He told me, "Nichole, Jesus is rejected every day, but it does not stop Him from fully being who He is."

I instructed her to learn from Jesus and apply this truth by living out fully who she is, even when that girl was around.

Rejection only limits you if you allow it to. God has tons of experience with this, yet He is still God. When a person rejects Jesus, it has nothing to do with who He is. Likewise, rejection most often has nothing to do with who we are.

Contentment with Your Child

Unfortunately, rejection does not always come from people outside the family unit. One of the most significant rejections a child can ever face is from a parent.

Sometimes parents try to live vicariously through their child, often leading to rejecting who the child is. When a parent is obsessed with living his/her dream through his/her child's life, the parent may reject the child and his dreams. This is not good.

Attempting to live through your child is a setup for failure. When he/she fails to meet your expectations, the disappointment you feel may spill out toward your child. If your child does not do what you desire, he/she may feel like he/she will not be accepted and celebrated. Your child will feel rejected.

I do not think most parents purposefully try to live through their children. Regrets from our own lives can lead us to do this, but we have lived our young lives. We must not contribute to perpetuating the life cycle of unhappiness in the next generation because we did not do what we wish we had.

One day I was hiding in a closet working on a fundraising letter for a student of ours. (I was in the closet because we had a house full of young adults, and I needed a private place to work.) Tyler, who was around eight years old, came in crying. I asked him what was wrong. He began telling me that he did not feel he had a place in this family if he was not in ministry when he grew up. I quickly told him this was not true and asked him what he wanted to be when he grew up. He told me a chef.

I thought a moment and prayed a bit. I told Tyler I would love for him to be a chef. A chef has amazing opportunities: working in a fancy restaurant, cooking for people in soup kitchens, creating cookbooks, making his momma some good grub, etc. But I told him that he must do what God has for him to do, no matter what that is.

I questioned him as to why he thought there would be no place for him if he were not in ministry; I felt like a horrible mother at that moment, wondering why he thought such a thing. He told me he just thought this because we were all ministers. It also sounded like people continuously asked him if he wanted to be a preacher like his dad (which often happens to pastors' kids).

I learned something that day. Children need to *know* they are accepted and loved no matter what they choose to do. Tyler felt a spirit of rejection that day, even though it was not real.

Sometimes it's not about living through our children. We just want them to do better than we did, so we hold them to higher standards. This can be damaging as well. We must remember God designed our little gifts with what they need to make a divine impact on this world. We must allow them to walk into the works He has for them to do. We must be content with whom God designed them to be, encourage it, and celebrate it.

Tyler did not become a professional chef, but boy, he cooks good!

. . .

Momma's Boys

In Matthew 20:20-28, there is a story I find quite funny. It's about a momma confronting Jesus about her boys' status in His *organization*. Momma Bear approaches Jesus and kneels. He asks her what she wants. She requests a better position in His Kingdom for her boys. Jesus tells her she does not know what she is asking. He goes on to teach a lesson about what it means to be great in His Kingdom.

What's funny to me is this woman's sons were disciples of Jesus Christ. They are part of the Twelve Disciples we read about to this day. But Momma was not content with who and what they were. Baffling, right?! What in the world was this woman thinking?

I think many parents do this. We are not content with God's lot in life for our children. This momma may have had a heart filled with good intentions, just wanting to help her boys get more and be more. I'm not judging her. But wow! Come on—they were part of the original Twelve. That is amazing! And it's not good enough for her?! Well, maybe I am judging her a little bit.

I wonder what her sons thought. Maybe they were happy she was jockeying for position. Or did they think, "Dear God, Mom! I am one of the Twelve Disciples the Son of God chose, and this is not good enough for you?"

Summary

Saying yes to God builds your (and your kids) confidence in Him. Rejection may throw a blow, but it will not be a knockout for the God-confident child. Let's be content with and celebrate whoever God has created our child to be.

5.9

COMMUNITY BLESSINGS

When we allow our children to walk in God-confident design, they will love others well and be a blessing to our communities. Children are not just the church of tomorrow; they are the church of today. Now! Now, they are a part of the body of Christ with a purpose in our communities.

We are all designed for community. Since community is essential in God's Kingdom, we must be in community.

One purpose of a Godly family is to bless the community. Shawn and I orchestrated, facilitated, fostered, and nurtured interaction between our whole family and community. We believe each family brings something unique to the body of Christ. We prioritized allowing God to work through our entire family within our community to the best of our ability.

At the beginning of life on the other side, God called our whole family to the nation of Romania. I remember, after we lived in Romania for a few months, I prayed, "God, what am I, Nichole, specifically called to do here?" There was so much need; we could not meet all of it. It was hard to know what to prioritize.

God spoke, "Just be a family here and allow others to watch—to see you."

My response: "What? What does that even mean? 'Be a family.'" Really?!

We did many things in Romania. God allowed us wonderful privileges: feeding the hungry, putting shoes on the shoeless, building a church of young people, leading thousands of people into praying a prayer of commitment to God, discipling Romanians and Americans, nurturing the missional spirit in others, and much more. But "just be a family" is what He chose to make the priority for me. Interesting!

One day one of the women who lived with us (several people lived with us during our time in Romania) told me that I love my kids too much. I asked what she meant. She told me I gave too much respect and love to them. She had never seen this.

I did not know what she meant, but I took note.

Fast forward to the year 2012—almost a decade later. I was ministering at a Women's Conference in Romania with my daughter Autumn. At the conference's closing, a woman walked up to me (with a translator) and told me she remembered our family from 2003. As she sobbed, she said she watched us then, and now (almost ten years later) seeing what God could do, well, she was moved to tears. How could a daughter and mom minister together and have such a relationship? She had never seen a faith passed down to a daughter and embraced like she was witnessing. Our family testified to her that God works in families to build heritage.

Team Ministry

We have embraced a team-ministry concept. The team included every member of our family. Why? Because God called our whole family to Romania, not just Shawn and me. God called every one of us to be His disciple.

Everyone has a purpose, including young children. Everyone is part of the story and part of the Church. Therefore, we were and are purposeful in including each family member in engaging God's community and mission together, just with different roles at times.

Keep Them in Church

Christian community is essential. We wanted our children to be involved in the body of Christ; therefore, we kept them plugged into a church. They attended services, small groups, events, and activities our local home church facilitated.

I knew how much gathering with God's people meant to me as a small child and how much I missed it when it was stripped away. I also learned how hard it was without a supportive community when we worked at the home for boys at the beginning of our marriage. God used my experience to inform the decision we made for our children.

Sometimes our kids attended church with us in adult service; other times, they attended church services geared toward children. Even when we were in Romania and there was not an English-speaking service, we coordinated with other English-speaking Christians and *did* church.

I say we "did" church, but we believe the people of God are the Church. The Church is not a building; it is a gathering of God's people who come together to glorify God and edify one another. We came together with others to worship and share the Word, often eating and conversing together. We did not have all the lights, music, and fluff that comes with Western culture. We had worship, the Word, and each other. Good times. Even though all our kids were under ten years of age at the time, we made sure to orchestrate a gathering together of God's people for them and us.

The Church is the body of Christ (made up of people). Our kids need to recognize they are part of the whole body of Christ, God's community. It is crucial for our children to connect to others in the Church in healthy ways.

Be the Church

One of the ways our whole family embraced community was by practicing home-hospitality. The marks of God on a family are found in the measure of their hospitality.

Over the years, several people have lived with our family. Some of them needed a family to belong to, some needed rest and nurturing, while some needed a transitional place. But we welcomed people into our home. (We were prayerful and cautious—not just taking anyone in.)

Weekly we hosted people in our home. We provided meals, fellowship, rest, and a living example of how a Godly family lives out their faith. We were the church to others. We have met amazing people and shared incredible experiences. We were even blessed to host Maasai warriors in our home. I mean, not everyone gets that privilege!

Our children were as much a part of this as Shawn and I were. We all sacrificed and were inconvenienced at times, sharing our food, bathrooms, bedrooms, time, emotional energies, finances, and space. But we also shared the reward of knowing some beautiful people, and we grew in knowing God through knowing them. What a blessing!

Young men learned how to be good dads and loving husbands by watching Shawn interact with us in our home and at work. They saw me, a mom, love her husband and children well. They watched us steward our home life.

God used the lack of our past (no one brought us into their home to allow us to learn from them) to fuel our efforts with the younger generation. God welcomed Shawn and me into His family; we could do the same for a few of His children.

Discipleship in Community

Through hospitality and openness, we demonstrated discipling for others (outside of our family unit) to our children. You cannot disciple people who are not in your life nor your home at times. Not everyone has to live with you, but you must be in each other's lives to fully engage the discipleship process. You can pastor, teach, encourage, coach, mentor, guide, or lead without this level of relationship, but it is incredibly difficult to disciple without it.

Our children became part of the discipleship process through our hospitality and intentional discipleship of people beyond our family. They learned to welcome and invest in others through our example and partnership with them in doing it.

Hospitality and *beyond the family* discipleship mark Godly families.

The Blessings of Community

The community of God comes with beautiful blessings. We pushed our children toward developing a community with God's imperfect people because we are stronger and better together. (A disciple of Jesus Christ cannot abandon the Church any more than he can leave himself.)

God created the Church to edify, sharpen, and love one another as we honor God with our lives. So much is gained by prioritizing and nurturing our family and expanding Church community.

Though we ought to guard against negative influences, good influences in the community will bless your family. We are so thankful for the many brothers and sisters who encourage and spur our children toward God. We are so grateful our kids have friends who walk with them in their pursuit of Christ, loving them and challenging them when they need confrontation.

Christ's community is life-giving. We celebrate together. We laugh, we dance. We sharpen one another. We stir up one another to good works. We encourage one another and endure with one another. We eat together, and we study the Word together. The community also walks with you through difficult times. We are there for each other when we need. We cry together. We pray powerfully together. We rebuild together. We face challenges together. We grow together. We are together through the good and the bad. We. We. We. Together.

God equips each member with gifts to share. You and your children are needed in the body of Christ because you have divine, strategically placed giftings.

I know how significant my children are in the house of God. They are "spiritual beings with eternal significance." What God placed in them to bring to His community and this world is relevant and needed. That is one reason we were compelled to make attending church a priority and being plugged into the community an absolute.

The churches we attend are imperfect (challenges exist) but equally valid, so is life outside the church walls. I am often baffled when people say they do not attend church because of the hypocrites they see. It is perplexing when they say they do not make their kids come to church because the children do not like it. I think to myself, "There are hypocrites in the world. There are things your kids will not like in the world, but you do not pluck them out of there."

Maybe there are times to pray to find a church where everyone can connect and grow. There is a time for a parent to dig, and keep digging, to understand what the child dislikes about the church you attend. Sometimes there may be more going on needing your attention.

Some people attend a mega-church, others a small church. Some attend home fellowships. Whichever way God leads your family to commune with your brothers and sisters in Christ, remember, the important thing is that you make connecting to your extended spiritual family, the Church, God's Bride, a priority in your family.

As a parent, I want my kids to have good, healthy, deep relation-ships with the people of God. I want them to learn to be productive members of the Church. Spiritual family is eternal; therefore, it is worth investing in.

Earlier in the book, I mentioned several instances when people in the church hurt me, and I could have remained offended. I will not mention others because they do not serve a purpose in this book. Even with much junk in the Church, we taught our children the importance of embracing the community of God. I understand that hurt can lead you into isolation or astray. I totally understand. More important to understand is our need for other members in the body of Christ and the need the Church has for us. You need the Church, and the Church needs you and your children. That is why we must face the challenges head-on and continue to grow in a community.

COMMUNITY CHALLENGES

God created a beautiful community, but we must be careful who is in our child's community as a parent. The community may influence and impact your child's life in positive or negative ways. We must remember we are the primary entrusted caretakers over our children and steward the community influences in their lives well.

Even in our foolish days, Shawn and I were careful with the community in which our children engaged. As we grew closer to the Lord, we considered more and more who our children were around and how much time they spent with them. We paid close attention to other leaders in their lives. We watched how peer relationships affected them. We made decisions for the benefit of our family—decisions some people disagreed with.

There is so much blessing in community and being part of a local church body! It is worth the time and the *trouble*. However, if you and your children invest in a church, you already know the challenges of *living* amongst many people. We must learn to play and work well with others.

One must learn and develop behaviors and skills to function well in a community. To overcome challenges within a community, a person must become well skilled in communication, listening, not complaining, humility, forgiveness, teamwork, and encouragement. When we do these well, we overcome the naturally occurring challenges that come from many people interacting.

As a family, we faced situations with fellow members of the body of Christ, that provided opportunities for us to exercise all the wonderful behaviors and skills mentioned in the previous paragraph. There are many articles and books which give insight on how to develop in these areas, so I will not go into them. I will go into some key areas we prioritized just as much as those, if not more, when engaging church community.

For us there were two main challenges we faced in church community. One was the area of discerning and overseeing leadership in our children's lives. The other was to learn to be resolute in unpopular decisions (that many in our church community disagreed with) we made for our family. Poor leadership and others' reactions we encountered regarding our stance on peer relationships provided challenging circumstances.

Of all things I could mention in this section, you may wonder why I am addressing these two areas: leadership over our children and our peer-relations guidelines people opposed. In my opinion, how we handled these two challenges made a huge difference in our child-rearing.

Do Not Be a Drop-off Parent

Dad and Mom, I want to re-emphasize, again and yet again, the importance of embracing the entrustment of being your child's primary guardian. Being active and engaged in the Church is critical for you and your family as Christ-followers, as I've endorsed. The Church, however, is not responsible for raising your child. The role of the Church does not supersede your God-given commission as a parent. Pastoral leadership is not anointed and appointed to be the head or heart of your household.

The Lord constantly nudged us toward being aware of and knowing who was speaking into the life of our children during church services—and what they taught them. Many parents are just drop-off parents. They blindly drop their children off at a children's service without a second thought; this is foolish.

It is important to be active and engaged in the children's ministry if your kids attend. If the church you attend does not allow you to be involved or share with you in some fashion what they teach your kids, I suggest you find a new church. Now, by being involved, I do not mean you should be able to govern, teach, or criticize everything you disagree with. I suggest that you make yourself available to know who is leading, what they are teaching, and if it is a safe place for your child to attend service.

As I write this book, my daughter is a director of a ministry geared and designed for children at a church. One of the things she implemented is a Parent Atlas. Weekly, she provides parents (in writing) what their children are learning. She attempts to engage parents whether they engage her or not. She helps provide resources, empowering parents to disciple their children. She understands that she and her teachers must teach the Word to the kids under their care.

She is also very much aware the leadership's role is to come alongside the parent and complement their efforts. She cannot facilitate every single parent as a teacher, critic, leader, or administrator. She can provide an open policy where information, resource, and the policies and procedures the church's children ministers abide by are available for parents. Parents should expect and appreciate this.

Leadership Challenges in Community

When Autumn was around twelve years old, she was involved in the weekly pre-teen service at our local church. One day she came home upset. She began to convey to me the leader in their class was making comments she felt were inappropriate and could cause division or hurt a child. I already felt a *check* in my spirit about this leader and had prayed God would bring to light what I should be aware of. I visited the class and noticed the leader did not preach or teach the Word (just ramblings of stories and opinions), but I could not place what else bothered me.

A few weeks later, I accidentally intercepted an email addressed to my daughter. This leader sent her an inappropriate email which went to my inbox by mistake. (I am saying it was a mistake, but I believe the Lord allowed it to find its way to my inbox.) The email was not sexual but crossed boundaries. We reported it; leadership did nothing. So we pulled Autumn from the class. We did not depend on the church hierarchy to decide what was best for our daughter; we decided.

Another time Josiah came very upset into the church kitchen. (I was cooking for an event we were hosting for our students; we worked at the church at this time.) He said, "Mom, how the hell can you let me sit under this teaching? They aren't even preaching the Word." Yes, my kid said hell at church. I reminded Josiah he had not read the whole Bible yet and may not know the whole counsel of God. I encouraged him to be humble and for us to discuss what the teacher said.

Josiah began to tell me the teacher was elevating Satan, giving him too much power, and putting fear into kids. Then he said, "I mean, come on, Mom, I listen to John Bevere. I need more." (Y'all, that kid cracks me up.) I told him I would check it out.

The following service I stood outside the room and listened. Josiah was correct. The teaching was unbiblical. Now this new volunteer teacher (from my understanding) was young in her walk with the Lord. Unlike the leader who was malicious in Autumn's story, this person seemed to be trying her best. She just did not know the Word.

I told Josiah he could attend adult service on Sunday from now on. If he decided to go to children's church, he needed not to complain but check everything against God's Word and ask me if he was not sure about something. I chose what was in the best interest of Josiah's spiritual development while explaining the need for patience and grace toward the volunteer leader. After all, they were kind to volunteer.

I share these stories for three reasons. First, I want to demonstrate that you may have to make the best decision for your child, even in a church community. Secondly, I want to point out that both children knew something was off because they were discipled at home. Autumn knew it was unkind to single out people and make them feel bad. We taught them to be kind to everyone, especially people others are not kind to. She could see other kids were saddened and felt left out. And she knew something was just off. Josiah knew the teacher was inaccurate because we talked about and taught the Word at home. He read the Word for himself as well. Would he recognize the error if he never heard the Word at home? Thirdly, I did not just assume my child was wrong and the leadership was right. (This happens more than you think.) We want to teach our kids to respect and obey leaders; however, this could be dangerous in some situations with some leaders. We listened to our children, prayed, and checked it out.

As you can see, we had challenges in the church. On a side note, I want you to know that the children's ministry this happened in is also one of the most significant positive influences of Autumn's young life. Overall, they do brilliant work and minister to thousands of kids. The pastors (whom we know personally) are beautiful people. Sometimes things just get missed, overlooked, or avoided by church leaders and parents. I should have dug more and maybe pulled Autumn out of that class earlier when I had a *check* in my spirit. This is my error. I could have checked out Josiah's new teacher and what they were teaching before he came to me. That is on me.

DISCERNING SPIRITUAL AUTHORITY

We taught our kids about spiritual authority and leadership. Parents cannot be with their children 24/7, so we must teach them to discern.

Spiritual authority should be valued and honored; it is biblical and beautiful. However, leaders in churches are often people who just sign up and have a background check. If nothing illegal comes up on the background check, we let them lead and watch our kids because we need help to pull off the service. We put unmerited trust in people giving them access to our most precious ones.

One of the main things we taught our kids is to listen to the *check* in their spirit. We must discern whether leadership is of God or not, and we must determine if what they teach is from God or not. We encouraged them to check everything through the Word of God. Even in churches, some people are untrustworthy. As they get older, parents need to teach their children to recognize which is which through prayer and discernment. The ability to discern is a vital skill in community. It protects.

Because we were in vocational ministry (most of their childhood), "spiritual authority" and leaders constantly surrounded our children. We taught them to discern between those two prayerfully. We taught them that Shawn and I, as their parents, are their over-mastering authority, even above the pastoral leadership. And as a parent, we have an over-mastering authority, which is God's Word.

We also taught them to respect government authorities unless they attempt to have you do something contrary to the Word of God. We taught them to respect teachers, coaches, and the elderly. Respect and obedience are different. They often walk hand in hand, but they are different; you can have one without the other. We taught them the difference.

You may think it's strange that I'm writing about this as a needed community skill, but it is crucial. Discerning leadership is vital in a church community. The inability to discern leadership is detrimental, in my opinion. How we discern distributes influence and weight. We give weight, significance, and importance to what people say when we believe they have a right from God to speak into our life.

As a parent, we are responsible for who influences the lives of our children. We are responsible for helping them discern how much weight they give to someone's words. As a parent, we cannot be present in every moment and hear what everyone says. We can only teach our children how to process what is said. Of course, our children may not listen, receive, or obey someone they should. Or they may give too much weight to a leader's words that they shouldn't. Mistakes are unavoidable but navigating them as they learn to distinguish between the two will help them sharpen the gift and skill of discernment they possess.

Untrustworthy people fill this world (including your church). Listen to the spiritual *checks* in you. Teach your children to listen to theirs. Do not dismiss your child's uneasiness with a leader. Do not let a leader override your divine wisdom as your child's parent. Do what you know to do as the parent. You are the one primarily entrusted.

5.12

FRIENDS AND FAMILY

Another necessary skill in community we focused on is developing good friendships. Our kids picked their friends, but as parents we decided how much time they spent with their friends. I cannot explain well enough how important it is for parents to guard their child's peer relationships.

Each of our children has developed many friendships. Most of them have been good relationships. Occasionally, an unbeneficial relationship would emerge. In those moments, we prayerfully and carefully put boundaries in place. Some friendships were allowed only within the context of visiting during church events. We did not allow our children to hang out with kids we thought may bring negative influences.

You can tell when someone negatively influences your child. If we noticed our child acted differently with a certain person or *changed* after hanging out with a specific person, we would talk about it with them, limiting the time they had with that person. How did we do that? We just told them they could not hang out with that person anymore, and they did not. Therefore, we did not have huge issues on an ongoing basis because of friendships. We nipped it in the bud, ending the relationship before deep ties formed.

Other times one of our children and another child were just an unhealthy combination. They both brought out the worst in each other. It's not always the other kid. Sometimes it can be your child contributing to the unhealthiness of a relationship. As a parent, we must recognize when our child is a negative contributing factor and make the necessary adjustment needed to end the unhealthiness.

It may surprise you to know our children did, and do, have friends that do not live for Jesus. These friendships have boundaries. Their closest friendships are with people who love Jesus and follow Him. We teach them to love all people, but there are different levels and types of relationships. There isn't a specific type of person we banned from having time with our kids. It was more about that *check* inside and how our children behaved with them and after they spent time with them. Overall, hindsight would suggest we made good calls.

Family First and Most

We ran our home so that our children spent most of their time with us and not their peers. Family is first. Community friendships have their place, but they are not as important as your family unit.

It seems like teenagers spend more time with their peers than their families during their teenage years. Over and over, the Holy Spirit reminded me to make time spent within our core community, our family, the largest interaction time for our children. I was to orchestrate schedules so that they spent more time with siblings and us rather than peers.

How much time do your kids spend with their friends? How much time do they spend with you? It has been said, "What your friends are today, you become tomorrow." Influence is powerful. Most children spend all day at school with peers, then come home and scan social media, play games, or are at sporting events or coffee houses. They may speak to a parent thirty minutes a day if that much. They spend weekends with friends. If your kids spend more time away from you than with you, maybe you should pray, think about this, and make changes.

HOMESCHOOL

Our children attended a private school for about four years before we homeschooled. As I shared earlier, Tyler was the conduit through which God led us to homeschool. Little did we know while living overseas in Romania, it would be in the best interest of our children to homeschool. But God knew.

When we returned to the States from Romania to work full-time at a local church, I prayed about placing the kids in private school again. The Lord led us to continue to homeschool. So we did. Over the years, I prayed every year before starting a new school year about putting them in private school. I received the same response from the Lord to continue homeschooling each year, until one year the Lord told me I did not need to ask anymore. He said if He changed His mind, He would let me know.

I had great difficulty resigning myself to continue to homeschool that particular year. I worked full-time as well as homeschooled our children. I felt the kids could have a better academic education if they went to school. I expressed my frustration and concern to the Lord, highlighting this overwhelming feeling. I shared with Him that I knew they were getting everything they needed academically according to our state educational guidelines, but I wanted them to have more. God did not see it my way.

I think we place a higher value than God does on certain things.

Academics are important. For some, God may lead you to focus intentionally on higher academic achievements. For us, God validated the value of academics but assessed other things as just as valuable or more valuable. Our kids learned many beneficial and profitable things because they homeschooled (providing them the opportunity to be around Shawn and me more).

My children often came to work with us. They worked alongside us. Josiah walked in his little blue flip-flops through the church halls with Shawn and me as we went from teaching and preaching to meeting after meeting. Josiah preached his first sermon to a room full of peers at twelve years old. At fifteen he spent the summer in Romania without us, helping to host missionary teams from around the world.

By the time Linzee was eleven years old, she could run an event better than most adults. She coordinated and facilitated local ministry efforts geared toward elderly and homeless people during her early teenage years. She also led several small groups—discipling younger girls.

As Tyler continued to seek truth and began to put his faith in God, he toured the nation with Shawn (and students from the ministry school we led), playing guitar for worship, and sharing his testimony to multi-generational congregations. He is the one who facilitated a place on Friday nights where Josiah and several other young teenagers preached their first sermons. He also influenced me greatly to step out and teach the revelations God gave me instead of writing sermons for others to preach. And something unique and beautiful for "one-on-one ministry" (for those struggling through or wanting to grow in their faith) began to develop in his latter teenage years.

Autumn preached right alongside me at the Beauty of God Conference in Romania when she was nineteen years old. She was the director for a local Sidewalk Sunday School, Crosstown, for three urban sites in our community before she was twenty. She ministered and coordinated ministry for people rescued from human trafficking in Eastern Europe as a teenager.

Homeschooling provided structure for a family learning and living in a team-ministry environment. We lived life together in every sense of the meaning. By watching us and working alongside us, our children learned through practical hands-on experience what reading books does not teach.

I acknowledge all parents cannot bring their children to work, but if you can, the experience your children gain could be more valuable or as valuable as what they find in books. It definitely will yield more time together as a family.

I Knew the Teacher

Homeschooling enabled me to know the teacher (me) and teach my children. Most parents do not know their child's teacher or what he/she teaches. We trust strangers to educate our children. Many children spend thirty-five hours plus a week in a school community surrounded by people parents barely know if they know them at all. Think about the sphere of influence this circle has in your children's lives. What are they teaching them? How are they treating them?

I want to clarify that I am not condemning you or saying you are a terrible parent if you do not homeschool your children. I have friends and family who feel their children attending public or private school is better for their families. Sometimes both parents must work for financial purposes, and children must attend school to learn. Some parents simply cannot homeschool their children for various reasons. Some simply do not want to. There is no condemnation for your prayerfully motivated, obedient choice. I am suggesting you pray about it. God may have a specific plan for your child's educational needs which you have not given an ear to. This subject is worth praying about.

What is your child learning in school? I attended public school. In eighth grade, my teacher attempted to teach us the methods of astral projection. She had the entire class lay on the floor in several circles, with our heads touching. She then proceeded to walk us through the method of outer body travel. True story.

During breaks between classes, people had sex in our common area, and students exchanged drugs in class. I was in high school way back in the eighties; things are worse now. What is your child witnessing or engaging in at school?

Things happen at private schools too. When Autumn was in the third grade at a Christian private school run by a local church, she received a "sex party" invitation. She also came home with many questions about terminology she did not need to know about at her age.

Now we don't operate out of fear, but faith (trust) in what He desires for our children's education. I hope you pray and obey whatever God leads you to do as a parent regarding your children's education.

SLEEPOVERS

I would like to mention the *guidelines* our family embraced concerning sleepovers. We came to a point where we did not allow our kids to sleep over at anyone's house (when there were other children present) until they were thirteen years of age. Even then, we were cautious. Why? During prayer, I felt the leading of the Lord in this. I kept revisiting this with the Lord because I did not know anyone else who followed these guidelines.

Before we decided upon these parameters, we allowed Autumn to sleep over at a friend's house when she was around seven years old. She called us around 11:00 pm that night to come to pick her up; she felt uncomfortable. Come to find out, she was left alone with her friend most of the day, swimming in a pool. She got sun poisoning. (Two little kids were left swimming alone all day!) Thank God the day ended with a call of discomfort from her and not drowning because of neglect.

As young children Shawn and I had terrible experiences in which we were exposed to things we should not have been. So this also reinforced this general rule. Then one day a man we knew from church looked at me and told me never to let my children sleep over anywhere. Out of the blue, he stared right at me and told me this. (He was later convicted and served time for the sexual battery of a minor.) I immediately thought, "Listen to wisdom where wisdom comes from." The Holy Spirit told me to enforce this guideline in my home, and my own experience informed me to do this, but it took this man's warning to shock me into obedience. We enforced the no-sleepover rule in our house from that moment.

I cannot tell you how many people we have counseled over the years sexually assaulted or *awakened* while sleeping over at someone's home. Yet we keep allowing children to be together alone at night with no one around. How many kids view porn at a friend's house for the first time? I have met quite a few.

You may think this is a bad idea or over the top. I am sharing what we did, not necessarily what you need to do. I do encourage you to ask the Lord about it. Most of us do not even think to pray about allowing our children to sleep over somewhere. Have you ever prayed about it? God's thoughts may shock you.

The Girl Was Mad

Not everyone agrees with the decision we made concerning our children. One woman from church wanted my daughter to sleep over. (She and her daughter were friends of ours at the time.) I explained our policy to her and that my daughter would not be coming over for a sleepover, offering an alternative of us taking the girls somewhere to visit and hang out. This woman became extremely and loudly upset.

The woman was angry! She expressed (loudly at me on a Sunday morning in a children's church room in front of God and everybody) that she understood the rule for others, but that by not allowing my daughter to stay the night at her house, I was saying I did not trust her, her daughter, or her family. I told her it was not about her or her family, but that we followed a personal rule. She was irate.

I felt sad; I did not want to hurt her, but I loved my kids more than I was concerned about hurting her. Not to mention, God spoke to me about it, my own experience validated the decision, and a man convicted of violating a child told me straight up not to do it. Sadly, I found out later that her sons were filming girls in the bathroom and had done inappropriate things with girls who came over. I am very glad I kept to our policy rather than appease her.

Community Summary

I've highlighted several areas regarding the benefits and challenges of community —especially in church communities. Community is good! After reading a few of the examples we faced, you may feel like locking your kids up and hiding them from the world. But that's not a good idea. We do not live by fear but by power, love, and a sound mind (2 Timothy 1:7). Community is a blessing for our children and us, but we must be vigilant.

Remember: I've shared what we did, not what you must do. You may or may never have thought of how you should steward these areas as a family. You may or may not have prayed about them. I would recommend praying about them. I picked these areas to highlight because we believe they were vital in developing the good fruit found within our family.

To sum it up: Discerning influences in a community is good. Relationships with healthy boundaries are good. Trusting the Lord with His instruction within community, even if a lady is yelling at you at church because she thinks what you're doing is offensive, is good. Learning in the way God instructs your family to learn is good. Embracing the privilege of being the one primarily entrusted with your child is good. God created us in and for community—it's a good thing! Just exercise prayerfully motivated caution.

CO-MISSION

Our children are privileged to partake in The Cultural Mandate and the Great Commission; we must make this known to them. They are your children and partners to reach this world with the Good News of Christ. You are co-missioned together.

Your family is divinely placed in a community to be on mission: to know God and make Him known within the home and beyond.

Arrows

Earlier in the book, I shared thoughts on Psalm 127:1-2. I want to continue considering the rest of this passage. Psalm 127:3-5 declares,

> "Children are a heritage from the Lord, offspring a reward from Him. Like arrows in the hands of a warrior are children born in one's youth. Blessed is the man whose quiver is full of them. They will not be put to shame when they contend with their opponents in court."

Arrows have four parts: the shaft (spine), fletching, arrowhead, and nock. When the psalmist wrote Psalm 127, arrows were not mass produced in machines. A person formed an arrow by hand. Each arrow was unique—a one-of-a-kind creation impossible to replicate. Your children are one-of-a-kind creations formed by God and you with a purpose to accomplish a thing.

We aim and shoot to hit the mark with an arrow; there is an intention in an arrow's creation. Often arrows are kept in a quiver, but they are created to launch out to accomplish a purpose. Sometimes you will retrieve them and place them back in the quiver until it is time to send them out again. However, their function is to *go out*.

Mom, Dad, you fashion and form your *arrows* throughout their young lives until it's time to send them out. You make sure their spine is straight but flexible. When an archer shoots an arrow, that arrow has a unique purpose. No other arrow will ever hit the target quite the same as that one. Even if the same archer shoots an arrow from the same quiver at the same target, it will not hit the mark precisely the same. It's impossible. When you shoot your arrow out, he/she will accomplish something unique to himself/herself. He/she will walk into the work the Lord has prepared only for him/her to do.

Arrows go out beyond us. They impact what we cannot impact. We guide and aim them, but they make the impact. They are fast and powerful and go farther than we can ever go. They are extensions of us, hitting marks and going into places and times we will not hit or go.

Our children will make God known to those we will never encounter. They will bring His goodness into dark places we will never light up.

Aim, Hit, Kiss

We launched out our little arrow, Josiah, when he was eight years old. And wow, he hit the mark!

Josiah walked into our bedroom one night and emphatically told us he felt like he was supposed to go on a mission trip to Romania. After prayer Shawn and I felt the Holy Spirit confirm this. We planned a trip and hopped on a plane to Romania.

One day we were visiting families, bringing food, and ministering the Gospel right alongside our young boy. We entered the home of a man who had been partially paralyzed for ten years by a stroke. It had been a decade since he could get out of bed. He could fling his arms around and move his thumbs and head, but that seemed to be it. He was also mute.

As we began to speak to him, sharing the Good News, he began to weep. We prayed with him, and he began flinging his arms across his chest to make the sign of the cross as best he could. He kept shifting his gaze toward a picture of Jesus on his wall. God's presence was palpable in that room.

I cannot explain with words the compassion and love I felt at that moment. It's like Jesus was standing right there. We were all experiencing God's grace and love.

Then the gentleman noticed Josiah. His eyes locked on Josiah as he tried to reach for him and pull his body up with his flinging arms. Josiah grabbed his hand and held it for a long time. The man just stared at him. According to the woman who let us in the room, this elderly man had not seen a child in many years—*forever* was her exact word (but in Romanian).

Then Josiah hugged him. He laid beside him, hugging him for a while. This man uncontrollably broke and wept and wept and wept. Something miraculous happened. Again, I cannot explain the healing power and compassion we felt in that room. But God used Josiah at that moment to minister to this man.

When it was time to leave, I kissed the precious gentleman on the cheek and thanked him for allowing us to spend time with him. He grabbed my hand with his crippled hand and tipped his head to me. He kissed my hand and thanked me with his eyes. There was such power, strength, and dignity in his eyes now. It is one of the best kisses of my life.

A mute man spoke much to us at that moment. People are waiting to hear the Good News of God, and the very sight of a believer—even if he is only eight years old—may be the best thing they have seen in a decade.

Josiah was ready to be launched into this moment. Even though we were right there by his side (and personally benefiting from this experience), it was Josiah who hit the mark in this divine moment.

We then put Josiah back into the quiver and brought him home.

Today on Mission
As Christ-followers, we do not wait until our kids are grown to

teach them to walk in who God calls them to be or do what God calls them to do. We do it with them now. We launch our little arrows out, retrieve them, and keep them safe in the quiver until it's time to hit a mark again.

We have not only taught our children that they have a voice and purpose for God, but Shawn and I also gave them opportunities and places to use their voices and walk out their purposes. From our earliest ministry efforts, our kids ministered with us. Together the whole family ministered. For example, when we ministered at events when Linzee and Josiah were two years old, they handed out balloons to people and simply told them God loved them. Sometimes they dressed up as clowns and handed out candy.

As children, they served and ministered to people in many places: soup kitchens, nursing homes, after school programs for youth, crisis pregnancy centers, homes for domestically abused women and children, homeless shelters, people rescued from human trafficking, the sick in hospitals, and kids at neighborhood Sidewalk Sunday School just to name a few. They have also served and ministered in the local church: cleaning the house of God, ministering from behind the pulpit, creating, planning, coordinating, greeting, cooking, preaching, praying, playing worship music, leading, and dancing in the house of God.

They have served and ministered overseas with Shawn and me. Our children collectively have been to forty-three states and eight countries. They have brought the goodness of God with them everywhere they have gone.

They have ministered in our home with us as well. Throughout their childhood, people have dropped by for help and prayer. Our kids have heard and been a part of every single one of these moments. If they were not in the room, they prayed and kept the person's confidence who showed up and poured out all their private business. They have made countless meals and cleaned countless dishes with me as we sought to give people a homecooked meal and family dinnertime experience.

All these things they did before they were eighteen years of age.

We taught them that everywhere they go, they carry Christ's light. The call on their life is to be a blessing: to love God, to love people, to share His Good News, to live in love and light, to bring and be His goodness in the lives of others, to be compassionate. It's that simple.

. . .

Excuses

Parent to parent, I'm telling you I know without a doubt that being on mission with our kids, giving them opportunities to fulfill their given God-ordained purpose alongside us, made a difference. Do not let stupid excuses keep you from providing ministry opportunities for your child.

Years ago, when we held weekly Sidewalk Sunday School within our city, we offered opportunities for other church members to get involved and come out and minister. One mother told me she was not bringing her child out because she did not want them exposed to what was out there. I asked her what she meant. She told me she knew there would be children cursing, and she did not want her child to hear that. She was afraid because it was a church event, they would think it was okay to curse. I'm not going to lie; I wanted to curse her out.

One, her kids attended public school where they heard cursing. And secondly, she cursed regularly. Surprisingly, I heard stupid excuses like this often. People would tell us how much they wished they could bring their family overseas to minister like us. We would tell them it was possible and that we could arrange a time to host them. They would immediately say something like, "Well, we would love to come, but we are planning a vacation to Disney World and have to go, but we wish it was possible."

Understand, I am not judging going on a family vacation over a mission trip. We take family vacations that are for bonding and having fun together. What a beautiful thing to do! But to use something like "my child may hear cursing" or "we cannot go because we *have* to take a vacation" as a reason for not providing an opportunity for your child to minister is ridiculous.

Side note: Each day provides an opportunity for a child to minister. Opening their eyes to this opens possibilities for them. It's not about a destination or event but engagement and awareness.

Let Her See the Need

When we began working at the boys' home at the beginning of our marriage, several people insinuated we were bad parents because of Autumn's exposure to "boys like that." I diligently prayed because I did not want the boys to affect Autumn poorly. The Lord showed me something. He said, "Nichole, keep the need before her. Let her see Me meet the need. She will never depart from Me."

I realized the Lord was showing me something significant. Autumn was under three years old when we worked there. Yet she could see the needs of the boys. She watched as Jesus healed them and restored some of them. Autumn watched God use her imperfect parents to bring order to chaos, counsel those who lacked guidance, and create a loving family environment for those who lacked one. She did not understand everything taking place, but she witnessed the Spirit of God moving in and through that home.

We cannot always prove God's existence to our children, but when they see His effect on people, they cannot deny Him. We were to exercise wisdom and be careful with Autumn (not foolish) as she was exposed to human need and witnessed Jesus meet the need. Living in this environment did not damage her; it drew her to Him.

This way became part of the Kingdom Culture within our home. Our kids saw need, and then they saw Jesus meet that need. They saw people sin, repent, and be set free. They also saw people sin and choose to keep sinning and stay in bondage. Those experiences helped compel them to Christ.

Same Spirit

There is something you have that your children do not have: the trust of God in partnering with Him in guiding your child into the fullness of His goodness. But you and your child do possess some of the same things. The same Spirit of God dwelling in you dwells in your Christ-following child. Like you, they are created, anointed, and appointed as God's image bearer. They have a purpose and mission today, just like you. Do not hinder them.

COVERED

Even if parents fully surrender and embrace God's design, community, commission, and entrustment (doing their absolute best), a child can still have a bad day or a challenging season. There will be times when they fail and sometimes sin. Falling short and missing the mark is part of every person's story. No one escapes transgression. The times in which our kids fall short is when we, as Godly parents, need to step up and cover our children.

I am not suggesting we do not allow our children to experience the consequences of their inappropriate actions. In the Garden, God clearly described to Adam, Eve, and the serpent what the results of their disobedience were, and each of them walked it out. Yet God covered their nakedness and shame.

Stop Telling Your Friends Your Child's Business

Shawn and I cover our children by concealing matters. We do this because of what the Word of God says. Proverbs 11:13 says, "A gossip betrays a confidence, but a trustworthy person keeps a secret." Proverbs 12:23 states, "The prudent keep their knowledge to themselves, but a fool's heart blurts out folly." And Proverbs 17:9 reveals, "Whoever would foster love covers over an offense, but whoever repeats the matter separates close friends."

Shawn and I desire to be trustworthy and prudent parents who seek love and unity with our children. We keep private what our kids walk through as much as possible. There were moments when we turned to a counselor when we needed outside help. We do not, however, gossip about our children.

As disciples of Christ, we learn from God's example (as seen in the Garden and throughout Scripture) how to treat our children when they do something they should not have done. We cover them. We cover them by concealing matters while allowing our kids to experience the consequences of their actions.

If possible, parents should shield their children when they sin. Sometimes you need to talk to a counselor or friend when you are at the end of your rope as a parent. There are moments when we must reach out for guidance and support from Godly community. For example, it can be tough to walk it out alone when a child is in addiction. Thank God for confidential support groups.

Sometimes you have a three-year-old who has decided to start biting, and you have tried everything you can think of to help halt this behavior. You call a friend and ask what they did to get their child to stop. This is good. We can share what works and does not work for us. Thank God for friends with new ideas.

Other times you need a confidant for yourself as a parent because you are in a dark place because of what you are dealing with in your home. I am the confidant of a few people. We talk and pray about what their kids go through. The kids know their parent confides in me.

There is a difference between seeking counsel for support and simply gossiping. Gossiping about our children is ungodly and does not build a Godly home. Over the years, I've heard parents openly reveal personal details concerning their child which should have been kept in confidence or trusted to a close friend or counselor.

One mother sat in Starbucks loudly telling her friends how disgusting her son is because he looks at porn on his phone all the time. She went on and on about what she found. Everyone in Starbucks could hear her. At the time, her son was in his mid-teens. I cannot imagine the embarrassment he would have felt if he had heard her.

Sorrow enters my heart when I see children exposed for their negative behavior on social media. A mom posted a picture of her son's unclean room because he did not clean it. She ranted about how she put it out there for the whole world to see so that he would be embarrassed. She boasted how she is a good mom and would not allow him to get away with it. All I thought was, "Wow. Obviously, he did get away with it. It's not clean. And you are seeking attention and acknowledgment by resorting to social media so other moms can chime in on how awesome they think you are—for embarrassing your son."

My attitude toward the mom isn't probably the most gracious on this matter, but I wonder how this mom would feel if her son posted the sink full of dirty dishes she did not do or if he told people about the things said between her husband and her during a heated argument.

Flippantly revealing a child's circumstances makes you untrustworthy, unwise, and divisive. It's not good. Children do not like it. Think about it this way: Would you want your child to reveal all your business to his friends?

Reaping

Throughout my discipleship journey with the Lord, I have witnessed how He covers people, including Shawn and me. God is incredibly gracious and patient. He seems like He will do everything possible to bring a person to a place of repentance and healing privately.

Sadly, sometimes when people do not yield to God, they are exposed publicly. Your sin finds you out. Galatians: 6:7-8 states,

 "Do not be deceived: God cannot be mocked. A man reaps what he sows. Whoever sows to please their flesh, from the flesh will reap destruction; whoever sows to please the Spirit, from the Spirit will reap eternal life."

Right about now you may recall that the entire Bible reveals stories about victories and personal failures. It is important to note that the Bible was written throughout time, long after the people written about left this earth. With my family's permission and input, this book

you are reading now is written decades after most of our struggles. It is a joint decision to share our story to help others.

Also, it is important to note that when your kids are young, they are not who they fully are. Children are still learning and growing. A child at fourteen is not who they will be at twenty or thirty or forty years of age. When you gossip about your kids, people will not forget. God forgives, but people, unfortunately, remember that junk. Concealing a matter protects and preserves a young person's ability to be who they are called to be in the future without judgment from others. And it's just not kind to spread gossip about your child.

Dad and Mom, cover your child. Conceal their matters. You will be a trusted refuge for them to run to.

LET'S TALK SEX

B efore we wrap up this book, I want to share a general account regarding how we dealt with sexuality in our home. Sexual references are everywhere; confusion abides in our culture. Our culture cannot even seem to agree on what gender is. The last time I googled, I found articles listing over fifteen sexual orientations—very confusing. Because this *sexual stuff* is so prevalent, we have included a chapter on this subject.

In creating Kingdom Culture within our home, we follow God's design for sexuality. We taught our kids there are two genders: male and female. We taught them God designed a male and female for many things, including sexual relations with one another. We also taught them to love and treat all people with respect. Humans choose what they trust and whom they follow. God designed us with the ability to choose. If someone chooses something not in line with God's design, we do not accept it as God's way nor judge them for their choice.

When Shawn and I had "The Talk" about sex with our children, we began the conversation by saying, "Sex is a good thing. God made it, and it is awesome." We then preceded to tell them sex is best in God's design. Depending on their age and their questions, we answered as honestly and openly as possible. We also did a health and sex education curriculum for most of our kids during homeschool. Then we had The Talk again and again in more detail as they grew older and asked more questions. We have had countless conversations regarding sexuality and sexual activity.

We approached sexuality and sexual activity from an "it is good" perspective and not an "it's dirty" perspective. We made sure our kids knew it is a good thing God created. Therefore, it's important to trust Him with how He ordained it. He created it; He knows best.

We taught our children that we honor God with every part of ourselves. We did not back down from teaching God's way regarding sexuality or sexual activity.

Pornography and Prostitutes

When dealing with the topic of pornography, we did not deal in extremes. We were honest with our children about the effects of long-term pornography use. We were also honest about the normal sexual curiosity most humans have, especially when they become teenagers. We did not shame them for being curious.

We did block access on their phones to adult content. (However, people can get around this if they want to.) We did random phone checks on what they were viewing. Occasionally, we asked them how they were doing in this area. We offered accountability.

If they crossed a line, we had an open conversation about why and what encouraged this. Teenage years are hard. Available, easily accessed sexual images present challenges for adults—how much more for kids with raging hormones. Even though some of these conversations were uncomfortable, we did not avoid dealing with them.

How a parent handles a child's pornography viewing can cause a wedge in their relationship; we did not want that. We encouraged our kids to honor God and other people with their hearts and eyes. We urged them to choose to trust Him and not the lust in their heart. We told them they were not missing out on anything of significance by not viewing porn.

We encouraged our sons to only view what they would be okay with their spouse or child displaying to the world. For example, we would ask if they would be okay if their wife posed naked and men or women carried her picture around on their phones and lusted after her. Would it be okay if someone lusted over their future daughter? And, vice versa, we asked our daughters.

We reminded our children that the people they viewed in pornography are people (God's image bearers)—someone's real-life daughter and son. To view someone in this way is to dishonor them. They are God's daughter, God's son.

Avoidance

Avoidance is a plague. As a parent, you cannot avoid something away. Not dealing with something will not erase it. Dodging a *thing* may enable it to become stronger, bigger, and more treacherous. In my opinion, avoiding what needs confrontation is one of the worse things a parent can do.

Avoidance is an attractive temptation when you do not know what to do or say or if it is an uncomfortable circumstance. When a parent does not know how to handle a situation, it is easier to pretend it will get better or that it does not exist. This is not a good idea. What we do not deal with will continue to grow. Left for three years, a tiny weed that can be easily pulled out by the roots when it first appears will take a tractor to pull it out.

We just purchased 9.6 acres of land which was abandoned for three years. The amount of effort it takes to pull out the three-year-old weeds is ridiculous. It is hard even to imagine that three years ago I could yank that weed out with just my two fingers.

In parenting or life in general, do not let the weeds grow. If you do not know how to deal with the weed in your child, get help then yank it out before it requires a tractor.

Porno-Star

Years ago, I met with a woman who was aging out of the porn industry. She had worked in the porn industry for years but was at an age where they no longer required her services. She chose to work in this industry—no one forced her. According to her, it was financially advantageous.

We had an interesting conversation. My heart broke as this woman discussed with me how porn is filmed. Sadness filled my heart as she spoke of where she was in life. She was at a crossroads, deciding if she would put her trust in Jesus.

I met with her because someone asked me to meet with her. People ministering to her were looking for a welcoming place if she turned her life over to Jesus. Sadly, they were not sure if their community would welcome her.

One of my students interrupted us during our conversation, asking me if I was okay. I told him I was. He then whispered in my ear, telling me that he was not sure if I knew who she was. I assured him I did; he was shocked, so I reassured him. He then shook his head and walked away.

I thought how awkward. A person he knew from porn and possibly lusted over in a movie was standing right there in flesh and blood form—broken and lost. Our student's face said it all—awkward and awakening.

I told my children about our meeting while not breaking her confidence. To hear this person's experience was eye opening.

Human Trafficking

As I mentioned earlier, our family ministered to men and women (used for the sexual entertainment and purposes of another) rescued from human trafficking. The first time I walked into the home for those rescued, I was taken aback; I felt sick. All the movies and documentaries I watched showed beautiful, trafficked girls who looked amazing even though they were in slavery. I realized that most advertisements bringing awareness of these heinous activities typically featured thin, beautiful images of young girls. The people in this home did not look like the people in the movies.

I know movies are not real, but they affected my thought process more than I was aware. Do not misunderstand me; the people in this home were lovely, but brokenness covered them. So much brokenness, it was difficult to see past it. They carried such pain and looked so worn out. The physical scars that several of them bore were minimal compared to the emotional scars. (So much sadness.)

The exploitation of people is evil. Not everyone viewed in pornography is performing by choice. Some are slaves, just like the people we had the privilege of spending time with inside that home were at one time: slaves to a system, slaves to another's unhealthy appetites, and slaves of people who are non-honoring of humans and God.

We made sure our kids knew this. (Most of our children visited this home with us.) There is a cost to somebody when you use a person for your lustful purpose via phone, movie, computer, magazine, or in person.

Pornography is a plague.

Fornication

We taught our kids that sexual intercourse is for marriage. When my kids were teenagers, I would often jokingly but seriously tell them, "Keep all your goodness to yourself. That's for your spouse." Or "Do not be tempting or teasing. Keep your hands to yourself; them hands are for your spouse."

When they began dating, we guided our children with wisdom such as "Do not be alone together. People do not have sex in public." "Do go out and have adventures. Go out in groups with friends." "Your girlfriend is precious; cherish her." "Pray with each other. Study the Word together." "Do not be overly touchy with each other. Hormones have a mind of their own." "Be wise." "We do not awaken love until it's time."

Like their faith walk, how our children handle their sexuality will be their choice. When it comes down to it, your child, and only your child, will choose how he/she wants to handle his/her sexuality. We can only impart wisdom and help set our kids up for success by encouraging, educating, and exercising our God-given authority in our home to protect them. And pray like their purity depends on it.

God's design for sexuality is under assault. It is a huge topic needing much attention and discussion (way more than I've included). I hope you glean from this small account how and why we have handled sexuality in our home with our children. It may seem old fashioned to some, but we must follow the Word of God in all things if we are indeed His disciples.

5.18

OUR HOPE

If you have made it to the end of this book, good job! We appreciate the time you have invested. It is our privilege to share the how and why behind how we ran our home and raised our children.

Our story is a story of a loving, intentional God who redeemed our past and gave us a future. It is of a God who taught us to be loving and deliberate with our family community. Our marriage is not perfect, but we persevere in love and with purpose. Shawn and I are not perfect parents, but we are persistent in honoring and loving our children well—as Christ loves us—to the best of our ability.

The Red One has redeemed and restored our lives. He has filled lack, brought peace to chaos, transformed our selfishness to love, and blessed us.

Everything good in our lives is because of Jesus.
Everything and everyone.

We pray with all our heart that you say yes to Jesus. He will change your life and your whole family if you let Him. If you yield to Him, you will be positioned to establish and nurture YOUR family from a place of

design rather than default,
love rather than lack,
promise rather than potential,
and thriving rather than surviving.

We hope something we have shared inspires and helps you on your journey as you, too, become a Godly family.

May you thrive in His design, His love, and His promises.

From our home to yours: May the Red One make you a family full of heritage and Hope.

Nichole and Shawn

NOTES

1.1

1. John 1:1-3

1.2

1. Matthew 28:18-20, Luke 24:44-49, Mark 16:15-18, John 20:21-23

1.4

1. Isaiah 50:7

1.13

1. Matthew 13:24-30

1.15

1. Dear one who struggles to conceive, it may anger you that I cried when I unexpectedly conceived a child. I am close in relationship with several people who struggle with infertility, and I have witnessed the effect stories like mine may have. I don't want you to think God does not believe He can trust you with another human. If you struggle with the ability to conceive, it is NOT because God does not trust you with another human. I don't know your circumstance, but I know God birthed nations out of barrenness.

   There are humans on this planet thrown away like trash who could use a dad or mom like you. There is the first birth through flesh and water, but there is a second birth through the Spirit. This Spirit confirms to us that we are adopted and children of God. Equal heirs. I'm thankful for my first birth but even more grateful for my second birth (Romans 8:15-16). There are unopened gifts in the form of abandoned, neglected children all over this world. These precious children are ready to expand your capacity to love. Ready to reveal God's goodness and grace to you. They are ready to receive the benefit of the spirit of adoption, the same Spirit at work in your life, and cry out to a dad and mom. To be part of a family, your family.

   If you struggle to conceive, you are doing NOTHING wrong. God is NOT waiting for you to be perfect. I'm not prideful enough to think I can answer the "WHY?" for you. What I want you to know is the value of your motherhood and fatherhood are not determined by whether a child passes through your body or not. It is determined by the love, nurture, acceptance, provision, and protection you shower on another tiny human. You cannot be better or do better to earn another human being from God. Those little human gifts arrive in all forms, with adoption reflecting the Spirit of God Himself. Sometimes God one hundred percent chooses your gift; other times, there is a world of gifts from which you can have a part in choosing.

2. Casual Christian, This Compilation ©1992 Forefront Records, Released: January 1, 1992, Degarmo and Key Collection

1.21

1. https://biblehub.com © 2004 - 2021 by Bible Hub; #1820 damah, #1097 beli, #1847 daath #7911 shakach
2. Ibid. #2377 chazon, #6544 para

2.6

1. A phrase from the lyrics of *Hold Me Jesus* by Rich Mullins. These words encapsulate well the struggle we often face.

2.8

1. New Kings James Version (NKJV) Scripture taken from the New King James Version®. Copyright © 1982 by Thomas Nelson.

3.3

1. Italic added for emphasis.

4.2

1. Strong, James. *Strong's Exhaustive Concordance of the Bible.* (Hebrew #2142, #2145)

4.7

1. Strong, James. *Strong's Exhaustive Concordance of the Bible.* (Greek #2776)

4.9

1. Strong, James. *Strong's Exhaustive Concordance of the Bible.* (Hebrew #5828, #5826, #5048, #5046)
    In this section, I will expound on the context of *'ezer kenegdo*. Although I will explain *'ezer* and *kenegdo* separately, the full concept is *'ezer kenegdo* combined. *Kenegdo* only occurs once in Scripture (that I could find), making it mysterious (to me) and leaving some lack of clarity. Women are definitely a mysterious creation! Ha! Also, I must mention Skip Moen here. Many years ago, his teachings provoked me to study the passage of Scripture this phrase is found in. I never had encountered this concept before that time and without stumbling across it I may never

have. (Side note, you may find that *'ezer* has difference spellings when translated into English.)

4.13

1. Strong, James. *Strong's Exhaustive Concordance of the Bible.* (Hebrew #1129)
2. Strong, James. *Strong's Exhaustive Concordance of the Bible.* (Hebrew #1004)
3. Strong, James. *Strong's Exhaustive Concordance of the Bible.* (Hebrew #3027)

5.3

1. Author of *Sinners in the Hands of an Angry God* is Jonathan Edwards
2. Author of *Sinners in the Hands of a Loving God: The Scandalous Truth of the Very Good News* is Brian Zahnd